Choice, Pathways and Post-16

Choice, Pathways and Transitions Post-16 is about the complex transitions from compulsory schooling, through the period of post-adolescence, of one small group of young people in South London, analysing the choices and constraints which frame their identities and experiences. The young people talk about their education, training and employment 'choices', all set against a general backdrop of governmental ambition to increase participation in post-compulsory education as a means of producing a 'learning society'.

The choices made by these young people bear only a passing resemblance to the one-dimensional, calculative, individualistic, consumer rationalism which predominates in official texts. Indeed, this study suggests that for some young people, occupational status and work is not a priority. Many post-adolescents are trying to postpone or keep their work identities on hold; and the authors reveal that they are also involved in constructing other identities through their consumption patterns and increasing fetishism in relation to fashion, style and concern with the body and the self.

This ground breaking book is the first comprehensive analysis of the transition to post-compulsory education and training within the dynamics of an education market setting. Its controversial findings will be of great interest to practitioners in education, policy-makers as well as to researchers and undergraduates.

Stephen J. Ball is Professor of Sociology of Education and Director of the Centre for Public Policy Research at King's College London. He is editor of the *Journal of Education Policy* and has published widely on education policy. **Meg Maguire** is a Senior Lecturer in the School of Education, King's College London; and deputy editor of the *Journal of Education Policy*, and author of a range of texts on the teaching profession and women teachers. **Sheila Macrae** is Research Fellow in the School of Education, King's College London. She has worked with young people for many years, first as a teacher and then as a researcher.

Studies in Inclusive Education Series

Series Editor: Roger Slee
Dean of the Graduate School of Education, University of Western Australia

Choice, Pathways and Transitions Post-16

New Youth, New Economies in the Global City

Stephen J. Ball, Meg Maguire and Sheila Macrae

London and New York

First published 2000 by RoutledgeFalmer
11 New Fetter Lane, London EC4P 4EE

Simultaneously published in the USA and Canada
by RoutledgeFalmer

29 West 35th Street, New York, NY 10001

RoutledgeFalmer is an imprint of the Taylor & Francis Group

© 2000 Stephen J. Ball, Meg Maguire and Sheila Macrae

Typeset in Baskerville by Steven Gardiner Ltd, Cambridge
Printed and bound in Great Britain by Biddles Ltd, Guildford and King's Lynn

British Library Cataloguing in Publication Data
A catalogue record for this book is available from the British Library

Library of Congress Cagaloging in Publication Data
Ball, Stephen J.
Choice, pathways, and transitions post-16: new youth, new economies in the global
city / Stephen J. Ball, Meg Maguire, and Sheila Macrae.
    p.   cm. – (Studies in inclusive education series)
Includes bibliographical references and index.
1. Youth – England – London – Longitudinal studies. 2. High school
graduates – England – London – Longitudinal studies. 3. Postsecondary
education – England – London. 4. School-to-work transition – England – London.
I. Maguire, Meg. II. Macrae, Sheila. III. Title. IV. Series.

HQ799.G7 B24 2000
305.235'09421 – dc21   00-022532

ISBN 0 7507 0860 3 (pbk)
      0 7507 0861 1 (hbk)

Contents

Figures and Tables

Figures

Tables

Appendix 3

Series Editor's Preface

Declaring their work to be an 'exercise in compromise . . . a struggle with our data, our selves and our words' (p. 142), the authors of this book display rare maturity and confidence. Do not confuse my use of 'confidence' with conceit, for it is precisely the opposite; a humility born out of extensive insight to which I refer. Many of us seek to conclude our work by reassuring our readers that our theory works, that we have dotted the i's and crossed each of the t's, hastening to rule a line under this project and move comfortably onto the next. Stephen Ball, Meg Maguire and Sheila Macrae defy that academic habit by highlighting the limitations of their work. This is not a signifier for commonplace, and understandable, research exhaustion, a shadow-boxing with the potential critics who lie in wait to broadcast what the researcher knows that they have conveniently ignored or glossed over. For this reader their lapse into 'conventionality' and an inevitable 'reductionism' is a sign of the sophistication of the research. Their representations of 'youth' remain far from 'overburdened', caveats are offered throughout the text to reveal the limitations and possibilities for interpretation. I will now attempt to clarify these initial reactions to this extremely important text.

Choice, Pathways and Transitions Post-16 is a multi-layered text wherein we are invited, rather compelled, to engage with the authors across a spectrum of issues and fields. This is a book that traverses disciplines and research interests and will as a consequence speak to a number of different audiences. The title immediately captures the imagination of those located within the church of 'Youth Studies'. Upon opening the cover we encounter researchers who grapple with social theory writ large, with research methodology, and with the formation and interpretation of youth and their encounters with post-compulsory educational 'choices' and thereby, the problematic of education policy as it articulates with diverse groups of young people. The extensive interviews with the cohort of young people in South London reveal the growing tension between 'young people' as they are presented in post-compulsory education policy scripts and the complex identities of youth which simultaneously defy and invite generalization. They are both reflexive in their exercise of individual agency and also subjected to Bourdieu's notion of 'inculcated disposition'.

The researchers sift through their data to identify profound tensions in the current play of social theory in general and youth and education policy studies in particular. As they argue in their conclusion, a chapter designation they would almost certainly reject, 'Conceptually and theoretically we need to avoid simplistic binaries and find a way between the dissolution theorizing of Beck and Giddens and a reassertion of a simple categorical structuralism' (p.145). Accordingly the subjects of this study resuscitate 'modernist' tools such as 'family', 'values', 'race', 'gender' and 'class'. However, the tools are reconstituted through 'their changing bases in time and space' (p. 18). Here is where Ball, Maguire and Macrae advance theory rather than rehearse it. Complexity is not the foe to a good theory; it provides the platform for it. The recent contribution from MacDonald (1999, p. 202) eschews commentaries that characterize a postmodern world fractured into 'a patchwork of microcultures, ... a multiplicity of tribes'. 'The older frameworks of sociology constructed in terms of class', he adds, 'are of little use'. Through his Melbourne-based study of a group of 150 young people he moves to frame his analysis within 'fields of relationship between actors' (p. 203). As the authors of this text assert the field is in need of extended consideration, debate and re-theorizing.

There exists a sense of continuing struggle in this book. Indeed, it is put before us repeatedly as we are told of the authors' consciousness of methodological choices and the consequences of these research decisions for the readings of these South London young people that may ensue. The struggle is between the gathering and the writing up of data and how those processes render the subjects in so doing – between description and inscription. Great care is taken to write the researchers into the text and thereby reveal the struggle between 'fieldwork, textwork and headwork' (p. 142). In this respect the authors contribute to an ongoing project to engender epistemic, political and methodological transparency within the critical qualitative 'tradition', that defies the current crop of critiques of 'new' sociologies of education (Foster, Gomm and Hammersley, 1996). This is a text I would offer to new and established researchers alike as they approach the interrogator's table to declare their 'reflexivity'.

So what is the fit between *Choice, Pathways and Transitions Post-16: new youth, new economies in the global city* and a series entitled *Studies in Inclusive Education*? On the surface we enter dialogues between the authors and their cohort about stories of inclusion and exclusion played out at this 'end-stage' of schooling, this site of educational transition. The stories texture the individuals to apprehend and challenge the notion of 'singular self' (p. 150) and weave the elements of a life in which education is but one, albeit substantial, component. Schooling forms its substance through a highly interactive process mediated, not wholly, by the young people themselves within new geographies and socio-scapes. Teachers, education administrators, government advisors and bureaucrats have much to learn from these vignettes about the world of and for young people and the varying proximity of education to those worlds. We witness young people rebuilding 'self-esteem and personal efficacy undermined through school careers' (p. 140) as well as education as the reinforcement of self-esteem inherited through privileged cultural dispositions and distinctions.

Inclusion and exclusion, temporary and extended, is at the heart of the study. Again, this is complicated by the perceptions and reflections encased within the narratives of the participants in the study. This text compels this reader to revisit notions of inclusive education to resist its reductionist urge towards universality and essentialism. We are invited to critically engage with ourselves as researchers and authors and open our data to broader ranges of theoretical possibilities, rather than close it down to make our texts work for each other. Finally I wish to pay tribute to the humility of the research posture and to the respectfulness with which the researchers interact with and reflect upon the young people who breathe life into this text. I will no doubt return to this book repeatedly as I continue to think about the formation and conduct of research.

Roger Slee

References

Foster, P., Gomm, R. and Hammersley, M. (1996) *Constructing Educational Inequality*, London, Falmer Press.

MacDonald, K. J. (1999) *Struggles for Subjectivity. Identity, Action and Youth Experience*, Cambridge, Cambridge University Press.

Foreword

Research produces discomfort and independent, critical research can produce acute discomfort. At least that is the effect which I hope this vital and engrossing account of the lives of a small group of post-adolescents growing up in London will have upon those politicians, policy-makers and educational professionals who can be persuaded to read it.

Current policy in education, training and employment, for example, is driven by the theory of human capital which, according to the authors, has a fatal flaw. It fails to recognize 'the complex interactional, intellectual and situated processes that constitute learning; it is socially disembedded' (p. 9). The same criticism could not be levelled at this study, which succeeds in conveying the embeddedness of these young people in their families and communities, and within the wider changing class structure and labour market of London as a global city.

The research reported here, which began as a project within the Economic and Social Research Council's programme of research into The Learning Society, is small-scale, intensive and multi-dimensional. It is also relatively unusual in a field where 'longitudinal' has come to mean 'anything over twelve months', in that the same young people were interviewed at various times over a four-year period and intensive efforts were made to keep in touch with those young adults, who very quickly after leaving school became difficult to trace.

The accounts of these young people's lives are theoretically grounded, sophisticated and self-critical. The authors are aware, for example, that they are providing only glimpses into complex lives: 'We have access to only part of who they are, might be, or might become' (p. 20). A sharp, critical approach also pervades the text; for instance, Anthony Giddens' notion of a diversity of options open to all is gently chided – 'reflexivity will get you only so far if you leave school without qualifications' (p. 22).

The book draws on a wealth of relevant literature, has original contributions to make to that literature and yet remains accessible throughout. The main chapters are constructed around the detailed narratives of particular sets of young people, a device which allows a range of conceptual themes to emerge from the similarities and differences of their stories. Rachel, for instance, was the 'golden girl' at school, academically able but also a gifted sportswoman. Her story exemplifies some of the authors' key points: the complexities of young people's lives; the limitations of choice; the endless processes of classifying and being classified; and the possibility of setback even for ideal students. Before her A-levels, Rachel reflected on her choice of university:

> I like the universities that are hard to get into. I don't want to go somewhere that takes anyone with the basic A-levels because, like I say, I like a challenge and I want the best so I can improve myself all the time and be with people who want to improve themselves as well (p. 81).

Her examination results were not, however, as good as predicted and the golden girl had to learn to re-classify herself.

In contrast, the learner identity Wayne acquired at school works as a mechanism of self-exclusion:

> Most people, you know, they have been in school for so many years, they just want to get on with their lives now. They've had enough of sitting in classrooms. They're bored. They just want to get a job and some money. They want a fresh start, a job, a new life, not more writing and learning things that nobody cares about (p. 135).

Wayne's story is not, however, presented as a pathology of exclusion and deprivation, although he is clearly outside any official definition of the Learning Society. Nevertheless, he slowly constructed a fragile new future for himself in the new twilight economy of a DJ in clubs. The book breaks new ground by describing young adults such as Wayne who are developing lifestyles rooted in leisure and pleasure, who are 'stridently avoiding the future' (p. 147) on the periphery of new urban economies, and who are so wonderfully different from those 'individual, rational calculators, [the] human capitalists' who stalk the pages of government White Papers on education.

An indication is all that can be given here of the richness of this text which, among many other themes, deals with the 'cut-throat' quality of the 16–19 education and training market (p. 13), and the 'continuing importance of social class and race and gender differences but also their changing bases in time and space' (p. 18). The researchers also retain the ability to be surprised by their data; witness their admission that the family (and particularly mothers) remained a significant factor in the lives of both Rachel and Wayne and most of the other members of their sample. The book is at its best when, for instance, it catches in a memorable phrase 'the choreography of decision-making within families' (p. 144). Many readers will, I suspect, recognize and may even be embarrassed by their personal recollection of the dance steps recorded by the authors.

Finally, the book contains a valuable discussion of the analysis and interpretation of the stories presented. Any higher-degree student, perplexed by the 'obdurate diversity' of their data, would be well-advised to read Chapter 2. The text is also eminently quotable and I predict that it will launch a thousand examination questions. But the reach, quality and significance of these findings deserve a better fate. The main themes – identities, space and place, leisure and pleasure, class, and post-adolescence and the family – deserve the close attention of politicians, policy-makers and all education professionals who are currently trying to construct a new framework for post-16 learning.

Frank Coffield

Acknowledgements

We should like to express our thanks to all those who made this book possible. The Economic and Social Research Council (ESRC) funded the two studies upon which the book is based: 'Education Markets in the Post-16 Sector of One Urban Locale' (award number L123251006) and 'Choice, Pathways and Transitions: 16–19 Education, Training and (Un)employment in One Urban Locale' (award number R00023726).

We have many other debts. Chris Fox for all her work throughout both studies in transcribing several hundred interviews; Caroline Gill for her calm, reassuring and efficient help with administration; Vikki Charles for her persistence in tracking down and interviewing those young people who were 'difficult to find'; Krzysztof Blusz, Freddie Spitz and Zoe Thompson for their help with interviewing the young people when they were in Year 11; the many members of staff at King's College for reading and providing critical comments on our draft papers; Frank Coffield for his rigorous scrutiny and support of our work; the members of the ESRC Learning Society Programme for their ideas and suggestions as our research developed; Phil Hodkinson for his comments and advice; and to all the others, too numerous to mention, for their expertise and insights. To each of these we offer our grateful thanks.

We may not name the young people, staff and parents whose contributions were the greatest of all. We can only thank anonymously the Head Teachers of Northwark Park and the Pupil Referral Unit for allowing us to conduct the initial fieldwork in their institutions. We are also indebted to the many members of staff in a wide range of institutions, as well as to a small number of parents for their time and thoughtful contributions to our work. Above all, the book rests on the interest and generosity of the young people who patiently worked with us over a period of four years and whose resilience and optimism are an example to us all. To them we express our enormous gratitude.

1   Landscapes of Choice – Horizons for Action

This book is about the complex transitions from compulsory schooling, through the period of post-adolescence, of one small cohort of young people in South London. We describe and analyse the choices and constraints which frame the identities and experiences of these young people as reported by them in a series of narrative interviews conducted over a four-year period 1995–9.

Time and Place

All the young people whose narratives appear in this book were born between 1979 and 1980. Some were born in London to teenage single mothers or to 'new' middle-class professional couples, the first from their families to go to university, struggling to manage a mortgage, two jobs and child care. Some were born in different nation states, such as Somalia, Ethiopia and Bangladesh, and became refugees. Some were born into minority ethnic families and communities who had moved to the UK in the early 1970s from the Gujerat or from Hong Kong, for example. Others were third- and fourth-generation members of communities which had settled in London after the Second World War. All these children and their families eventually settled into the Northwark/Streetley area of South London. Some were housed in post-war council housing estates, some lived in newly-gentrified Victorian terraced houses, some were 'looked after' by the local authority. They all ended up attending Northwark Park Comprehensive School or the local Pupil Referral Unit (PRU) where we first met them in 1995. In a number of ways these young people are 'Thatcher's Children' (Pilcher and Wagg, 1996). They came into the world as she became head of government in the UK. While there is a complex and shifting range of individual circumstances which circumscribe the social and material worlds of these young people, in this first chapter we want to foreground some of the political and economic processes and transformations of the last twenty years which are common to them all. These young people were born at the start of a 'revolutionary' period, which has had very direct consequences for their lives, their choices and their identities: what Desai (1994) calls the 'sheer audacity of Thatcherism' which transformed 'the immediate environment in which ordinary subjects went about their everyday business and never even thought about it' (Desai, 1994, p. 28).

This introductory chapter will provide a brief overview of the politics, economics and society of the lifespan of our research subjects. However we do not describe this historical specificity using theoretical devices like de-industrialization and globalization (Bettis and Stoeker, 1993; Hoogvelt, 1997), critically useful as these may be. The general impact of authoritarian populism and the New Right, of neo-liberal economic policies and deregulated, globalized capital have been fully articulated elsewhere (e.g. Hall and Martin, 1983; Bartlett and Le Grand, 1993; Hutton, 1995) . We focus here on the more immediate consequences of eighteen years of Conservative government for the lives, values and social perspectives of the young people in our study. In other words, we describe the social landscape in which our young people are located. We privilege four inter-related themes which are critical in understanding the context in which their post-16 choices and decisions are made. These four themes provide the border-lines which structure the scope and space, the 'horizons for action' (Hodkinson et al., 1996) of the young people's relationships, opportunities and identities. They are: the rise and spread of the culture of individualism and economics of individualization (Beck, 1992); the intensification of social and economic polarization; issues round consumerism, leisure and identity; and the alleged demise of class politics alongside the ascendancy of new work and labour market identifications.

The Culture of Individualism and Economics of Individualization

'In the space of one generation there have been some radical changes to the typical experiences of young people' (Furlong and Cartmel, 1997, p. 8) and some of the effects of these changes are evident in the extent to which young people now see their decision-making as individual 'choice' rather than the product of structured constraints (Giddens, 1991; Beck, 1992). Crucially here 'individualism' has to be separated from 'individualization'. Giddens (1991) has argued that risk and uncertainty are experienced subjectively and individuals are held more and more accountable for their own survival in a time where change is the only certainty. In the late modern period, the self is constantly engaged in a process of self-construction and reconstruction as part of a contingently reflexive life-time biographical project which responds to new risks and new opportunities. Or as Beck (1992) puts it: 'The individual himself or herself becomes the reproduction unit of the social in the lifeworld' (p. 90). One consequence of these new risks and new opportunities, Giddens argues, is that some of the older certainties and collective identities have weakened. Beck (1992, p. 89) suggests that there is a ' "freeing" relative to status-like social classes'. Contemporary experiences and a diversification of life-styles have replaced older traditional social relationships – this is what Giddens and Beck call individualization; a concept to which we shall return throughout this book.

Beck refers to individualization processes creating new social identities, which in consequence lead to a reconfiguration of social relationships and patterns of social welfare. This is the basis of reflexivity – reflexively organized life-planning which presumes a consideration of risk as a central feature in what Wilkinson (1996, p. 226) calls a 'cash and keys' society. 'Interdependence is turned from being a social process into a process by which we fend for ourselves in an attempt to wrest a living from an asocial environment'.

The culture and ideology of individualism interpenetrates – feeds and is fed by – social changes which encourage greater reflexivity and individualization. Thus, here we want to signal the way in which the political and economic culture of neo-liberalism, of the market, with its stress on individualism, connects with the 'individualization' changes in social identity and social attachments. Working together, the ideology of economic individualism and individualization as a reflexive project of identity-formation, mute and obscure the continuing class-based nature of structural inequalities. 'Class differences and family connections are not really annulled . . . they recede into the background relative to the newly emerging "center" of the biographical life plan' (Beck, 1992, p. 131).

Since the late 1970s, UK policy and practice, in virtually every field of government, have increasingly been dominated by economic liberalism (Gamble, 1994; Ball, 1998). A series of international economic crises and subsequent high levels of inflation and unemployment in the UK of the 1970s and 80s were 'explained' by the Conservative neo-liberals as consequences of too much state intervention, too little space for free-market capitalism and more generally of the 'failure of social democracy' (Kingdom, 1992). The antidote was a return to the common sense of the entrepreneurial, individualist tradition or a 'return to nature' as Kingdom (p. 82) puts it:

> What the Thatcher decade represented was a repudiation of the Party's twentieth-century tradition on economic policy, and an explicit abandonment of the national economy as a proper object of government policy.

Further, through the insertion of micro-economics into the public sector, such as selling public housing stock, allowing choice of school and opting-out of company pension schemes, devolving budgets from Local Education Authorities (LEAs) to schools and from Health Authorities to general practitioners, a culture and a politics of individualism was articulated to underpin what Gamble and Kelly (1996) call the 'new politics of ownership'. A shift from 'a culture of commitment to relative public good to a defence of relative private interest' (Grace, 1994, p. 53) was evident. Key ideas of competitive individualism, that 'It is possible to comprehend the nature of a person without reference to society' (Kingdom, 1992, p. 6); and of the 'freedoms' offered by market egalitarianism, have been sedimented in the national social consciousness for over two decades. A new kind of politics has been interpolated. 'The political subject is henceforth to be an individual whose citizenship is manifested through choice among a variety of options' (Rose, 1992, p. 159). It is not surprising then that the hegemony of 'the cash and keys' society and the '*social surge of individualization*' (Beck, 1992, p. 87) have made their mark upon the beliefs and attitudes of young people who have grown up in Thatcher's Britain. As Hall (1988) points out, a crucial factor in the success of Thatcherism was that its key ideas formed part of a coherent outlook in society.

With the new politics of ownership has come the celebration of individual rights and 'the moral duty of the parents to choose the best for their families. Family thus becomes the private solvent for any imputation of public guilt' (Lloyd, 1996, p. 39). However, some families value more highly or are 'better' at 'choosing' than others and have greater financial and cultural resources to support their children in the post-16 arena, as elsewhere (Ball and Vincent, 1998; Reay and Ball, 1998). Sets of individualized tactics such as moving house, developing church affiliations, skilful networking, paying for costly cross-city travel, etc. are clearly more available to some individuals, families and social groups than to others. Concomitantly, 'bad' choices become a matter of individual responsibility – and 'responsibilitization' of the self (Rose, 1992), an 'instilling of a reflexive hermeneutics' (p. 149), goes hand in hand with the freedom to choose.

In all of the recent major studies of youth transitions from school to work, as with our own, one consistent finding emerges (Bates and Riseborough, 1993; Bynner et al., 1997; Chisholm and Hurrelmann, 1995; Du Bois-Reymond, 1998; Foskett and Hesketh, 1996; Furlong, 1992; Hodkinson et al., 1996). Young people constantly reiterate that they *do* have choices, that luck, hard work and sheer determination are the bases of 'success'. This is what Rose (1992) calls the 'instrumental autonomy' of the 'enterprising self'. That is, 'a calculating self, a self that calculates *about* itself and works *upon* itself in order to better itself' (p. 146). As Rees (see Chapter 10) explains, 'Life is hard. It's no good feeling sorry for yourself'. The young people in our study were most likely to blame themselves for any lack of success, either because of stress or a failure to 'see' their best interests, or competing 'interests', or not enough hard work while they were at school. At the same time, the greater diversity of their life experiences and prolonged and extended opportunities to participate in education and training provision, tended to obscure the structural and material continuities which patterned their 'choices' and life decisions. The young people see themselves as individuals in a meritocratic setting, not as classed or gendered members of an unequal society. This critical and central tension within what Roberts et al. (1994) call 'structured individualism' is a thread which runs through our book and is a key issue to which we return in our final chapter.

Social and Economic Polarization

In many ways our second theme, social and economic polarization, also derives from the economics and practices of individualization and individualism. While discourses of individual responsibility and freedom to 'choose' have been rehearsed repeatedly in the politics and policies of neo-liberal governance over the last twenty years, the 'downside' of the new 'freedoms' of the market and the growth in social polarization has only just begun to be acknowledged (Oppenheim, 1993; Hills, 1995; Hutton, 1995). Hutton (1996) has characterized the UK as the 'thirty, thirty, forty society' where the bottom 60 per cent are 'disadvantaged', 'marginalised' and 'insecure'. He describes a society where 'segmentation of the labour market . . . is sculpting the new and ugly shape of British society' (Hutton, 1995, p.108). His point is that, in the new labour market formations which are emerging, there is a central core of prosperity and security contained within a periphery of part-time, contract workers and those with low skill–no skill credentials or, as Castells, (1998, p. 161) puts it, there is 'a sharp divide between valuable and non-valuable people and locales'.

In these uncertain times, families are likely to struggle to preserve any advantage they may hold in an attempt to reproduce those advantages for their offspring, leading to what the Treasury Report (1999) calls 'the increased concentration of opportunity' (p. 5):

> Over the last twenty years not only has the gap between the richest and the poorest increased, but the amount of movement between income groups has been limited. What is more, damaged life chances perpetuate across the generations.

Rather than a trickle down of wealth, what has actually occurred has been an increase in child poverty and economic polarization (Oppenheim, 1998). According to government statistics a third of all children were living in poverty in 1992–3 (DSS, 1995). Child poverty and other early disruptions to family life tend to have long-term repercussions, as the Treasury Report suggests. While such family disruptions and the 'immediacy of *crisis and sickness*' (Beck, 1992, p. 89) are not unique to urban settings, it is in inner cities that the highest concentrations of the marginalized and dispossessed are to be found. Between 1981 and 1991 'the degree, intensity and extent of poverty increased markedly in Inner London and other large metropolitan areas' (Maden, 1996, p. 20) and 'in the list of England's thirty most deprived areas, all Inner London boroughs are there' (Maden, 1996, p. 21). Six London boroughs are listed in the worst ten areas of deprivation in the UK where deprivation is measured in relation to employment, housing, education credentials, race, crime, lone-caring etc. London is thus a cockpit within which to view, in a concentrated manner, many of the inequities and polarizations arising from contemporary policy-making (Grace, 1978). Poverty, the 'new hybrids between unemployment and employment' (Beck, 1992, p. 89), family stress and other social exclusions (see Chapter 4) distort and disrupt the lives of many young people in transition from youth to young adulthood, and yet this may all be disguised to a degree by the processes of individualization and the superficial homogeneity of youth patterns of consumerism. For some of the young people in our study, poverty and insecurity are a significant part of the contexts in which their choices, identities and 'horizons for action' (Hodkinson et al., 1996) are located.

While we want to acknowledge the specificity of space, region and locale in the ways that choices are negotiated and navigated and thus we highlight the role of the urban as a place marked by acute polarizations in terms of poverty, housing, lifestyle and occupation, somewhat contradictorily, we also want to call attention to the power of the urban in relation to the manufacture of desires and dreams. The density and diversity of the modern 'global city' provides a place where new identities can be forged, where new economies and new cultural formations flourish (Ball et al., 1999). This too, is a point to which we shall return (see Chapters 3 and 10 in particular).

Consumerism, Leisure and Identity

The new identities which young people are busy forging as they make the transition from youth to early adulthood is the third theme of our overview. The current identities of the young people whose narratives are explored in this book cannot simply be understood in terms of the older traditional categories of class or gender. Very few of the young people referred to their social class or gender in any direct manner – although some of the minority ethnic young people saw their race as a key aspect of their identity. Nonetheless, these are 'starting points' which 'limit and condition' what we are and what we do (Craib, 1998). The young people are indeed classed, 'raced' and gendered. But they are also involved in constructing other, not necessarily alternative, identities through their consumption patterns and increasing fetishism in relation to fashion, style, and concern with the body and the self (see Chapter 5).

Youth identities are bounded by and to consumerism and 'the economy of symbolic goods' (Lee, 1993). Young people are what they consume – they consume what they want to be (Polhemus, 1994; Redhead, 1993). In the 'atrium culture' (Ferguson, 1992), lifestyle and identity – or identities – blur. Indeed, Shields (1992) goes as far as to suggest that consumption 'serves in the reconstruction and realignment [of] community around the tactility of the crowd practices and the "tribal" ethos of new urban spaces of consumption' (p. 111). These young people are less likely to vote or engage in politics at any level than the older generations (Bynner, 1994). Indeed, politics seems to them to have little relevance to their lives at all.

However, as always, some are more able than others to participate in the experiential commodities of youth consumption. Going clubbing, drinking, smoking, recreational drugs, fashionable clothing and other life-style accessories do not come cheap (see Chapter 6). Some resort to 'cheaper imitations and look-alikes' (Shields, 1992, p. 100) or rely on 'freebies' from better-placed friends (see Chapter 8). Many young people, in this study as elsewhere, are involved in poorly-paid, part-time, 'flexible' employment (Clywd, 1994; Lavalette, 1996). Indeed, some spend more time in their 'part-time' jobs than they do at their full-time studies – a fact which is sometimes sidelined and ignored by policy-makers keen to expose young people to the rigours and demands of the 'real world of work'. This is very much the underside of the extension of youth and post-adolescent experience.

Work and Labour-Market Identification and 'Learning'

The final theme to rehearse in this chapter addresses the status of work in contemporary society. Occupation, status and identity are inextricably interwoven – we are what we do – and not to work is in many ways to become excluded, a 'non-person'. However, here we want to register two caveats. First, occupational status and work may not be that important in the lives of 'the young'. Indeed, evidence is suggesting that many post-adolescents are trying to 'postpone' or keep their work identities 'on hold' (Clarke, 1999; Du Bois-Reymond, 1998). Other sources of identity and identification deriving from music, fashion and leisure may be more central to how they think about themselves. Second, the fact of occupation may be more important in terms of economic security to specific constituencies; the status of occupation and its interpenetration with identity may well be primarily a middle-class phenomenon. So while the primary concern of youth researchers (e.g. Banks, 1992; Brice Heath and McLaughlin, 1993; Bynner et al., 1997; Ferri and Smith, 1997), 'remains the economic transition from school into the labour market and the unequal occupational opportunities that befall young people as they progress towards adulthood' (MacDonald, 1997, p. 20), they may be mis-reading the primary concerns of young people themselves. Nonetheless, in our society where work is central to inclusion, access to work and concomitantly education and training provide the major 'contexts of opportunity' through which to tackle what Mandelson (1997) has called 'the scourge and waste of social exclusion'.

The relationships between work and identity play around and upon young people in another more general sense. That is, through the 'rhetoric and reification' of a continuing demand for an upskilled, technologically literate and flexible work force which will contribute towards national economic competitiveness. This rhetoric is embedded in policy condensates like 'life-long learning' and the 'learning society'. In respect to this, the current Labour administration display some distinct continuities with policies developed by the previous Conservative governments (Cockett, 1996). On the one hand, 'The philosophy underlying the proposed reforms is perhaps not as focused on market solutions or as ideologically driven as that of the previous administration' (Bartlett et al., 1998, p. 1). On the other, there is perhaps an even closer connection and a blurring of distinctions between education and the needs of the labour market – the point of the first being to service the requirements of the second (Ball, 1999). White's (1998) discussion of the Third Way represents this as 'employment-centred social policy' – 'a prime example of the dual commitment to the values of opportunity and personal responsibility' (p. 6). (Again there are links back to our previous discussion of 'individualization' and 'responsibilitization'.) In effect, social and educational policies are collapsed into economic and industrial policy. As David Blunkett explained in his 1998 Labour Party Conference Speech:

> We recognise the very real challenge facing manufacturing industry in this country and the way in which we need to support and work with them for

skilling and re-skilling for what Tony Blair has described as the best economic policy we have – 'education'. (p. 5)

Within all this 'learning' and the 'learning society' is a new and powerful normativity, a moral economy – the government Reports and Papers which address post-16 education and training seek to establish a 'new culture of learning' (DfEE 1999, p. 1). Learners are encouraged to see themselves as a constantly renewable skill resource, the acquisition of skills ensuring 'national competitiveness and personal prosperity' (DfEE 1999, p. 1); 'people are to be treated first and foremost in relation to their potential contribution to the economy', as Coffield (1999, p. 9) puts it (see Chapters 2 and 4 for further discussion). In a sense you are your skills. This is strongly represented, in one respect, in the commonly held view, right across our study sample, that qualifications are the key to obtaining and progressing in work. However, many of those outside of education and training post-16, the 'others' to the 'learning society', carry with them 'learner identities' (Rees et al., 1997) often severely damaged by their experiences in compulsory education. More learning is the last thing they are interested in (see Chapters 5, 8 and 10).[1]

'Landscapes of Choice – Horizons for Action'

Just as the understanding of a society requires a metanarrative, so the understanding of an individual self, identity or life requires that it be inserted in that metanarrative.

(Craib, 1998, p. 28).

The purpose of this first chapter has been to describe some of the metanarratives or 'borderlines' which surround and 'make up' the young people in transition, in our study. The same 'batterings of world history' (Mann, 1995, p. 53) exert pressure on them all, but do so differentially, producing very different 'horizons for action'. It is within and across this social, economic and political landscape that the young people 'choose', 'plan' and construct their narratives. In the following chapters it is these narratives which are foregrounded.

Notes

1   However, it may be that within at least some parts of the 'new urban economies' referred to above, it is 'who you are' and 'what you can do' rather than what qualifications you hold that matter in getting work (see Chapters 6 and 10).

2 The Research and the Young People: Working in the 'Ruins'

In this chapter, and using pseudonyms throughout, we introduce our research sample and the research setting – the local education, training and employment market – and discuss some of the issues and difficulties arising from the conduct of the study. We also clarify the style and stance of our writing and interpretation of data. The book you are now reading represents one of several possible ways in which our research could be written up. It constitutes the outcome of a variety of compromises and involves 'a deflation of pretences' (Wexler, 1992, p. 1) and at times a resistance of resolution. Most obviously it does not do anything like full justice to the sheer volume of data we collected. Only some aspects of the lives of some of our respondents are represented here. We have written about others in different ways elsewhere but there is considerable scope for further work on and with our data base. We deal only in passing with the providers' perspectives on the post-16 education and training market. (See below for a fuller outline of the research design.) As indicated in the previous chapter, the general backdrop against which our study is set is the ambition of government to increase participation in post-compulsory education as a means of producing a globally competitive, high-skills economy, what is referred to as the 'learning society'.

Despite the obvious attractions of human capital thinking, as educational researchers we have a number of difficulties with this calculative, instrumental, abstract and generalized conception of learning. It seems to fail to recognize the complex interactional, intellectual and situated processes that constitute learning; it is socially disembedded. (See Schuller and Field, 1998 for a fuller discussion of the weaknesses of human capital theory.) Apple (1986, p. 5) offers a different view of learning:

> We do not confront abstract 'learners' . . . instead, we see specific classed, raced and gendered subjects, people whose biographies are intimately linked to the economic, political and ideological trajectories of their families and communities, to the political economies of their neighbourhoods.

Our research is much closer to Apple's conception of learning than that of the UK government. In our view, learning is about social biographies and identities rather than human capital. It is about self-realization rather than futurity. It is about meaning and difference, about struggle, disappointment and imagination. It is 'located in social participation as well as in the heads of individuals' (Coffield, 1999, p. 17). The young people in our study are complexly raced, classed and gendered and we have tried to retain and reflect this complexity, as far as we are able, in our writing about them. We also work to retain in our analysis and interpretation of data, the embeddedness of these young people in their families and communities and within the local political economy of Northwark (and London more generally).

The Setting

The local and London labour markets are a key backdrop to the choices and opportunities available to these young people. Crucially, in London in the 1980s and 1990s:

> The expanding sectors of employment differ from the contracting sectors in several important respects. In particular they have a much lower proportion of male jobs and fewer jobs open to workers lacking formal qualifications (except in private consumer services . . .). These growing sectors are short of the skilled and supervisory manual jobs on which males lacking school-level qualifications have traditionally relied to provide more secure and reasonably paid jobs.
>
> (Gordon and Sassen, 1992, p. 110)

A polarized economy has developed. As Lash and Urry (1994) indicate, there has been 'a dualist pattern of employment change, of the growth of professional–managerial jobs on the one hand, and of a large McDonaldized workforce on the other. The former in part produces the latter . . .' (p. 196). The young people are themselves located differently in relation to these sub-economies; some are headed for the former and others for the latter. Some could go either way. Some are, for the time being, out of employment or education altogether (see below). However, a point we reiterate in this account is that the stories we present are unfinished and open-ended. Essentially, they represent snapshots of lives in progress.

In April 1995, a partnership consisting of the local Training and Enterprise Council (TEC), Northwark, Mersley and Burbley was formed to provide an all-age careers guidance and employer support service. The 1995 census of employment showed that, although the area had 13,879 firms employing 201,078 people, some 90 per cent of these companies employed fewer than twenty five people and over 60 per cent employed between one and four people. In common with the rest of the country, the manufacturing and construction sectors had shrunk considerably during the 1980s although in Mersley, manufacturing was still comparatively strong. In the Northwark area, the main employment opportunities were in: business and finance (34 per cent), retail and distribution (24 per cent), health and social work (9 per cent), other social, personnel work (8 per cent), hotels and restaurants (7 per cent), manufacturing (5 per cent), transport and storage (5 per cent), education (4 per cent), construction (3 per cent) and public administration, social security (1 per cent).

In 1996, 1,704 students completed Year 11 in Northwark (see Appendix 1, Table A1.1). Of these, 74 per cent remained in full-time education, a figure which had remained consistent over the previous three years. Proportionately more students stayed in full-time education than nationally (68 per cent) (see Appendix 1, Table A1.2) and in the London area generally (73 per cent). Six percent more females than males remained in education, up from 3 per cent the previous year. As in the two previous years, fewer white students remained in education than students from other ethnic groups and this corresponded with the national situation. Of those staying in full-time education, 60 per cent remained in school and 40 per cent moved to college. There was a decline of 2 per cent in the number of young people going into work and training which appeared to be in line with the national trend.

Our local market extends over an inner-city/suburban setting based on the Northwark area of London (see also Gewirtz et al., 1995) and is defined in terms of the expressed interests and choices of a cohort of Year 11 students from one comprehensive school – Northwark Park – and one Pupil Referral Unit (PRU) (see below).

Northwark Park school lies at the boundary between Northwark and Streetley LEAs. The former comes in the top thirty nationally in the Department of the Environment's rank order Index of Local Authority Deprivation, while the latter is in the top twelve – of approximately 300. In fact, this particular local, lived market extends to encompass several different, small LEAs that organize their schools' provision in a variety of ways. The main players in this market are two 11–18 secondary schools, five Further Education (FE) colleges, a tertiary college, a denominational sixth form college and two TECs. Three other FE colleges, another sixth form college, and an 11–18 denominational school impinge upon the margins of this market (see Figure 2.1). We have engaged with the main groups of actors in this market setting: providers, that is, those offering education, training or employment (48 interviews); intermediaries, that is, those offering advice or support, including teachers, careers officers and parents (46 interviews); and 'consumers' or choosers, that is, the young people themselves (244 interviews).

The schools and colleges (FE, sixth form and tertiary) in our local market have distinct, widely shared ethnic and class identities based on a combination of location and patterns of attendance. They are part of a complex, social and ethnic geography which reflects what Keith and Cross (1993, p. 26) refer to as 'the city as, in part, a nested series of overlapping locales through which the different processes and scales of racialisation [and we would add social class] are realised'. The locations and identities of the colleges interact with complex raced and classed choosing to produce a movement to the south and west of students, both black and white, away from the inner-city schools (like Northwark Park) and colleges into the suburbs (cf. OECD, 1994). In some of the suburban FE colleges this produces a marked mismatch between the student population and the local

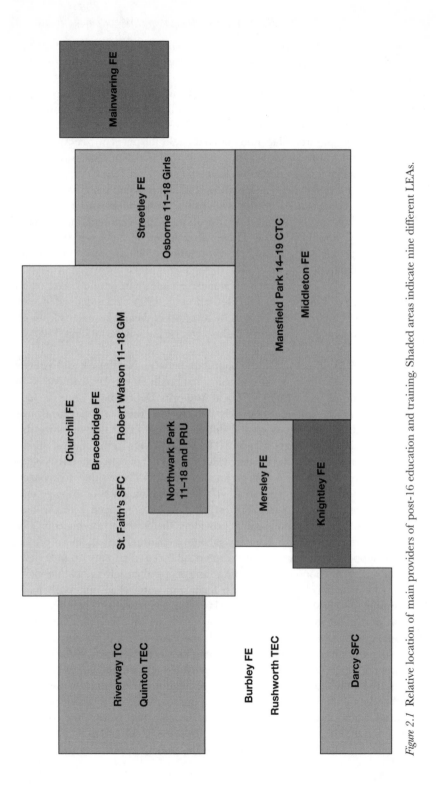

Figure 2.1 Relative location of main providers of post-16 education and training. Shaded areas indicate nine different LEAs.

residential population: Northwark is approximately 80 per cent white whereas Bracebridge College has approximately 80 per cent minority ethnic students; Mersley has a minority ethnic population of 16 per cent whereas Mersley College has 50 per cent minority ethnic students. This drift has knock-on effects for the reputation of the receiving colleges which drives local choices further south and west. However, these patterns of choice rest, in part, upon a resilient misperception of the actuality of the suburban settings.

> You would hardly find a student from say, Madely, that goes all the way East to Streetley College. They would be an extremely rare bird. That is partly to do with academic standards and it is partly to do with objective standards. It is also partly to do with perceived standards, class and other things. Burbley is seen as a much more middle-class and, quite frankly, much whiter college. So a lot of white, middle-class parents want their kids to go there, instead of Bracebridge College. So there are class issues, race issues even in the competition between Colleges. There is also the perception that Burbley is less inner city, more rural. But that, as far as the college is concerned, is a misconception because it's right in the middle of the town and surrounded by high rise buildings.
>
> (Marketing Manager, Burbley College; white, male)

> I think we probably outdo the number of black students with regards to comparison with Burbley itself because, as you know, Burbley is a very quiet, middle-class area. It would probably be that we have more black youngsters than the population as a whole. So they have come from outside. We have got a lot of youngsters from outside Burbley. If you go to Bracebridge, where I have been once or twice, you see a lot more black youngsters there than the population would suggest. But you expect that, you know, because they take students from Streetley and Studley.
>
> (Marketing Manager, Burbley College; white, male)

Overall, the market presented here can be characterized in a variety of ways. It might well be thought of, as one respondent described it, as a 'cut-throat' market (Deputy Head of Faculty/Bracebridge), or put another way, from the point of view of the providers: 'it's grow or die' (Student Counsellor, Bracebridge). This cut-throat quality, which is generated in part by the proximity of multiple providers, in part by the entry of new players and in good measure by the FE funding regime, is evidenced in a variety of ways in the market behaviour of, and relationships between, providers. Markets reward shrewdness rather than principle, and privilege the values of competition over professional values (Gewirtz, 1993; Ball et al., 1997; Ball, 1998).

> Look, it's dog eat dog nowadays in Northwark. We'll take them on inter-mediate (GNVQ) courses even if we know they are not up to it because if we don't, someone else will. . . . And we know they will drop off. So we

encourage them to transfer routes and we are providing strong pastoral support to ensure that we retain them for a second bite at the apple. We've got to hold our numbers, you know [laughs].

(FE college tutor)

Education markets, like other markets, are driven by self-interest. As one respondent explained: 'the College cannot afford to take a moral stance' (Deputy Head of Faculty, Bracebridge). On the one side is the self-interest of consumers who choose and on the other, that of producers aiming to thrive, or at least survive (Gewirtz et al., 1995). The cut-throat quality and the values of competition increasingly in play in this market encourage and make possible a particular variety of actions and tactics. Various respondents identified new forms of inter-institutional behaviour emerging in the context of market relations (Ball et al., 1997). Northwark Park is itself a player in these competitive relations, seeking to retain as many as possible 'good' students in its sixth form in order to maximize income and retain its 11–18 status (see Chapter 6).

The Young People

Our study is small-scale, intensive, multi-dimensional and longitudinal. Our original sample comprised a total of 110 students: 81 from Northwark Park, an 11–18, mixed comprehensive school and 29 from the local PRU. In the Autumn term of Year 11 these students completed a questionnaire outlining their interests, ambitions and tentative intentions for the following academic year. An analysis of this information allowed us to select a smaller group of students for in-depth study. This sub-sample was constituted to represent the range of Northwark Park students in terms of sex, social class, academic attainment, 'ethnicity', and destinations and routes from school to work. It included some young people who had already opted out of formal education. To an extent, the attendance of the PRU students determined their inclusion in the study. Some were on roll but did not attend, others 'disappeared' after a few sessions and, despite the efforts of teachers and education welfare officers (EWOs), were unreachable. Others were fairly regular attenders and it was mainly, although not exclusively, these who formed the sub-sample.

The sub-sample consisted of 59 young people: 42 from the school and 17 from the PRU. (Appendix 2, Table A2.1 presents details of the school career and family of each member of the sub-sample. Appendix 2, Table A2.2 is a summary of the ethnicities of the sub-sample.) They were interviewed once in each of the Spring and Summer terms of Year 11 (1996) and at some point in their first year post-16 (1996–7) and again at two or three points in the second and third years (1997–9). You will notice that the numbers of young people presented in the tables below vary somewhat. This variation relates to the problems we have had in maintaining contact with some of the sample. In the second phase of our study Vikki Charles was employed specifically to trace and interview those young people who moved, left home or otherwise disappeared for periods of time. She proved to be a very effective 'tracer' and at the time of writing we are in contact with 54 of the original 59.

In this book, 24 of the study sample are represented: 16 females and 8 males; 9 minority ethnic young people; 1 refugee; 4 who have been looked-after by the local authority; 7 from one-parent families or having no parents; 19 from Northwark Park and 5 from the PRU.

One of the difficulties we have had in constructing our various accounts of the research is that of communicating a sense of the diversity and dynamism of the cohort (see below). At different points over time the pattern of destinations or routes within the cohort varies considerably. Career decisions are often unstable or transitory in nature and not predictable. 'The future of a career trajectory is partly unknown' (Hodkinson et al., 1996, p. 4). The degree of instability and unpredictability varies across the cohort with most stability evident within the A-level/university route. This posed problems for data collection and analysis. There was no guarantee that our interviews would coincide with 'turning points' or key decision-making moments. In many cases our interviews, especially the school-based ones, were full of doubts and indecisions, changes of mind, vague possibilities. For those young people whose preferred option was, or would have been, work and a wage, their uncertainties are a product or symptom of their 'liminality' (Bettis, 1996). They realize only too well the lack of 'good' job opportunities in the locality but their damaged 'learner identity' makes more education seem like an impossible or unpalatable option. These doubts and uncertainties are also evident in the actual trajectories of many of the students – courses started and dropped, jobs found and lost, training programmes begun and interrupted.

We have tried to convey something of this instability in a time series of destinations for the cohort as a whole and in some of the individual narratives presented. Table 1.3, in Appendix 1, shows a summary of the 'starting points' of the young people post-16 (1996). Appendix 2, Table 2.3, shows their domestic careers (Wallace, 1987) at that time. Tables 2.1 and 2.4 in Appendix 2 summarize their career and domestic pathways respectively at the end of the following June 1997. Tables 2.5 and 2.6 again summarize these pathways some eleven months later, at the end of May 1998. Table 2.7 shows the self-described ethnicity, career and domestic pathways of 50 of the original 59 and Tables 2.8 and 2.9 summarize these career and domestic routes in February 1999. Tables 2.17 contains details of the same information eight months later, October 1999, and Table 2.18 has a summary of their domestic pathways at that time. It is not possible in these tables to show the amount of movement across categories between census points. Furthermore, although numbers within categories may appear relatively stable from one count to another, it is not always the same people who make up the numbers. For example, of the 50 who commenced employment or a course of study in September 1996 only 29 were in the same employment or had completed or were still on course in June 1997. Of the 11 who commenced Network Training at that time, only one completed it and of the seven who started work when they left school at 16, only one was in the same employment one year later.

Table 2.1 Summary of career pathways, June 1997

Career pathways	Females	%	Males	%	Totals	%
	32	54	27	46	59	100
A-Level	8	25	4	15	12	20
GNVQ Advanced	1	3	0	0	1	2
GNVQ Intermediate	5	16	2	7	7	12
GNVQ Foundation	4	13	5	19	9	15
BTEC	1	3	0	0	1	2
GCSE re-sits	1	3	0	0	1	2
NVQ Level 2	4	13	2	7	6	10
NVQ Level 1	3	9	4	15	7	12
Employed	3	9	2	7	5	8
Not in paid employment	2	6	5	19	7	12
Unknown	0	0	3	11	3	5
Totals	32	101	27	100	59	100

In the following academic year, 1997–8 there were 39 starters and 27 finishers in the same job or course. Everything suggests that the instability will continue as the young people change jobs, leave and re-enter further and higher education, take on family commitments, etc.

One of the themes that weaves through the substantive chapters which follow is related to the dependency, support and obligation which are invested in the relations between the young people and their families. By the age of 19, 27 of the 50 were still living with their parents (see Appendix Tables A2.3, A2.4, A2.9 and A2.18). Several of the young people formed relationships and moved in with their partners, only to return home again when the relationship had run its course. In six cases, young men have been accepted into young women's family homes by parent(s) unwilling to allow their daughter to leave home to live with her partner. To date, no young woman has left home to live with her partner's family.

Interpretation and Writing

Our various attempts at analysis and interpretation have been continually confronted by the obdurate diversity of our data. That diversity refers both to the variety of trajectories and positions occupied by the young people in the study as well as to the range of data, over time and across topics, amassed for each of the young people. As indicated, all have been interviewed three, most four times, many five or six times over a period of almost four years and the accounts generated are 'complex narrative achievements' (MacLure, 1995, p. 16). We have also interviewed 17 parents. The interviews have branched out from work and education choices in the first instance, to cover family lives, relationships, sexuality, finance, health, religion, politics, leisure, music and drugs.

Our analysis has been in Glaser and Strauss' (1967) terms 'ever-developing' (p. 32); the 'joint collection, coding and analysis of data is the underlying operation' (p. 41). As the outcome of this process, the substantive chapters of the book

Table 2.2 Summary of career pathways, October 1999

Career pathways	Females	%	Males	%	Totals	%
	27	54	23	46	50	100
Higher Education	4	15	5	22	9	18
Full-time employment	11	41	7	30	18	36
Part-time employment	1	4	3	13	4	8
Not in paid employment	11	41	6	26	17	34
Unknown	0	0	2	9	2	4
Total	27	101	23	100	50	100

are written around 'analytic sets' of young people. This is a device we have adopted as a way of representing, analysing and interpreting data. It seems to work. It blends fairly detailed narratives with a degree of conceptual focus. That means that the narratives are selective in relation to points of comparison and contrast between the young people in each set. The stories in each case are not complete or exhaustive but focused on themes and points of comparison. Each set addresses a range of issues via patterns of similarity and difference identified in the narratives elicited from the young people. Thus, the emphasis is upon themes which are picked up within and between the sets. This allows us to do some conceptual development work and to generate theoretical descriptions. One of the tasks we have set ourselves is to find and develop a 'language of description' for representing and interpreting this diversity of lives. This language draws on existing theory, other research and our own home-grown conceptualization work – which rests upon the disciplines of data coding (Strauss, 1987). Each of the sets provides the opportunity to highlight specific concepts and life-experiences but we are not suggesting that the groupings are mutually exclusive or that the allocation of young people to the sets is simple or absolute – one young person, Lucy, appears in two of the sets. There are some themes and concepts which are generic and recur and some of the distinctions between young people are very fine indeed. The presentation is thus heuristic, a tropic device which has weaknesses as well as strengths. We want to achieve a kind of analysis which is subtle and flexible. That is to say, the groupings of young people, as represented in the sets presented below, are not intended to essentialize them. To be clear, the sets are not categories or types. Indeed, they are very much a retreat from such a style of analysis. In other publications we have used other tactics and devices for data presentation and interpretation, none of which we were entirely satisfied with (e.g. Macrae et al., 1997; Ball et al., 1999). We have been trying out forms of presentation and representation, but do not claim any erasure of authorial conventionality (see Chapter 11). The problems of analysis and presentation were also exacerbated by the fluidity, change and instability of the life courses of many of the young people, and the processes of their 'growing up' – they have changed, emotionally and physically in the course of the research – some are literally unrecognizable from the young people we first met at school. They are not the same people they were when we started the research. Alongside the processes of individual maturation and change, the policy context is also changing; for example, change of government, the introduction of the New Deal, new arrangements for co-operation among providers. The researchers' relationships with the young people have also changed overtime. We are not the same people we were when we started the study. All this is very different from the snapshots of lives and learning presented in many other studies.

Some of the difficulties we have faced in interpretation and representation were created by us, inasmuch as there is a number of 'attitudes' of writing that we have hoped to avoid – not always successfully. For example, primarily and particularly, we wanted to avoid either portraying the young people as simply victims of their circumstances or pathologizing – 'othering' – them. Our interpretations suggest a sense of struggle or creativity within the sample – sometimes 'making out', sometimes just 'getting by' (McCrone, 1994) but not just giving in. Not all the young people are successful in their struggles, some may be seen as leading sad, sometimes desperate lives but different sorts of purposefulness are apparent throughout. We try to convey this, and the diversity of the sample itself and young people generally, while not losing sight of underlying and persistent patterns of difference or inequality. Thus, we do not assert or celebrate diversity for its own sake; in a sense, quite the opposite. We want to examine and communicate the continuing importance of social class and race and gender differences but also their changing bases in time and space. The use of and opportunities of space are themselves a basis for differentiation and inequality within the research group. The young people in our sample inhabit a number of different 'socioscapes' – 'networks of social relations of very different intensity, spanning widely different territorial extents' (Albrow, 1997, p. 51) (see Chapter 8).

We also increasingly felt it necessary to eschew the overly simplistic characterizations of young people evident in policy documents: as individual, rational calculators – that is, human capitalists. While some instrumentalism and economic rationalism is strongly apparent, this is unevenly distributed across the sample as the 'making out'/'getting by' distinction suggests. While some of these young people are clearly 'planners', others are stridently avoiding the future – either unwilling or feeling unable to contemplate the longer term. Furthermore, the decisions and strategies of those who plan do not appear to be solely or even primarily related to the calculation of economic returns. These also have to be understood as 'investments in the self' – part of a process of identity formation. More generally we need to be aware of Weber's warnings about the difference between formal and substantive rationality, and his point that 'the application of rational calculation to the furtherance of definite goals or values is problematic' (Giddens, 1971, p. 184). Hodkinson et al.'s (1996) concept of 'pragmatic rationality' is a much more useful one (see Chapter 11). This may be related to a further point of difference from policy discourses about youth. As noted already, the majority of our sample of young people continue to be part of, and dependent upon and obligated to, their families. The idea of a straightforward youth–adulthood transition is now too simple, too crude. These are clearly 'post-adolescents'; post-adolescence is what Zinneker (1990, p. 28) calls a 'new institutionalised stage'. Thus, 'adolescence is being extended and parental responsibility prolonged' (Brannen, 1996, p. 115).

Generally, we are attempting to represent these young people as rounded and socially embedded characters. Our data allow us to do that to an extent but equally we cannot pretend to be able to construct holistic accounts of them. We have only glimpses into complex lives: they select, revise and re-order their experiences in interviews and then we select, re-order and interpret these experiences in our analytic work. Our agenda is not theirs: 'entering other people's lives and representing their stories is far more complex than many assume' (Larson, 1997, p. 469). There is a fine and very difficult balance to be sought between abstract interpretation and conceptualization and the retention of 'authentic' meanings. We have had many squabbles and differences within the team over the 'meaning' of some of our transcript materials – often a very constructive process. We 'read' the transcripts differently and have different sorts of emotional responses to them. In some cases our interpretations and understanding were informed by personal knowledge of and relationships with the young people. There is no 'obviousness' to the interpretation of these lives (see Hodkinson, 1999).

Our interview procedures and our interactions with the young people also changed over time. While all interviews were based on *aides-memoire*, those conducted when the young people were still at school were more prescriptive than the later ones. In these early interviews we, rather than the young people, were defining both content and coverage of issues (in order to collect basic information) with the result that some of the topics which interested us, failed to capture the imagination of some of the young people. Several young men were particularly monosyllabic. Our agenda constructed them as having nothing to say. The later interviews, however, were more open-ended and the vast majority of the young people were extremely co-operative and able to talk fluently on a wide range of topics relevant to their lives. Not infrequently, they introduced issues which we might not have considered and we were then able to explore these with other young people in subsequent interviews.

After they left school, most interviews were conducted in the family home. On occasions this could be inhibiting, especially when a parent, sibling or partner was around. It was difficult, and often impossible, to broach certain topics (for example, some aspects of the young person's social life), when other family members were around. Some interviews took place in the family sitting room where the television was being watched by friends and/or siblings of the young person. Sometimes, family and friends joined in the interview, sometimes they ignored us and carried on their own conversations. It never felt appropriate to ask if we could move to another room. Interviews were also carried out in cafes, restaurants, in the street, at bus stops and in leisure centres. Six people were involved at various stages in the interviewing of the young people: Sheila Macrae and Meg Maguire did most, but Vikki Charles, Krystof Blusz, Fred Spitz and Zoe Thompson also did some.

It may have achieved the status of a truism but it is probably worth restating here that we do not simply see the interview transcripts as 'voiced' or 'expressed' from a singular essential identity. Rather, we take it that the self is discursively and interactively constituted. These narratives are self-constructions which are not merely representational, but also conventionally and unconventionally per-formative. We might see the interviews working – for some young people – as 'technologies of the self', offering the possibility 'of no longer being, doing or thinking what we are, do or think' (Rabinow, 1987, p. 46). Furthermore, we remain aware that, to paraphrase Foucault, these interviews may be 'a space into which the speaking subject constantly disappears' (Foucault, 1986, p. 102). Even in the simplest sense, these young people live 'other' lives at other times, and these are only partly accounted for in these 'texts' (cf. Macrae and Maguire, 1999). We have access to only part of who they are, might be, or might become.

There is a complex and difficult set of ethical issues involved in this research and its writing; we are not referring just to the ethics of representation. The more that the young people we interviewed came to trust us, the more frank they became about their lives and behaviours – although we tried to maintain boundaries. Some of these behaviours were technically illegal or potentially dangerous. Some disclosures raised issues which needed addressing in practical ways. We have given advice and provided information when it seemed appropriate – although the 'right' thing to do was not always clear. We have tried to make sure that the young people knew what we were doing with their 'talk' – to maintain an informed consent – although, from their comments, it was not always clear to us that they understood what they were consenting to. We have certainly edited out the more indiscreet or potentially damaging or salacious of the 'revelations' elicited. Furthermore, in addition to using pseudonyms, changes have been made to some details of the young people's lives in an attempt to preserve anonymity.

Generally within our interpretative work we intend to relate these individual lives and struggles to the changing socio-economic context, as Wright-Mills puts it: 'to grasp history and biography and the relations between the two in society' (Wright-Mills, 1970, p. 12); 'to understand the larger historical scene in terms of its meaning for the inner life and the external career of a variety of individuals' (p. 11). For example, de-industrialization on the one hand, and the expansion of the service economy on the other, and the consequent changes in the class structure and labour market in London as a global city, are key contextual features of and conditions within which these young people are constructing their lives and forging their identities. Harloe and Fainstein (1992) employ the term 'global city', referring to London, New York and Tokyo, as shorthand for a set of complex economic changes 'that really marks them off from other large cities and links their evolving urban and social structures most closely to changes in global economic organisation and its consequences' (p. 245). (See also Ball et al., 1999.) However, the relevance of these key contextual features is not the same for all young people, as we try to demonstrate.

The last point to be made about our interpretative work and writing relates to the previous one. We want our interpretations of these young people's lives to be clearly located within the particularity of both the 'local' and the London (Ball et al., 1999). The particularities of London as a global city are often taken to stand for trends or patterns that can be spoken of and applied generally to the whole of the UK. Local and regional idiosyncrasies are ignored. Here we want to recognize the specificity of London and the 'opportunities' it offers for new kinds of work for young people. However, the city is a contradictory space in many senses. It consists of several interpenetrating economies old and new, varieties of ethnoscapes (see Chapter 8), changing patterns of opportunity and constraint. These are specific to global cities like London, but may well be reflected, perhaps on a smaller scale, in many other Western urban settings. In attending to these new economies we are not intending to underplay or displace the effects of de-industrialization and its human consequences either generally or in relation to the specific setting of our research. Nevertheless, it is important to see the changing relationships between the urban economy and urban education in all their aspects. To reiterate, the city is not available to all young people in the same way and the new urban economies produce new inequalities.

Concepts and Choices

The choices made by the young people in our study, with the exception perhaps of those going on to A-levels and higher education, bear only a passing resemblance to the uni-dimensional, calculative, individualistic, consumer rationalism which predominates in official texts. Our analysis of these choices identifies patterns and points of significance similar in many respects to those explored by Hodkinson et al. (1996) and we have made use here of their career decision-making model and, like them, we also find Bourdieu's concepts of habitus and cultural capital key analytic resources. However, our sample offers a broader cross-section of post-16 routes (their research concentrated upon the Training Credits system and employs in-depth case-studies of 16 young people). The work of Rees et al. (1997) has also been a conceptual resource in the interpretation of data, particularly the idea of 'learner identities'. And, more generally, we need to acknowledge the central importance of identities formation within the transitions with which we are concerned and draw upon a range of recent writing on the unstable and multiple nature of identity – without acceptance of which, we cannot understand 'the fragility, permeability, difficulty, agony and yet poetic energy of most human lives which result from attempting to live with and through the contradictory combi-nation of a variety of possible social classifications, possible identities' (Corrigan, 1990, p. 114). We take it as axiomatic that: 'identities are always relational and incomplete, in process' (Grossberg, 1996, p. 89). This is all the more so, given the age of our research group. Again, related to identity and career decision-making, we have made use of Bettis' (1996) concept of liminality. Also Wallace's (1987) discussion of domestic careers has been influential, as has Irwin's (1995) work on dependence and obligation. Bourdieu's (1986) work on 'distinction' is also woven into and through the text as we link 'choice-making' to the practical mastery of distributions – the competencies of attribution and classification, or 'a "sense of one's place" guiding the occupants of a given place in social space towards the social positions adjusted to their properties' (p. 466).

Our attempts at explanation in this study draw upon a dual epistemology. On the one hand, in a Weberian mode we are striving for an *understanding* of the decisions made by young people. This rests upon an attempt to explore and represent the intelligibility of action descriptions. In these terms Boudon's (1982) criterion for explanatory adequacy is pertinent; he observes that 'the description of another's actions proposed by the researcher is only really satisfactory when he [sic] can convince his reader that, in the same circumstances, he would have acted in the same way' (pp. 145–6). On the other hand, set against this methodological individualism, we see the lives and actions of young people bounded and influenced by real, but changing, social structures (positions, distributions, relationships and accesses) and patterned by socialized frames of perception and thought. We do not see social reality as reducible to individual action and hope to avoid what Boudon calls the 'fallacy of composition': what is possible for some individuals is not possible for all! The use of 'habitus' in particular allows for movement between these positions (see Hodkinson et al., 1996 and Ball, 1998). But there is also a paradox which runs through our analysis. For while habitus gives emphasis to the reproduction of practical consciousness, dispositions and 'already realised ends' (Bourdieu, 1986), we shall also be highlighting some young people whose consciousness and self-identity is 'a reflexively organised behaviour' (Giddens, 1991, p. 5). As Giddens puts it: 'The more tradition loses hold, . . . the more individuals are forced to negotiate lifestyle choices among a diversity of options' (p. 5). We will return to this paradox at various points in the substantive chapters and again in the conclusion. While we find Giddens' concepts helpful in some respects, we are also critical of them and end up in an analytic position somewhat different from that of Giddens, as signalled in our use of the term 'structured individualism'. Reporting on transitions from school to employment in England and Germany, Roberts et al. (1994) conclude that:

> The young people's own experiences did not normally make them feel that there were rigid boundaries to their opportunities. In any case breaching the boundaries was improbable rather than impossible and the boundaries were not the same for everyone. Like the young people's careers, the bounds of their probable opportunities were individualised and varied according to the multitude of configurations created by different combinations of family and educational backgrounds, gender, place of residence, and prior training and employment experience (p. 51).

In other words, the 'diversity of options' referred to by Giddens (1971) is not the same for all (see Chapter 3). Some boundaries and boundary markers remain as very powerful constraints upon opportunity and identity. Reflexivity will get you only so far if you leave school without qualifications. Racism, sexism and homophobia also operate to circumscribe the 'diversity of options' available to some young people.

Reading this Book

The chapters which follow are not presented in a particular sequence and can be read in any order. They have some common themes and there are various cross-references but some call up specialized literatures; for example Chapter 9 on teenage pregnancies and Chapter 4 on social exclusion. Some of the published and conference papers from the project, which are referred to in the text, cover different ground and refer to other young people from the study sample. We are, at the time of writing, continuing to collect data about these young people, and will write about them further. We may come to see them differently and write about them differently!

3 Making and Escaping Identity
Amma and Michael, Rena and Delisha

One of the tensions which runs through this account of post-16 'choice' is that between a view of the individual as 'thoroughly social and cultural but at the same time unique and creative' (Branson, 1991, p. 93). On the one hand there is the danger of 'a process of infinite reduction' (Jones and Wallace, 1992, p. 14) and on the other, the danger of reifying complexity and re-articulating structural simplicities. We want to recognize both the individual construction of social identities and the different structural possibilities and conditions for such construction. Identity needs to be understood as something 'created in response to a set of circumstances' (Tsolidis, 1996, p. 276), as forged out of categories of perception and acquired dispositions, and as the product of the logic of individuality (Grossberg, 1996, p. 97). That is, the individual is seen as both 'cause and effect' as 'both subject and subjected' (Grossberg, 1996). This recognizes that, 'it may be that subjectivity as a value necessary for life is also unequally distributed' (Grossberg, 1996, p. 99). The social, personal and material resources needed to live a reflexively organized biography are not equally available to all. The 'new democracy' of individualization which 'compels' people 'for the sake of their own material survival to make themselves the centre of their own planning and conduct of life' (Beck, 1992, p. 88), may rest upon an exaggeration of the extent to which 'the traditional parameters of industrial society: class-culture and consciousness, gender and family roles . . .' (p. 87) have been 'dissolved'.

Nonetheless, this chapter gives particular attention to the resistance to aspects of identity, to the displacement of traditionalism and essentialism. The emphasis is upon the making and re-making of identity, and the tensions between reflexive individualism and culture, family and community. Identity is socially and culturally 'located' in time and space and inflected by rejection, displacement and desire. Post-16 'choices' are bound up with the expression and suppression of identities. These choices are one aspect, of varying importance, of the sort of person you may become.

There are four young people in this 'set'; Amma, Michael, Rena and Delisha. Three of the four narratives illustrate the instabilities which marked the 'careership' of many of the young people in our sample. Each of them, in different ways, illustrates the contingencies and conflicts which are inherent in such careership

Table 3.1 Amma, Michael, Rena and Delisha

Amma	Michael	Rena	Delisha
Single parent mother, hotel worker	Single parent mother, unemployed	Mother, factory worker father, driver	Mother, care assistant father, factory worker
Three A*–C, five D–G grades from Northwark Park	One A*–C, two D–G grades from PRU	Six A*–C, three D–G grades from Northwark Park	Two A*–C, one City and Guilds from PRU
Part-time FE course in Hairdressing	Full-time BTec	Full-time NVQ Hairdressing and City and Guilds Beauty	Full-time Computer Studies
Part-time shop assistant	Part-time hairdresser	Part-time hairdresser	Part-time steward

and in the processes of identity. Here the question, 'How shall I live?' relates decisions about education and work to much more profound personal meanings and struggles. Again, families and family life are an important backdrop to these key and difficult decisions. All four are from working-class families and all four are engaged in Further Education courses.

Amma

Amma is black and lives with her mother and two brothers. Amma achieved three GCSE A*–C grades at Northwark Park. Her move from school to a College course and subsequent 'dropping-out' vividly points up some of the interplays and tensions between the structure of opportunities, choice and identity formation. Like many other students, Amma's initial preferred option was to find a job. She had done work experience in Year 10 and 'loved it':

> I thought I was ready, so even though I felt that it would be a big jump I didn't really feel that I wanted any more education. I know that you should want to stay in school or go to college. Everyone says you should get qualifications, but I didn't really feel like that. I felt that I was ready to work there, you know. [Two years later as we shall see Amma is thinking about going to university.]

But the 'need for qualifications' as 'everyone says' and an absence of suitable occupational opportunities made immediate entry into full-time work a non-option. Staying-on in the Northwark Park sixth form was also closed down. Amma left school with a very clear sense of her learner identity and her position in the educational scheme of things. The Northwark Park staff made a point of targeting students they hoped to retain in the sixth form but Amma received no such attention.

I think if I was an A-level type of student then there would be pressure on me, but because I am not, no one has said nothing to me about staying. No one has encouraged me to stay or nothing, so. But I think because I am a C and D kind of person that is why, they really want the type of A-level people to stay and give the school a better reputation so that is why I think no one has said nothing to me about staying because I wouldn't do nothing to improve the reputation. I am sort of in the middle and I think they want the best ones to stay.

I felt really bad after I did my GCSEs and it didn't hit home until somebody had said to me, 'Amma you did really bad'. So that has made me feel that I don't really want to show anybody anything until I know that it is done perfect. I don't want anyone to feel that she is a failure. It's so discouraging. I wonder if people know how hurtful they can be.

Amma's interests are in the performing arts and a course at a FE college seemed the way to go. Her area of interest is long-standing and is rooted partly in her sense of her personal skills and partly in her ongoing involvement with a dance troupe.

Am: [I want to do] a BTec in performing arts. I want to do everything, the directing, filming the other side of the camera and being in front of the camera and stuff, everything.
Int: Where does this idea come from, Amma?
Am: Well I have always wanted to do it and I guess the media has had a lot to do with it.
Int: Tell me about that.
Am: You know you watch these programmes of how they make films and sometimes being on the other side of the camera is even better than being in front, you know. You get to make all these important decisions, you know, and I like being in charge quite a lot. And I would like the fact that I would be giving orders of where I want things to be, how I want things to be set out, you know. I would like that idea.
Int: You feel that you might be a natural leader do you; you like responsibility?
Am: Yes, I think I will need a lot of help a lot of assistance. Definitely.
Int: So this idea of doing Theatre Studies has come from watching television and from watching programmes on directing and stuff like that. How long have you been thinking of this?
Am: I have always wanted. I knew that I always wanted to do something in media and I always like that, because it was a way of expressing yourself.

Amma's mother is not convinced: 'She feels that there is not really a future in that. She would like something more, like, secure, something she understands, like a doctor or a lawyer [parental fantasising?] you know, but she says whatever I want to do she will go with it'. But Amma was aware of the difficulties involved in getting to work in the arts, the competition for jobs and the need for talent and dedication. These things had been reinforced by the Careers Adviser. She had a fall back position:

> Yes. I want to do dance as well, because I want to fit that in as well as the drama, and so hopefully I will do courses in dance as well, I just want to do a bit of journalism so I want to take an A-level in media and then, hopefully, I would like to do some kind of training in journalism.

She phoned twelve colleges from a list provided by the Careers Adviser and obtained a number of brochures. She was differently impressed by the brochures and ruled out several possibilities at this stage. She was particularly concerned, drawing on the brochures and 'grapevine knowledge' about the ethnic and class make-up of the colleges, about 'finding the right distance' (Bourdieu, 1986, p. 472). Thus:

> Riverway, it sounds very upper-class and I am thinking to myself, well how many black people go there? And so I look around I look in the pages to see whether there are black people in there. There probably are, but I can't remember. There was probably about one black person maybe. . . .
>
> I know that a college like Streetley where there is, like, so many black people there, I don't think, I don't think I would be happy. I don't think I would get good results or nothing, I think I would probably fail, because sometimes being in, being with too many black people, I think you need a mix, you really do. Too many black people, sometimes black people can you know, stop you from doing your work and it really depends upon the black person. . . .

In Amma's 'attributive judgement' colleges being too white and too black are both problems. As it turned out she applied to four colleges, including Riverway, but finally decided to follow her older sister to Vernon College to do a GNVQ in Media Studies. Her class was overwhelmingly black and she quickly became unhappy with the learning environment of the college and the course. 'Nobody really wants to learn if you know what I mean. And everyone has got this kind of attitude with them. That is what I didn't want to get into'. She was very disappointed: 'Whether they are black, white, Asian you know, no one has really got that drive'. And as early as November of the first term she was saying: 'I just don't even want to go in because it is like, you know, it is, you know exactly what is going to happen and what their attitude is going to be. And sometimes I don't know if I'll last'. She felt distinctly ill-at-ease:

> The stress of the place does my head in. It really is a stressful place . . . people are rude but a bit more mature rude, you know. . . . Yes it is definitely not cool to be seen to need support. That is like a sign of weakness, you know. And if you show that, then your life isn't worth living because some of these people, you know, are just looking for people's weak spots. And working hard is not cool and like a sign of weakness.

Amma found herself an outsider, unwilling to accommodate to the dominant student culture, to be policed by style and cool. In a sense she resists resistance. She does not see herself in terms of young, black, urban hyper-performativity.

> The way I dress maybe. My mum has always said to me I should try to be individual which I try to be. But when you walk into that college it is like a fashion parade. As soon as you walk into the common room, eyes are on you. Is that a Gucci top she is wearing, no, forget you. They're not interested in you unless you have brand names. You're rubbish and not worth talking to . . . whatever. Just joining the student union seems like a white thing to do and it is not very cool to do it.

Amma was critical of her own lack of understanding of colleges and of the lack of support from school and the Careers Service.

> I realise now that I don't even know what most of the colleges do. It really is difficult making sensible decisions, you know, when you only have patches of information. I realise now that I didn't even know the questions to ask. It's terrible. I think I should have talked to a lot more people rather than leaning on what my sister said, or what her friends said, you know. I think information definitely, just knowing more about what is out there and visiting all the places. I left my choices late and very limited and this is what I ended up with. I mean I can't blame it all on the school. But it is like I was really naive to what was going on around me.

Here Amma's reflexivity is expressed in an awareness of what she has not had/got, as well as what is counter-productive. Her identity is being extended/worked-through in relation to stifled aspirations and a sense of gaps she needs to fill.

> I didn't know how to find out about these things. And like when I spoke to teachers in Northwark Park nobody knew. They said, 'yes there must be colleges like that but I don't know where they are'. And if you remember they weren't really into advising pupils, not really. It was just like, 'stay for sixth form, go to college', whatever. It wasn't, well I think this college would be good for you. Or, 'have you thought about this one'. None of that. At that time yeah, because one thing college taught me to do is, like, where to get resources from, like when I was in secondary school, I didn't know where to get the information from, you know. The Careers Officer, you were lucky to catch her.

Amma's experience of choosing points up the dysfunctions of information flow in the highly competitive post-16 market. As it turned out she confronted a mismatch of lifestyles, Amma felt uncomfortable, out of place at Vernon. And embedded in this discomfort are other possibilities of identity, particularly here different realizations of black identity.

There is a certain kind of stereotype within black people that they think of black people, so to be a black person from one black person's perspective, you listen to R and B music, you wear, like, a certain kind of clothes. You have your hair a certain way, do you know what I mean. You talk in a certain way. . . . I had big arguments with my friends at Northwark Park: 'Amma how many white people have you been hanging around with?' . . . It is like you are some-body else, you are not really, really black, you know. Really silly, but when I was younger I honestly felt that I wasn't all black because it really does get to you, you know, you start believing that. . . .

This resonates with Hewitt's (1990) discussion of 'new forms of self-definition – and anti-definition', an escape from essentialism, which results in the erosion of 'once narrowly-defined notions of a tightly homogeneous culture' (p. 194). Amma does not want to avoid her colour, as we shall see, but neither does she want to be a simple racial subject. She exemplifies Hall's (1992, p. 254) unpacking of what he calls that 'necessary fiction. Namely, that all black people are good or indeed that all black people *are the same*'. She is struggling with the social semiology of 'racial' division. All of this is important in Amma's second attempt at a college course (see below).

Amma's mother is a significant figure in the background here. She continues to support Amma morally and financially – paying her travel to College, for instance. 'It is £10.60 a week and that was a bit of a shock to me'.

Amma left Vernon in November and took a part-time shop job for Christmas, followed by switchboard and office work obtained from a Recruitment Agency. Amma 'uses' the city as a resource for part-time work and also finds an opportunity for international travel – her socioscape is extending (see Chapter 8). In February she began work-experience with a dance group, again did office work, and travelled to the USA with the group. 'I learned a lot that might be useful in the future. It was the best thing I did last year'. At the same time, with advice from a member of the dance company, Amma was again looking at college brochures and made appointments to visit three colleges to talk to course tutors. This time she did not want to make a mistake. She began her choice-making early, and among other things was very attentive to the ethnic mix of the colleges: 'Every time I see a lot of black students I feel, okay, am I going to be able to learn here?' She opted for Queensdown College and a BTec National Diploma. 'I spoke to Harry who ran the BTec National Performing Arts. . . . I spoke to the dance teacher, and she was very helpful. . . . There was a couple of students sitting on the side and I spoke to them, and they were like "yeah, yeah it is really good", the teachers are very co-operative as long as you show that you are willing to work'. Because her GCSE grades were inadequate Amma had to do a dance audition. At the same time she got a new part-time job in a department store. She dramatically contrasts her experience at Queensdown with Vernon. She feels 'comfortable' at Queensdown:

First of all it's a mixed college and there is predominantly white people there, but there is black people there as well. The first thing I noticed when I went to that college was that everyone was different, everyone was different, I couldn't see that there was two people the same and it worked. You know this was the first day and everyone was getting on with each other, it was just such a nice atmosphere, I felt like, I don't know how to explain it, it was just that feeling of, I have found my place, you know. I don't need to go anywhere else . . . in this place I have people that I can really talk to . . . you can learn things from them and they listen and you can try ideas out on them.

I don't know where that idea came from about if you don't do certain things then you are not seen as black. I don't know, but it is so narrow, you can only do certain things and that, as if black people can't have a whole load of different perspectives and views and opinions.

Choosing a college is in some respects about choosing a way of representing yourself. Could we even say that Amma seeks to escape from an 'excess of belonging' or even from the oppression of coherence or the modern logic of difference, into a concept of identity without belonging? What Amma appears to be striving for is an ontological freedom. A paradigm case of the individualization thesis, of making a project of one's biography? Perhaps. In finding 'her place' Amma seems to be talking about a setting in which identity can be worked up/played out/extended/re-examined – related to her interest and involvement in performance? Amma's imagined future is now becoming clearer.

I hope to, when I finish this course, to go to university. At the moment I am not sure which course but it will either be a dance or drama course combined with like some kind of business management. That is definitely what I want to do . . . I don't want to be a performer or actress or actor, I just want to be behind the scenes making things come together . . . my aim from now, until I reach university and onwards, is to do as much performing as I can, just to get that kind of experience and then I am going to start writing to companies for work experience . . . if I manage to get all the experience I need, I will have a good idea of what kind of job I want because there is so many other jobs other than director and producer that I might find interesting . . . I have already got some university prospectuses and I was surprised at how many do accept BTec. . . .

But again Amma is alert to the ethnic mix and curriculum orientation of her possible destinations:

Whenever I go somewhere I look for the kind of cultural, ethnic things they have going on because although the course may be good I want to feel comfortable . . . because when it is a predominately white college you just get thrown into what they are doing, whether you like it or not, you tend to just go with the flow . . . I need to be around black people because I am comfortable that way, I have white friends and all that but black people are important because I am black.

Again Amma is sensitive to the issue of ethnic mix. Like other Northwark Park students she seems most at ease in ethnically diverse settings. And like almost all of the rest of the potential university students in our cohort, she wants to stay in London. And yet, for Amma, there are still serious doubts, at least about university. Certainly through all this Amma's 'learner identity' is dramatically re-formed, if not totally re-made. Nevertheless, her habitus continues to feed into a disposition of perception which makes going to university seem like an impossible way of acting – not a thing that people like Amma do – which can mean self-exclusion. She says:

> I can't see myself with a degree. I don't know why, I can't . . . sometimes even at the back of my head there is always a kind of something saying that I am not getting there . . . a kind of a barrier stopping me . . . I don't know if it is me stopping myself, or somebody else. . . .

Amma's narrative can be read in a variety of ways. One obvious reading is that of triumph over adversity. Her individual drive is clearly important here in finding various jobs, refining her goals and interests, learning from bad experiences; although she sees her 'laziness' as a problem. Amma makes a strident critique of the formal sources of advice and support she received, or rather did not receive (see also Chapter 6). Nonetheless other informal support from her mother, from her new College and from her 'mentor' in the dance company are of enormous importance to her. We can also read this as a story of chance. There are many aspects of her account, which are not detailed here, which indicate the serendipitous nature of her 'careership'. Hodkinson et al.'s (1996) 'turning points' (structural, external and self-initiated) are clearly much in evidence and Amma exemplifies Strauss's (1962) point that 'these points in development occur when an individual has to take stock, to re-evaluate, revise, re-see and rejudge' (p. 71). There is a mixture of planning and ad-hocery or reactivity in all this (with some similarities with Michael, below).

Amma is perhaps one example of a young person who crosses 'the bounds of her probable opportunities' (Roberts et al., 1994, p. 51). Her resistance to, and exploration of, identity seem to produce for her a less essentialist view of the world and an agentic stance. In exploring 'herself' she can exceed her own expectations.

Michael

Michael is white, he lives with his single parent mother who does not work, he has a younger sister and brother, he is gay. He is a gentle and polite young man, always well-dressed, with a ready smile. He has highlights in his hair and is of slim but muscular build. He attended the PRU and achieved three GCSE passes, including one A*–C grade. Michael finished his compulsory education at the PRU as a result of being bullied in his secondary school and refusing to return. He feels that he was not supported by his secondary school. Like Amma, his area of 'career' interest is very clear and long-standing, and like Amma his post-16 'career' can be understood, subjectively, as an attempt to 'express' 'himself'.

> I have been thinking about it since I was 11. My mum used to make clothes and everything and I used to help her. I just had an interest in clothes. I knitted a cardigan, and jeans, loads of clothes I made myself . . . I have an interest in art as well and I started putting together an art portfolio and I'll take it to college and show them what I am doing . . . I like doing my hair. I like anything to do with fashion, I like jewellery, clothes, hair.

Michael's vocational commitments are very much bound up with his identity, who he is, how he looks. He wears his interests on his sleeve, literally. He is making himself up, so to speak, through the clothes he makes and buys, through his hair style, and through his body-sculpting at the gym.

On leaving school Michael's initial plan was to attend college to do a Fashion and Design course. However, he found most of the courses he wanted to do were expensive and available only to 18-year-olds, so although he was offered several places, including one at the London College of Fashion, he decided to train and work in hairdressing until he was 18. 'It [choosing] went on for ages, I didn't know what I was doing . . . I was really stressed about it. I had a word with my mum and we talked about it and we decided that I was going to stay working until I am 18 . . . and then I'll go to College'. He was already working in a salon three days a week while at the PRU but through a hairdressing journal found a better-paid job with Network Training. 'It's five days a week and I go to the [Hair] College . . . I get about £80–90 a week plus £5–15 a day in tips'. Michael sees the job and especially the (Hair) College course as a way of making 'lots of contacts. I have got a lot of phone numbers already which is really exciting. So I am building up for the future all the time'. He sees his future in fashion design. 'When I've done the College course I'll be able to design clothes'. His imagined future and his route to that future are clear and continuously in sight. But Michael finds the 'reality' of work more demanding than he had anticipated. 'I knew it was going to be hard. It is a bit harder than I realized it would be. You are more independent. . . . I knew but I didn't really know'. He has to come to grips with being responsible for himself and for others; 'It is different':

> When you're at school or whatever, you're sort of protected . . . It's not real life. . . . I still have dreams and that but you begin to see that the ones you had earlier were just that, just dreams. You have to be more grown up, more mature . . . I try to act grown up but I often don't feel it.

A number of young people in our sample talked about their fears of adulthood and not being ready to be 'responsible' for themselves (see Chapter 8 and Wyn and Dwyer, 1999). But while all this is more difficult than school, in other ways it is easier. 'It's easier because the people that I mix with and work with and whatever are people like me'. This was a phrase Michael often repeated. He had felt out of place at secondary school, 'because there is too many different sorts of people all together'. In Michael's case his exploration of identities is focused upon his sexuality. Like Amma, he is 'at home' in contexts where simple binaries – common place schemes of classification – can be played with or dissolved.

With independence, there are new freedoms. 'You get to meet a lot more people. . . . You can stay out all night, all weekend, go to parties. I can choose my own clothes'. Altogether Michael has a sense of moving towards his goal. 'I am more settled. I know where I am going, I know how I am getting there or whatever. I've got my life planned out now'. What was a split, disrupted, unfulfilled identity is now coherent, it makes sense. Within his work and study environments Michael feels affirmed.

After a few months in his training placement he moved to a salon in the West End because, 'It was all so slow. I thought I'll be here for years and I'll still not be a proper hairdresser'. But while he enjoyed the new location 'it got really busy straightaway. They didn't have much time to train me. . . . I was like working hard and not getting proper pay because I was a junior stylist but I wasn't getting trained'. He moved again to another central-London salon. Social networks and personal contacts were beginning to work! 'I had a friend and he was a hairdresser. . . . I didn't bother telling him I was training . . . and they were hunting for people to come and work for them . . . so I was nervous at first there but I knew what I was doing'. Michael now works two days a week – 'I get £100 per day' – and attends a North London college three days a week. Interestingly he chose the college because:

> Well it looks nice, it is, like, trendy and has really like modern ideas and decor and the people are like nice and helpful and it is really just like the sort of place I would want to go with the things I want to do and whatever. It's my sort of place.

Like Amma, Michael has found an institutional habitus in which he feels comfortable. He is now saving for a Certificate in Fashion course at a prestigious London college, 'it lasts about a year and they give you the basics and everything', and his ambition to become a fashion designer is firming up:

> I would like to go and work for a big shop . . . Christian Dior or something like that. . . . I would probably be starting off just like helping other fashion designers, carrying materials and stuff like that . . . most people start that way and just build themselves up . . . you just learn things from watching people and meeting people.

A number of the young people in our research cohort, like Michael, Wayne (Chapter 10) and Rachel (Chapter 6), are moving through new forms of work in sectors of the labour market – new economies – which are concerned with the commodification of style. We might think of these young people as 'new-style workers'; working upon themselves and for others in the fetishization of image and the marketing of experience. There is a peculiar fusion of identity work involved here – a self-imaging process. The new, urban, post-industrial, labour markets engender both opportunity and risk for their participants – while excluding some 'others' altogether (see Chapter 8). They are also increasingly important proportions of overall urban and national economic activity in Western societies. They have their own internal hierarchies and structures. Modelling (Rachel), DJ-ing (Wayne), and hair-styling (Michael) each offers some potential for a 'glossy future' or they may equally well produce low-wage, serial unemployment. Luck, tenacity and talent are important (see below) but 'success' also depends on who you are and who you know – differently distributed forms of capital.

For Michael, the steps between where he is and where he wants to be are filling in, becoming clearer. His time horizons, his imagined future are extending, being 'filled out':

> If I can't do that I will probably go on and do like another five years at college . . . and get a degree or something there. . . . As long as I feel I am learning things I don't mind how long I take, or what I do. . . . I know it can take years . . . people who are very successful in big fashion houses . . . have just started like me and worked up. You just need flair, hard work and a bit of luck.

Much of Michael's social life in clubs, bars and restaurants mirrors and reinforces his interest in fashion and his identity as rooted in the performance of self. He is working on himself, and his embodiment, as a project of self – who and what he is and wants to be.

> There's one called Legends and we go there on a Thursday night . . . and we are always nervous about getting in . . . they only let gorgeous people in . . . most of the time I drink vodka and cranberry juice. . . . Me and my friend are going away this year to the Dominican Republic. . . . I like Prada, Gucci, I bought a pair of Patrick Cox shoes just before Christmas £250. . . . I wear these like jeans, they are like printed newspaper, I got them and the jacket to match, the trousers are like £407 and the top for £208 something like that. . . . I go to the gym a lot, I spend a lot of money at the gym. I spend a lot of money going out, socialising. . . .

But he continues to live at home and is invested heavily in his family, in particular in his relationship with his mother:

> I pay her at the end of the month, I pay her so much rent and then I help out with the bills and put some money towards the telephone bill and I give my sister pocket money and stuff. . . . I've taken my mum to the theatre . . . out to dinner things like that. . . . I took her shopping at the West End as well for her birthday, splash out a bit. . . . I take my Mum to places that my Dad should be taking her to. . . . We do family things, take my sister out. . . . .

Nevertheless: 'We argue about lots of things, we argue about money, she also knows that I am gay . . . she doesn't really accept it . . . she does most of the time'. When asked to envisage life in five years time Michael was clear about one thing:

> If I do leave home my mum will come with me. . . . I eventually want to have a big, nice house, I don't want to have children . . . so instead of the children I will have my mum.

Michael's transition to adulthood and into working life is a combination of planning and experimentation. He is very strongly personally invested in his 'working life'. His interests, his fantasies about the future, his leisure and life style and social relationships are tightly bound together in his emerging identities. He is accomplishing an identity, even perhaps making a project of himself in a positive and highly motivated fashion. 'I don't really think about my relationships . . . I will concentrate on my work and everything more than anything else and just enjoy myself as I go along . . .' His accomplishment, expression of self, is its own reward. For Michael (and Amma) liminality and social class are, for the time being, obscured – 'certain paths and fantasies are open' (Walkerdine, 1997, p. 98).

The transitions from school to work, from adolescence to adulthood, from dependence to independence are of course tightly interwoven in and through the lives of young people 'growing up'. Their sense of changing identity, efficacy and self-esteem is made and unmade, reinforced and undermined, in social, domestic and economic arenas. 'Identity is always a temporary and unstable effect of relations. . . . Identities are always incomplete, in process' (Grossberg, 1996, p. 89). This is pre-eminently the case in post-adolescence – but at any point in time and in particular settings there is a limited set of possible identities to be expressed, instabilities to be managed or resolved, social relations to be coped with or avoided, 'people like me' to be sought out. This is all very different from the simple, de-socialized and disembedded, rational–calculative discourse of the reports and policies which frame post-16 education and training. Rather, it relates to what Hodkinson et al. (1996) call a *pragmatic rationality*: a decision-making process which is embedded in 'a wider choice of lifestyle' and the influence of social context, a process which 'must be seen as part of the ongoing life course'; and which places decision-making as 'part of the interaction with stakeholders' (p. 137). (We give little attention to the latter in this volume, see Ball et al., 1997; Ball et al., 1998; Macrae et al., 1996; Macrae et al., 1997.)

Rena and Delisha: Between Identities?

If, in the simplest terms, Michael and Amma are 'looking towards' their identities; Rena and Delisha are 'caught between' identities. While Michael and Amma are seeking places to be 'at home', Rena and Delisha are struggling against the predictable comforts of home. Rena and Delisha are, at first glance, very different young women, with different backgrounds, lives and views. Yet they are both 'caught between'. They both perceive and experience their lives and their futures in terms of hopes and possibilities, frustrations and constraints. Their hopes and fantasies about the future are set over and against 'real lives': Rena's family's expectations of her marriage to a Gujerati boy and having children, and Delisha's 'dead end' office job. Both young women are in FE.

Rena is from a Gujerati family long established in the Northwark area and is the youngest of three daughters. She left Northwark Park with six GCSE A*–C grades and began NVQ Hairdressing and City and Guilds Cosmetic and Make-Up courses at Burbley College. She is the only Asian person on these courses. On the face of it she is over-qualified for these courses but is very committed to a career in Hair and Beauty. It is something she had always been interested in: 'My mum she wants me to do something, because my older sister is doing a degree in Business Studies and she wants me to do something like that as well. I don't want to'. Like Amma and Michael, she was keen to leave school. 'I've been in school too long. . . . I want to be with different people in a different sort of atmosphere . . . you can be your own person there [at college]'. Burbley offered the courses she wanted and quickly gave her a place. It was the only application she made though she perceives the college as having a 'bad reputation' and 'really easy to get into'. 'It is known as a doss college but for that course it is really good because they have got really good salons and all that'. Rena's father was dubious. He thought the college 'too far' and was worried about the one late night; 'the trains after seven come every half hour' and had to be persuaded to let her enrol. She now has a mobile phone and telephones home when she leaves college late. She was also taken aback at interview, which she attended with her father, by the lack of ethnic mix:

> I felt really out of place because like everyone who was there were white people and I was the only Asian girl and there is only one black boy, so I was like oh my god, I was really nervous. . . . I was scared about going and not having any friends too.

Ethnic mix is again important but, for Rena, not decisive. On the basis of an initial assessment Rena was started on NVQ level 1. 'I was really annoyed with that, it was really basic'. As 'class rep' she protested and was moved to Level 2 in which 'there's a lot more training, they get down to cutting and all that'. Rena attends college three days a week and works in a salon run by a large company two days a week. She also works in the salon on Saturdays, for which she is paid. Despite her six GCSEs she finds the written work hard. 'I have started to slack a lot . . . I have become really lazy . . .'. Like Amma, Rena sees laziness as a basic character fault. The failings of schooling are internalised and personalised: 'I just can't be bothered to do written stuff'. Nonetheless, in 1997 she was 'Hairdressing Student of the Year', won a competition and successfully completed her City and Guilds. But she continued to find the courses 'going really slow . . . I have told the teachers, all of us have complained' – a point also made by Michael. She returned to college for the second year of her Hairdressing course and had a job offer from her training salon for when she has finished: 'I would probably start with £80 a week'. [The 'local' wages are very different from those in Michael's central London salons.] The course itself has suffered high wastage. Only eight students remain from two full-time classes which started: 'Can't be bothered with it, half of them. Some of them have gone to salons just to work full-time'. Rena is wondering about her future, whether to do more courses. But her family 'think I'm going to work, they want money coming in, they want me to give them money'. Money is a constant source of friction between Rena and her mother. And Rena is very well aware that her personal aspirations will continue to be limited by the expectations of her family and her community:

> I want to travel and do artistic stuff. I don't want to be based in one place. . . . I would love to get into the film industry . . . I don't think my Dad would like it if I went overseas. . . . We have to do like a nine-to-five job and get married by 21, 22. . . . There was a point where they pressured my sister. . . .

In some small ways Rena leads a double life. The world of college and the expectations of her white friends are in tension with home and family. Identities are in conflict. Her parents do not know that she smokes. If they found out 'I would die. They will probably disown me, actually they will feel gutted'. She is frustrated because 'I haven't really got [a social life] . . . we are not allowed out, so there is no point in even asking mum and dad'. She does go to the cinema on College half-days but 'my mum she would be like, where are you getting the money from. So I don't bother telling her, just do it . . . they are still living in the 1960s'. She has recently begun a relationship, without her parents' knowledge, with a boy who is not part of her community. Rena's chosen career remains a problem: 'What I am doing it's not really . . . I have to do well for them to be actually proud of me'. She faces similar dissonances at college: 'When you see an Asian you think whoa, they are doing hairdressing?'

When asked to look ahead two years Rena saw herself 'probably engaged or married. Hopefully getting my own business together . . . but I don't see it myself . . . I don't see my mother-in-law and father-in-law letting me do that.' Rena is fatalistic about her family's and community's expectations that she will marry and focus herself on a domestic life. Here her possible future, in her chosen 'career', sits uneasily with her likely future. Rena's cultural and social identities are unstable. As to the former she might well fit the construct of a 'Britasian' (Sing-Raud, 1998): 'I don't feel that English, not really, no. I don't feel totally Indian.' She manages 'a kind of life' between the norms and expectations of an increasingly generic, cosmopolitan world of 'youth' – fashion, films, music and boyfriends – and the entrenched local and communal expectations of her parents and relatives. Her social and cultural/domestic identities are on a collision course. She is engaged in a set of very specific, but not uncommon, negotiations and 'strategic and positional identities'. In several respects her choice of career and her lifestyle are transgressive. Her plans for the future are, at this time, fantasies set over and against the realities of marriage within her community and a domestic rather than a working life.

Delisha is dual heritage – her mother is white, her father African-Caribbean. Her parents are divorced and she lives with her mother, two younger sisters and two younger brothers. She has had a chequered educational career, to say the least. Delisha was excluded from several schools before attending Northwark Park, and was excluded from Northwark Park for 'violent behaviour' six months before her GCSE examinations. This followed three suspensions for bullying, theft and smoking marijuana at school. She says 'I was a bully at school . . . I just wanted everybody to notice me at the time . . . I had the whole school eating out of my hands and if someone troubled me, I didn't have to fight; there were these two boys and they used to beat them up for me'. But now she protests that: 'If I could change, I would've been totally different . . . I would've studied more . . . I have seen people that I have actually bullied in the past and said "sorry".' From school, Delisha spent three months in an Intermediate Treatment (IT) Centre but found that 'the education was very poor' and 'I didn't have any respect for them as teachers'. However she gained a C in Maths, B in English and a City and Guilds Certificate for Photography – the only courses on offer. She began post-16 on a TV and Video Production course at Knightley College – 'you didn't need any GCSEs' – and stayed for six months before being excluded for fighting in the library with a friend. 'It all started to build up and I saw her one day in the library and picked up a chair and threw it and hit her'. There followed six months as a stockroom and trainee sales assistant in a Knightsbridge shop, earning about £800 a month. 'I enjoyed it at first, but I wasn't used to working, I wasn't used to the hours but when it was pay day. . . . I left there because I was only a stockroom assistant and I would end up as one of those old sales assistants. . . .' She was confronted by an unpalatable future. The retail labour market in Inner London does present particular opportunities for work for young women like Amma and Delisha. The gendered nature of such work gives them certain advantages over their male counterparts; there are different 'opportunity structures' (Roberts, 1968), but also embeds a set of 'career' limitations. Delisha is now studying at Northwark College for a BTec National Intermediate Certificate in Computing and she works part-time as a crowd steward at sports events:

> I am not enjoying it at all, I hate it. I don't like college, everyone is young; they are just like school-leavers now. They are just, like, running up and down. They just make me feel old. I should've been finishing my A-levels by now or done a bit to go to university and I am back in college and won't do my A-levels for another two years. . . . .

Like Rena, Delisha reports a heavy drop-out – 'After Christmas, about a third of my class disappeared' – and a difficult learning environment – 'they just muck around, you have got a smokers corner, chatterbox corner' [but] . . . I want to stick at it. . . .'

Despite her determination to finish the course Delisha remains fearful of her future. Not in the sense that she will not find a job, but rather that she will. 'I don't really want to be doing it but most of my family are secretaries . . . in the long run that's where it leads, house, car, mortgage, kids'. This is very different from the world of many of her friends:

> Most of them are making their money other ways . . . by selling drugs or most of them are into nicking from banks and post offices . . . A few of my friends have come out of prison a couple of weeks ago and are back at it. . . . One of my friends was pimping at one time, he was making like four or five hundred pounds a night only off four prostitutes. . . . My friend Shelley's been to Holloway [women's prison].

Currently Delisha is trying to find her way between two worlds – one straight and one criminal – both of which attract and repel her in almost equal measure. She knows what she does not want but is perhaps unsure about what she does want:

> I don't want to go to gaol. I don't want to, I just prefer to do it the honest way. If I can't do it the honest way, then maybe if I am drove to it, I might do it one day, but that is a very big might. . . . I've seen what you can do on the streets, I want to see what you can do for yourself working like and then it is up to me whether I want to make decisions to do this or that . . . . After I have finished this course I might go back to college, I might go to work, I don't really want to work nine to five for twenty years. . . . I would like to do something like owning my own network sales company but I don't know. Realistically [in two years time] I think I will just have an office job, I will be earning money but it will be spent on clothes, as usual. I will just be partying.

Again Delisha's world is one of instability and risk, opportunities (of sorts) and difficult choices, and the different expectations of family and friends: 'My Dad would love it if I worked in a nice office'. She is faced with a choice of lifestyle, of biographical project. In a sense she is reinventing herself and searching for herself. Like some of the other young people quoted here, she is learning by making mistakes, but also, like them, she displays a developing reflexivity. 'I know that I could accomplish a lot but it's just destruction. I am just too interested in everything. It is like I haven't seen everything'.[1]

Thus, while we are keen to stress the continued importance of forms of class difference and class reproduction, Delisha's story in many ways again exemplifies Giddens' point that, in the context of contemporary changes in social and economic structures, 'individuals are forced to negotiate lifestyle choices among a diversity of options' (1991, p. 5). And yet both Rena and Delisha also have ambitions that they deny. They seem to know what is not possible in a world of possibilities. They are aware of limits and constraints. They seem to know what they cannot be – these are their 'horizons for action'. They see predictable futures, however resistant they are to them, stretching out before them: 'personal perceptions of what was either possible, or acceptable' (Hodkinson et al., 1996, p. 9). These do 'not even require active consent merely the non-occurrence of refusal' (Connell, 1989, p. 297). Despite their transgressions they are still hemmed in by circumstance and likelihood – a certain obviousness. Again the abstract 'individualisations' of Beck and Giddens are confronted by the practicalities of family and custom, social expectations and the fixities of labour market structures and the demand for qualifications. However, in the same way the continuing importance of class differences have to be set against and take into account the agency and activism of the young people portrayed here.

Work and education play a very different role for these two young people. They 'mean' something very different. They have different implications for identity. For Rena, education and work are potential 'escape routes'; ways of eluding or at least postponing rather fixed family and community expectations. Her interests and commitments here threaten her family affiliations. They offer an arena of experimentation. They are in some senses dangerous and transgressive. She is attracted by the lifestyles of her college friends. For Delisha, education and work hem her in. They draw her into a conventional trajectory and closer to her family in terms of lifestyle, behaviour and aspirations. They are, in a sense, an arena of safety where dangers can be avoided. But she has little interest in or respect for her college peers or the lifestyles of her family. For both young women education and work offer them possibilities, however reluctant or ambivalent they are to take them, to 're-make' themselves, to alter established socio-cultural trajectories. Here, choices are enormously complex and very weighty. We might say that lives are in the balance. The choices these young women make are 'embedded' in very different and significant social and familial relationships. They are not rational choices in any simple sense, nor educational and vocational in any simple sense. They are about, and invested in, identities and opportunity. They are framed and formed by key events, moments and influences – various significant others. They evolve and change in a nexus of fearfulness and aspiration, hope and possibility.

Unlike Amma and Michael, Rena and Delisha have not found work, learning contexts or identities with which they can feel totally comfortable. Rather, they are confronted with ways of being and becoming which are in tension. In a somewhat inchoate manner they are looking for means and contexts and relationships within which they can explore/express/invent possible selves and lives. These explorations may involve disappointing significant others (friends or family) and taking risks with their futures. For all four of these young people, identity-work is hard. 'Being yourself' and 'becoming somebody' is troublesome, troubled and on-going.

Clearly again all of this makes the notion of 'choice' post-16 highly problematic and highly complex. The social trajectories and 'learning careers' (Bloomer and Hodkinson, 1997) of these young people, and many of the others in our cohort, are constituted as much by chance and risk as they are by rational deliberation and effort. False starts seem almost the norm, set-backs are common, and the social and domestic aspects of 'choice-making' are often more important than the educational. Certainly for these young people the learning environment, the habitus of institutions, is a significant part of their response to learning challenges – 'learning identities' can be re-made or undermined by post-16 experience. Post-16 education is also an arena within which there is the possibility of production of, and experimentation with, social identities. This is a key period of social maturation and personal change. Bloomer and Hodkinson's (1997) point that 'As young people leave school, their entry into Further Education forces many to reconsider who they are' (p. 88), certainly bears reiteration here. However, it is also important not to overplay the significance of education and work in the lives of these young people: 'their lives are about much more than this' (Hodkinson et al., 1996, p. 145). Leisure activities are also a primary site and resource in making social identities (Ainley and Bailey, 1997, p. 79) (see Chapter 5). Furthermore, as a backdrop to all this, complex relations of dependence and social obligation within families are being played out (Irwin, 1995).

Notes

1   Delisha did not finish her college course. She worked as a market researcher and a traffic warden and then, through the New Deal, got an office 'admin' job which she enjoys; this is linked to an NVQ course. She still lives at home and continues to 'flirt' with a more 'dangerous' life.

4 At Risk of Social Exclusion
Debra and Ayesha

Exclusion

In our study there is a core of young people whom, for now, we will call 'socially excluded' (see Table A2.10). A brief review of some of the key features in their biographies to date demonstrates the complex and interrelated factors which can precipitate social and economic exclusion: unemployment, low pay, discrimination, lack of support, interrupted schooling, lack of formal qualifications, reduced self-confidence as well as poverty and material disadvantage are all recognized elements involved in exclusion (QPID, 1998). Many of these factors as well as other variables such as the powerful influence of early family disruption have 'strong associations with several of the outcomes in adulthood' (Hobcraft, 1998, p. 2). There is no simple cause and effect relationship at work but nevertheless there are patterns of continuity in exclusion over time and across generations.

A number of writers and reports have identified a growth in social exclusion (Bynner et al., 1997; Oppenheim, 1998). Blair, in the Labour Party's Green Paper (DfEE, 1998), made the point that in the UK 'between 1979 and 1994–5 households in the top fifth of the population saw income rises in excess of 50 per cent; but the incomes of those in the bottom fifth barely rose in real terms' (DfEE, Webpage). The Rowntree Report (Hills, 1995) found that the income share of the poorest fifth of households fell from 10 per cent in 1978 to 7 per cent in 1990. Since 1977 the proportion of the population with less than half the national average income has more than trebled (Hills, 1995). As a result, MacDonald (1997, p. 20) believes that 'young people now grow up in social, economic and political conditions radically different to those encountered by their parents' generation in the post-war years of relative economic prosperity and social cohesion'. These changes and insecurities are marked in the number of social transformations which have occurred in family life, in education and training, in social welfare policy and notably in the labour market. In consequence, for some time social policy has targeted youth unemployment, the 'long tail' of low educational attainment and the lack of qualifications of up to one in twelve of all school leavers (Pearce and Hillman, 1998). Since the early 1970s, a wide and continuous range of policy interventions have targeted unemployed and allegedly under-skilled youth, via schemes such as Training Credits, Modern Apprenticeships and, latterly, the New Deal. Over the same period, research has consistently indicated that whatever the intervention under consideration, a proportion of young people has always been excluded, or excluded themselves, from these sorts of schemes (Bynner et al., 1997; Demos, 1999). Demos (1999) claims that 'despite six years of economic recovery in Britain there is still a growing constituency of poverty-stricken youngsters who are not in education and not in work and excluded from the welfare to work project' (Pandya, 1999, p. 25). Crucially, as Pandya also points out, the Government 'has no strategy to understand this group' although, at the time of writing, strong attempts are being made to generate a coherent 'framework' for post-16 learning which will target students as young as 13 who are in danger of 'dropping out' (Carvel, 1999), as well as providing a 'second chance' for school leavers with no qualifications (DfEE, 1999).

Our point in this chapter is to suggest that the sorts of damaging life-experiences, disruptions and personal dilemmas which form track-lines through the lives of some young people, are not amenable to end-on tactics of inclusion like the New Deal; the long-standing and, in some cases, 'intergenerational and life course transmission of social exclusion' (Hobcraft, 1998), call for different sorts of understandings and different types of strategies. With Halpern (1998) we are concerned that there appears to be limited consensus on what is meant by 'social exclusion' – on the scope of the problems which are to be included in exclusion and where 'boundaries' might be drawn. Social exclusion is indeed a 'boundary concept' which disguises any disagreement about what is implicated. At the same time it works as a banner round which it is possible to include a wider range of issues than just poverty and deprivation, for example. Any attempt to gloss over differences of interpretation and work towards a holistic version of social inclusion may simply work to manoeuvre 'sharper edged policies concerned with equalities and social justice into safer linguistic and policy territory' (Milbourne, 1999, p. 1). This slippage constitutes the contradiction embedded in the rhetoric of social exclusion (Halpern, 1998). But we are running away with ourselves. In what follows we examine some of these issues through our understanding and interpretation of the narratives constructed by Debra and Ayesha.

Debra

Debra spent her childhood living with her mother, who is of Irish origin. She lives in a small council flat in South London and is long-term unemployed. Debra's parents had a difficult relationship which finally broke down while she was at primary school. Her father has two more children with his current partner. They live in Denmark. Debra frequently talks about her 'cool' Dad and says she may go to visit him; that she is welcome at any time and that she can bring any of her friends. During the four years of the project she has never seen him. As she says herself, aged fifteen: 'My Dad left my Mum. He went out with a woman who had two kids and then he got back to my Mum again and then he left. I am not really a family person.'

Debra has always had a complex and at times stormy relationship with her mother. Her mother was abused as a child and has experienced a series of troubled relationships with men. She has always advised Debra not to trust men and not to get 'saddled with kids trailing behind you'. Debra is very matter of fact about all this:

> I don't really talk much to my Mum, I don't really get on with her much. . . . She used to hit me and that. I didn't like it and I hit her back once and she didn't hit me much after that.
>
> She used to hit me a lot and I just couldn't take it. . . . My Mum used to beat me and that.

While Debra was still living at home and attending Northwark Park (she had a rate of 73 per cent attendance in Years 10 and 11), she was in her own words 'a bit hyper and a bit of a loner'. She was a little over-weight, wore glasses, had protruding teeth and did not dress fashionably – she was isolated at school and perhaps isolated at home. In her first two interviews she told us that she loved animals – dogs in particular – and that she spent a lot of her time walking her dog on the local common. She would frequently talk to other dog owners and offer to 'train' their dogs for them. She saw this as her 'job'. She used to approach dog owners and give them her telephone number – in this way she found work for herself. When we first interviewed Debra she told us that she spent a lot of time with adults in her neighbourhood – older people 'down the market' or in local cafes – perhaps anyone who had time for her. These often seemed to be adults with social and emotional problems. She had no friends at school: 'I go around with myself. . . . I get on with more adults than people my age. . . . A slag that is probably what they would call me because they are jealous because I have got so many friends.'

School and Learning

Debra has always had learning difficulties although she has always attended mainstream school. 'I didn't used to read and write good but I am better now'. When she was getting ready for GCSEs she finally decided that she needed some constructive help in getting her folders ready and in trying to be clear about what work she needed to do. However, she was extremely disorganized:

> I went to [a teacher] and said, I'm in a spot. I don't know what I'm doing and I don't know what I have to do for the course work. He didn't give me much information either, so basically I went home and I have got a cabin bed, so, like all the papers underneath from first year up to the fifth year. . . . I just took every bit of paper out on English, Maths and Science, I don't know how to sort it out, so I just came into school today, my bag totally full of all different

stuff . . . and gave it to my teachers. . . . I just let them sort it out. I need them to tell me, but basically nobody tells me nothing and I can't do my work and that if I don't know, so I just left it for them.

She was very realistic about what school was like for people like herself. As she said (aged fifteen):

Nobody really enjoys school, especially if they are in Special Needs like me. School work is hard and I can't do it a lot of the time, so I get fed up with it, and wish I wasn't here, and I bunk and that because I find the work hard and boring.

Here it seems that Debra has totally exhausted her 'learning identity' (Rees et al., 1997). Sources of positive identity are unavailable at school and she has every reason to want to escape from those which are available. Schooling as experienced by young people like Debra may simply confirm an 'estranged or at the worst damaged' learner identity (Ball et al., 1999, p. 33). In the dash for certification, for students like Debra, it is not really surprising that they quietly exclude themselves by withdrawing from a less than worthwhile experience. Debra's withdrawal is maybe one way of repairing her identity and self-esteem which has been 'damaged' by her experiences of school with its 'hidden assumptions of student inferiority' (Wexler, 1992, p. 133). In the following extract Debra provides a powerful and reflexive account of what school is like for her, and perhaps for others like herself:

Well sitting in lessons every day and listening to teachers telling you what to do, that isn't really enjoyable, is it? And being cussed up and called names isn't really enjoyable, is it? And finding the work hard, isn't enjoyable either, is it? And teachers that don't help you, don't make it enjoyable, do it? So I don't get much out of this school, do I?

I got picked on a lot because I wore glasses. I had buck teeth, you know. I kept myself to myself. I probably enjoyed primary school days better. I got picked on at primary school but I don't remember much about stuff like that.

Here there are two different sets of relations: with teachers and with other students. Debra is thus doubly 'stigmatized' and 'othered' – socially and academically she is an outsider.

Managing Her Difficulties While She Was at School

When she was fifteen and still at Northwark Park she decided that she couldn't cope:

We had loads of little fights every day, her [mother's] moaning and stuff, and I just couldn't take it no more. It did my head in and I couldn't think or nothing. It was getting me down. I went to work one day and I brought the dog back late and decided not to go home that day. I think everything just hit me that day. I couldn't face it no more. I needed space.

She stayed with a friend (not from school) and after a few days she realized that she needed to get help with housing. Her friend lived in a neighbouring borough where there was a drop-in centre for young people in her situation. But she was ineligible for help because her mother's home was out of the catchment area:

> I went to this place called 'Friends and Neighbours' in Tarvin. It is in Streetley really so they couldn't take my case on. . . . It is for people that have trouble at home or run away from home. . . . Basically I have to go home because they can't do nothing because I don't live there.

She eventually went home and things returned to 'normal'. That is, Debra sometimes went to school. She got a few GCSEs (one at grade C and two D–Gs) and was kept on into the sixth form; a form perhaps, of pragmatic rational 'choice'-making; drawing on 'personal perceptions' of what is 'possible, desirable or appropriate'. As Debra herself puts it: 'There was nothing else, was there. I ain't got no Network, I ain't got no job. I ain't got no money. So I came back to school and I'm doing A-level Art'.

She has always enjoyed copying cartoons from comics and the newspapers – but other aspects of art, life-drawing, clay work, etc. did not interest her. She had to go into school for only a few hours each week:

> I just floated away from school. I didn't go to school. It wasn't nothing even deliberate; it just sort of happened. I'd been in school for five years and I got a bit bored with it, which I did anyway, so I thought, I'm not going. And one day led to another and then it was months. I didn't even think about it.

More Changes

While Debra was drifting away from school, she was drifting towards a social world which started to take up more and more of her time. At this point, her mother started a new relationship with an unemployed and 'illegal' immigrant. Debra spent more and more time away from home, going to raves and clubbing in North London. She slept at friends' houses and flats. She was sexually active – she had arranged to 'get the depo [*depo provera*] injection. . . . I've been getting it for quite a while now. I've had it about three times. There is no way that I can get pregnant because it is 100 per cent. You can't get pregnant.' She was also involved in a series of relationships with men who were all considerably older than herself. Many of these men used soft drugs on a regular basis – some of them were dealers in the locality. Debra, perhaps inevitably, started using a range of drugs:

I was smoking weed mostly all day. I went to a friend's house and they had some crack in a pipe and you put a light at the end of it and take it all in. The first buzz, I can see how people can get addicted to it if you are not strong-minded. It can make you addicted. It just made you go all cold; that is how it come through you. Like, if someone walks over your grave. It is like that, only you feel relaxed.

Her living situation deteriorated and just before her eighteenth birthday she was housed in an emergency hostel for young women in Central London. While she was in the hostel, 'A lot of the time I was with friends. We puffed a lot, a lot, I don't remember a lot. I went into a stage of just puffing a lot'.

I don't know. I was quite happy. Maybe I was depressed but I was quite happy in my own way. Nobody was going on at me, nobody was getting me down and that. Nobody was hitting me, no stress. Just me in my little room puffing and listening to the radio. It was peaceful and that. And the voices on the radio were some company. . . . I just puffed a lot. I just did it. I didn't know what else to do.

In this way, she escaped from all those things that bored, hurt, oppressed, damaged her self-esteem: her school, her home, her peers.

Housing

One of the problems which Debra has had to manage has been the issue of housing. In many ways, had she been eligible for help at an earlier point, perhaps her life would not have been quite so hard. However, as we have seen, while she was in the hostel, she was using recreational drugs on a regular basis. She was also staying out late and by now had entered into a new relationship with Leroy, a married man in his forties. He had been sacked from his job as a 'bin man' for the local council because of previous drug dealing offences. He has two teenage children and a son in primary school. Debra was not coping in the hostel and eventually was re-housed in a short-term tenancy where her partner stays-over most nights:

I had like a key worker that I had to see every few weeks. They said, have I got Irish in the family, which I have, so they got in touch with an Irish Company who help you with housing. . . . I moved into Billington Cross and I stayed with two other women. They have moved out now so there is only me in the house so I am having housing problems now as well because they want to get me out and want to take me through the courts to do it and stuff. And they aren't going to re-house me either.

The two other women were much older and quieter than Debra. They were both in full-time employment. Tensions between them, and Debra's noisy, erratic lifestyle, led to many disputes. Crucially at this stage, and supported by her key worker, Debra had registered for a GNVQ foundation course in Performing Arts at Bracebridge College, with a view to obtaining work as a dancer in nightclubs in Denmark, where her father lived. She also had a 'little, cash-in-hand job' in a local cafe serving teas and washing up – she was trying to get her life in shape but it started to disintegrate as her housing difficulties came to a head:

> So everything is just stress. I thought it was going all right. I got the flat, I got the job, forty pounds cash-in-hand, start College, everything going to work for me. And then, no job, no money and then the letter [saying they wanted to evict me]. So everything is just stress.
>
> He [landlord] like said, we are going to bring the bailiffs round, change the locks. I was really scared. I know I'm living on my own and all that. I didn't know nothing about housing and stuff and then I found out that I can get in touch with a solicitor. Now I have got a solicitor involved, he [landlord] is all nice to me. . . . I went to a few drop-in centres, they help you about housing and stuff and one Youth Advisor sent me to a solicitor just where I live. He is really nice.

What is evident here is that Debra's life seems to move between brief periods of 'stability' and crises – involving necessarily complex but intermittent support from various social agencies. What is also evident is the fragility of these brief periods of stability – and the powerful role of contingency in her biography.

Debra's Attitudes to Her Circumstances

Like others in our cohort, Debra seems to take an almost fatalistic attitude towards her life and the social world she inhabits. This stance has not shifted over time:

> I don't know, I take it day by day. I don't make plans because they are always messed up anyway. I am not the kind of person to make plans because when I make plans they never work and then I get upset, so it's not worth making plans see (age fifteen).

> Things never work out for me, so . . . I just take it day-by-day. That way, you don't get no disappointments, do you? I think I could get a dog even if the other things don't work (age seventeen).

> That's life, innit. You never know what's going to happen. You're going along OK and then, bang, it all goes wrong. You never know what's going to happen, so I don't bother no more. Just take each day as it comes (age eighteen).

> I live life everyday. I've always said that, you know. You never know what's round the corner, so don't make no plans because they will come falling down round your head. Take it a day at a time, I do (age nineteen).

In an extensive study of households in Kirkcaldy, McCrone identified two 'broad sets of ideas that people use to make sense of the future of their individual and collective lives' which he called 'getting by' and 'making out' (McCrone, 1994, p. 99). Making out

> involves taking a longer-term perspective, taking decisions in the short-term which have deliberately long-term implications, marking off, as it were, milestones of progress along the way, indulging in strategic thinking and behaviour. (p. 69)

As opposed to that is getting by, which is 'about coping in the short-term, say on a day-to-day or week-to-week basis'. Although McCrone also notes that

> Clearly people can be more or less strategic, and where the former is the case and where they have achieved their aims, we can say that they have 'made out'. In practice, however, most people behaving strategically, will still have their goals to achieve, which is why the idea of a process, of 'making out', is preferred. (p. 69)

However, while there are class differences between the two groups – planners and non-planners – every household employs 'coping devices to get by' (p. 73). McCrone believes that getting by can involve some 'intricate and highly competent routines' (p. 70) (see also Chapter 8 below).

Debra has a realistic view of her life and her world: 'I just want simple things, ain't it, no big, impossible dreams for me, just ordinary things'. She is attempting to get by and she certainly has had to negotiate some highly complex routines in order to sustain herself and her self-confidence.

Debra eschews any 'imagined future' – seeing beyond the immediate barriers of daily existence, money, shelter and friendship becomes impossible. And her pragmatically rational perspective is set against a work-based identity and does not fit the normative and structural 'futurity' of the learning society – the planning for future employment and investment in skills acquisition. Debra's life is driven by a different rationality and different material needs and constraints.

Choosing, Surviving or What?

In Debra's life to date, she has had to negotiate herself through a number of difficult sets of circumstances: her immediate family; her lack of success socially and educationally in school; her housing difficulties; her relationships with men. However, in all this she still retains a sense that going to college is important, that certification is potentially a step forward for her, if only she can get all the other things in place which will permit her to access the chance. But she is fatalistic – little evidence of a biographical project here?

I've been sort of surviving. There isn't a lot that people can do in this world. If you are surviving that is about it. There aren't many people that can do anything else but survive unless you are a millionaire or something. That's how life goes, innit. You survive or go down and die. There's not much choice, like I say, unless you are a millionaire and I'm not that. So I just survived (age eighteen).

Her mother now has a ten-month old daughter, Breeze, who sleeps in Debra's old bedroom. She cannot realistically go home even if she wanted to. She is worried, though, that her Mum may start to beat Jade. She is also worried because her last partner but one (Blade) has just informed her that he has herpes. It looks as if her current relationship with Leroy is in a fragile condition – he is about to go back to his wife. She is not yet sure what will happen about her short-term tenancy and her longer-term accommodation needs. She also has a fundamental organizational and confidence problem, a 'damaged' learning identity (Rees et al., 1997).

I'm not into the College. I'm just trying to get back into a routine of getting up in the mornings and be in College for five hours or so, you know. And I will see how that goes. I was scared to go to College. I didn't know if I had the confidence and that, but it wasn't just that. It was, would I manage to get up in the mornings, get up three mornings a week? I didn't have no routine did I. . . . But if you go to College, it's not just the course. Will I manage that, will I meet people who will like speak to me? No, it's not just that, it's the routine, getting up in the morning

Ayesha

Ayesha lived with her Indian mother until she was nearly fourteen. However, her Barbadian father had left their home when she was a little girl. Ayesha's mother has always worked long hours as a clerical worker in order to maintain the mortgage and pay the bills. They lived in their own house in South London and Ayesha attended a successful, local, comprehensive school until her early teens when her problems came to a head. She was pregnant. She was deemed to be 'at risk' and was placed with a black foster family.

Like Debra, Ayesha had been abused by her mother over a long period of time. Like Debra, Ayesha's parents' marriage had broken down at an early stage in her childhood:

She [Mum] beat me up . . . anything that I done wrong, like stupid little things.

At the age of four he [Dad] left. He wanted to come back. My Mum wouldn't take him back. I was really angry and crying. My Dad used to stand at the [school] gate and call me over and I would end up crying and the teachers would end up telling my Mum and at the end they had to get an injunction out on him which she did. My Mum thought I was a traitor and I used to stick up for my Dad.

Ayesha had enjoyed her primary school and her secondary school experience began well. However, the disruptions and abuse which she experienced in her family and at home caused her to stay out late and she started to get involved with a serious boyfriend. She was finding it difficult to relate to her Mum. She was doing much of the housework and looking after herself almost full-time: 'I've always looked after myself, done my own washing, done the shopping and that, so I've always been independent ever since I was a little girl'. Her attendance became intermittent and she gradually stopped going altogether. She discovered she was pregnant. She was obviously a very unhappy young girl at this time and started to run away on a fairly regular basis: 'I came back in March and I ran away again . . . and I had nearly finished school and Social Services decided that I should find myself a job. . . . They set a few goals for me.' As a minor who had been deemed 'at risk' Ayesha had a social worker and was given the support of local state-welfare professionals in relation to her finances, living arrangements and education and training needs. However, she was not happy with what was arranged for her. She had said that she was interested in the business side of catering, hotels, travel and tourism. The social worker arranged a training experience in a local kitchen, but Ayesha felt exploited. She was not getting any training and was not paid the overtime she had been led to believe she would get to compensate for her long hours – 7 am until 4 or 5 pm each day.

> That is what I spent my time doing the most, was the dishes and she said that, if I was to work later than after half past two, because that was the time I finished, I would get extra pay and I never got extra pay. I never got extra pay. . . . I am only 16, they are supposed to be helping me, training and teaching me. . . . And she [Training advisor] is shooting off her mouth and screaming at me and I don't like it.

As her social and emotional world became increasingly fractured and fragile, her educational world was sidelined. Her move away from mainstream education into the PRU may indirectly have started to close off curriculum options for her. Her formal education moved towards a less inclusive and more temporary type of provision. Her experience of post-compulsory provision was tightly located in on-the-job training – where the emphasis was on 'doing' rather than on much training – at least from Ayesha's perspective. Thus, 'being looked after' might well have reduced Ayesha's opportunities and compounded her educational disadvantage (Pearce and Hillman, 1998).

Running Away, Housing and Coping

Both Debra and Ayesha resorted to 'running away' as a tactic for coping with aspects of their family lives and social worlds. Ayesha repeatedly ran away from her foster home and described one early experience:

> It was OK. I was watching television. I had nobody breathing down my neck. I felt free. I felt comfortable even when I had no money and I was hungry.

> There was no food in the house. He [the friend she stayed with] expected me,
> everything had been paid for, he paid all his bills, except his phone bill which
> was cut off. I was a bit distressed about that and because I was hungry, so I
> had a few friends a couple of doors away and they said 'Oh, come in and have
> something to eat'. They gave me a change of clothes and I had a bath as well.
> It was very nice. So I was OK. I was perfectly fine.

While Ayesha was able to use this period of running away to gain some respite and
'feel free', she was obligated to have sex with the man who had made this arrangement for her. In fact, she said that frequently when she ran away she exchanged
sex for accommodation.

Ayesha has spent a period of four years, running away for short periods, staying
where she could, with people she hardly knew and getting involved in abusive
relationships and drug taking.

> He said, if you don't go I will chuck you out. Then I stayed for about two days
> and I found somewhere to go. So I decided that I should find somewhere else
> to live. . . . Then I went down to his Mum's place and I stayed there, but his
> Mum thought that I was homeless because they told her that I was seventeen.
> So she kept me for a couple of days and then her husband told her that I was
> lying and that I was only fifteen. . . . So there was an empty flat so I squatted
> in there for a little while.
>
>   But that took a lot of strain. I was always hungry and I needed a change of
> clothes and cigarettes and the pressure of doing it every day constantly got to
> me. So I went to another friend and she said, 'I know a friend who has got a
> flat', so I lived there for two weeks.

Ayesha took a lot of drugs during this period of her life; what she calls her 'wild
time'. Like Debra, she had tried a wide range of soft and hard drugs and found
'being out of it' was one way of coping with her feelings and depressions:

> I was taking more than an addicted person would be with drugs. I was worse
> than them and I just didn't even care. But I got off it so easily. . . . I ran away
> and I just didn't care what happened to me. . . . I just didn't care and I was
> just depressed and angry and I was just taking anything. But I got off it all and
> that was it.

In many ways, what has happened to Ayesha seems to have been that while some
of her basic needs have been attended to – she was found a foster home, she was
placed in the PRU, she was assigned a social worker, careers advisor and helped
towards a Modern Apprenticeship – in other ways, other tensions round issues
of self-esteem, confidence, insecurity, stability and family disruption seem to
have hardly been touched at all. Currently she is being supported through the
Independent Living Scheme (ILS) which is available to over-18s and helps with
accommodation and provision of cookers, fridges, etc. But again, she experiences

the process as one of too much control: 'I am on it [ILS] but I am not attending any of the meetings because I don't like people telling me what I should do with the money I earn, right. I don't like them telling me.'

Included Again?

By the time Ayesha had finished with her 'wild time' she was housed in a hostel for young women in the local area. Her social worker and a mentor had arranged for her to attend the local FE college and she managed to complete an NVQ Level 1. Her mentor had arranged a Modern Apprenticeship in the local college where she was also employed as a secretarial assistant. Ayesha has to work for four days and studies for Level 2 and 3 of a Business Administration NVQ one day a week. She has a wage and a roof over her head. In many ways this is a good example of 're-entry' and inclusion. Paradoxically, young people who have become involved with careworkers are more likely to get re-entered to FE; the 'ordinary' kids like Rees, Jolene and Daryl (see Chapter 8) go mostly 'unnoticed.' Nevertheless, Ayesha is aware of a mismatch between herself and other 'normal' kids:

> I just want to get this training over and done with. For me to actually get on with this job and get a good reference off my boss, I will have to grow up a bit more you know. I was grown up before, I just let it go because I thought, I am only seventeen and there is no point in me being a grown up when I was seventeen and I should be doing what normal kids do and having fun.

Her family life is still posing emotional problems for her. Her mother has been saying that she will relocate in Spain and sell up the family house. Ayesha feels disturbed about this for while she is realistic about her childhood experiences, her house, her actual home, provides a sense of belonging somewhere and is a point of security:

> My real Mum is going to live in Portugal in two weeks. . . . I was upset, I was very upset about it but then I feel that she is gone and she has never looked after me anyway. I have looked after myself all my life . . . my Mum she may have looked after me a bit, she may have put clothes on my back, food in my mouth, but she hasn't been there. She hasn't been there. . . . She was in but she didn't want to speak to me, she was too tired. I feel the same about my Dad. My Dad hasn't done anything, he hasn't got any proof that he's my parent basically because he has done nothing since he left.

If her mother does actually leave London, although her Dad is not far away, he is not really capable of much at all. Ayesha does ring her mother from time to time and still attempts to maintain a relationship with her, something which is not possible with her father: 'You know, my dad is drinking and he has always drunk, but he says that he doesn't drink anymore but I find out that he is a drunk and he sleeps every day and he is up in the night.' Ayesha persisted with her NVQ but failed part of the Level 2 requirements. She passed the Business Administration part but failed in the Computer Examination. She was still pressing on to Level 3 and was ambitious in this aspect of her life. She also made better housing arrangements and after her eighteenth birthday was given her own bedsit in the locality. However, she was now attempting to cope with a second miscarriage:

> I lost a baby last month. Yes, my second miscarriage. I was five months pregnant when I lost the baby so, you know, things have been pretty tough. Split up [from the father] once the baby died. Didn't know him very long . . . am trying at the moment to get over the baby and everything. It was my second miscarriage because my first miscarriage was when I was 14. That was when I was nine months pregnant. I was expecting a baby and then I lost it, you know. It is just difficult at the moment. This one brought it all back and it's just so difficult. I work hard. I go to work just to get my mind off things because I never went to work for two months.

She was very depressed and took time off work:

> I am not depressed or anything about it like I was two months ago. That was because I stayed in bed, starved myself, made myself ill for two months. . . . So, you know, I suppose at the end of the day I have to pick myself back up and get myself into work. I think that is the only thing that takes my mind off things.

Ayesha was still extremely hurt. She had recently been contacted by her first boyfriend from secondary school. He had proposed marriage to her after their second meeting and she was thinking of getting engaged and making a commitment to settle down with him. Underneath, she was still apprehensive and emotionally fragile:

> I've been waiting for men all my life, three or four months, waiting for them to call. They think they can pick you up when it suits them and then dump you again. I tell you, I've waited for men from my Dad to boyfriends and they never ring. They just let you down. . . . I don't know what is going to happen about my boyfriend and my ex because I've been in situations like this before and I know people just let you down, throw it all back in your face and hurt you and that. . . . I'm not rushing into anything because I don't want to get hurt again.

Like Debra, Ayesha sometimes displays a fatalistic and day-to-day attitude towards her life. She finds it hard to see much of a future for herself and tries not to plan too far ahead. Like Debra, in many ways this is a sensible tactic in the light of her life experiences to date. Both young women are heavily invested in getting by rather than making out and perhaps this is (for now) the best they can do – a pragmatically rational stance, which nevertheless involves many coping devices 'in handling day-to-day and week-to-week living' (McCrone, 1994, p. 70). Debra and Ayesha have to battle with extremely complex exigencies often in a short-term manner – for it is only the short-term (housing, jobs) which is available as part of their 'horizons for action'. Thus, both young women try to make a good emotional and social life for now – letting the future take care of itself.

Interestingly, and somewhat contradictorily, in the following extract we see that Ayesha is bound up in a personal dilemma. Her plans are thwarted by others so there is no point in planning for the future:

> That's part of the trouble. I don't feel I have any control, to tell you the truth, because other people are always telling me what to do and what not to do. I can't just do what I want, and so my plans always go wrong, and so I don't bother because it's just not worth it.

And yet, she does have plans or desires for a 'normal' biography, although again she is concerned that too much support has reduced her personal autonomy. Perhaps she wants to make out but is caught up, for now, in a culture of getting by.

> I don't think very much about the future because it's hard enough living just now, never mind thinking about next week, next month. No, I just try and take it as it comes. What's the use I think, what's the use. I used to think I'd like this and that, but no, it never happens. There's always someone who says, 'No Ayesha, you can't do that, don't be stupid Ayesha, how could you do that?' And so, no I can't take it much more to tell you the truth. I'd like a flat and a car but, I don't know. . . . Sometimes I don't think I'll ever be on my own, making my own decisions. Sometimes I think I'll never get away from people telling me what to do.

Social Inclusion – More Rhetoric?

Debra and Ayesha have both had to cope with some debilitating experiences so far in their lives. One of the striking aspects is the persistent and cumulative nature of the events that take place and the multiple disadvantages which both young women face (Pearce and Hillman, 1998). Both young women have had a difficult start; for various reasons they have probably felt rejected as children. Both have tried running away. There was not the appropriate help right at the start when it might have made a real difference. Running away resulted in both running into more problems – abusive relationships with men as well as abuse of drugs. In consequence, it was almost impossible to manage jobs, college or any sort of regular commitments. Without any regular income, housing became another difficulty to be managed.

At some critical moments or turning points, Debra and Ayesha were unable to access external support or advice. Housing was either not available because of their age or because of where they were living. Both young women have also been in need of contraceptive and sexual health support. Ayesha seems not to have had any support with the emotional stress of two late miscarriages. Debra found her mainstream schooling too difficult and her learning difficulties were never really constructively recognized. Ayesha was removed from mainstream and placed in a PRU, thus denying her access to specialist teaching and the full range of the mainstream National Curriculum. To a degree then, both young women were let down by mainstream education which could not respond to their complex and interrelated sets of individual needs. There was no on-going counselling for these young women with emotional and social difficulties, no systematic help with sexual relationships or contraceptive support.

On the other hand, Ayesha in particular has had support in relation to post-compulsory education and training – something which Debra has seemed to lack. Perhaps paradoxically, there is a danger here of what (Corbett, 1990, p. 3) calls 'the oppression of apparent kindness'; Ayesha believes that she has been on the receiving end of interventions which have sidelined her own decision-making. Young people who are at risk of exclusion may also be excluded from important aspects of citizenship such as being involved in choice-making processes. As Corbett (1990, p. 1) says, 'it is at transition to the world of adult autonomy, employment, training or continued education that a marginalised status becomes uncomfortably evident'. At this stage, some young people may be shoe-horned into some vocational pathway or another, although this may well cut-off later life-choices.

In a context where social exclusion policy and practice mainly deals with factors related to employment, such as the real need for qualifications and skills, this may work to marginalize other aspects of exclusion (such as inadequate housing, for example). If these are not addressed coherently and systematically, they can operate to counteract positive interventions on the employment front. In consequence policies of social inclusion which are reactive and not responsive to a range of dilemmas may not be successful. In part this may depend on whose definition of social exclusion is in play – for this will precipitate a specific policy response. Some definitions are professionally constructed and not mediated by the young people themselves. A young woman attempting to come to terms with a second late miscarriage on her own in a bed-sit will not be best placed for success at NVQ examinations.

A cursory consideration of the young people in our cohort (see Table 4.1) who can be considered as socially excluded reveals some commonalities. Many of these young people were intermittent school attenders and thus have very few qualifications (Bynner and Parsons, 1997). Many have experienced troubled family lives. Some of these young people may not have been well served by the National Curriculum, which proved irrelevant to their interests and needs and thus compounded damage done to their 'learner identities'.

In this chapter we have considered the narratives of two young women whom for now, we have called socially excluded, although their narratives make the point that social exclusion is not an absolute. Young women coping with inadequate accommodation or attempting to develop self-esteem or rebuild their lives after extended periods of homelessness and substance abuse are, understandably, less concerned about some of the technical demands of the 'learning society' than with their emotional lives. Work-place identities may just not be anywhere near as central and powerful as emotional and 'relational' identities such as daughter, mother, girlfriend. Social exclusion itself needs to be extended beyond the employment–training context to include critical factors such as family disruption, poverty in childhood and the loss of confidence and self-esteem which can often accompany these debilitating life experiences. There are some vexed issues here: can the state take over and rebuild emotionally shattered lives when 'kindness' is already felt by some as oppressive? One way forward might lie in the policies which focus on supporting families at an early pre-school stage and challenging poverty (schemes such as Sure Start which are currently being developed by the Labour Government's Social Exclusion Unit). Other tactics could involve a recovery and expansion of the pastoral work of schools which has been displaced by more traditional academic concerns.

Finally, in almost all the narratives we have elicited, there is a fragility and contingency involved in the sorts of identities which the young people in our sample are busy constructing for themselves. The identities which they (have to) construct are contingent on sets of structural and material factors and are embedded in the social fabric of their real social worlds – that is, their identities are bounded by time–space variables. Different and alternative identities co-exist at the same time. Ayesha has managed to hold onto a version of a 'learning identity' through her struggle to get proper training with a recognized accreditation; she is also struggling to accommodate to family disruption and her emotional needs.

In these stories, post-compulsory education and training, the normative rhetoric of the learning society and lifelong learning, have a somewhat hollow ring and seem divorced from the day-to-day worlds of young women like Ayesha and Debra. The temporal normalizations of the learning society are set in terms of making out and a great deal of forward planning – which clashes with the 'getting by' approach of these two women and the other socially excluded young people in our study. As Hodkinson et al. (1996, p. 156) say, there is a need to 'recognise that inequalities will not be lessened by paying attention to the young people themselves. Changes are needed to job availability, employer recruitment patterns, workplace cultures and labour market structures' – a critical point. A learning society which concentrates on individual 'deficit' rather than wider structural concerns may well be counter-productive (Coffield, 1996). If unjust social structures are sidelined and not addressed by policies of social inclusion the central dilemma will remain undisturbed.

Yet, to finish with Debra and Ayesha, both of these young women do see a need to continue with their education and training and actively are still doing their best to press on. They are struggling to get by in the hopes of someday making out.

5 Learning Fatigue, 'Choice Biographies' and Leisure
Aaron, Lucy and Anne

Culture and Labour Market Reproduction: A Tight Fit?

In the sociology of youth there has been a long-standing concern to document the connectedness between 'ideologies of traditional masculinity, the institution of waged labour and the process of working class culture in contemporary society' (Haywood and Mac An Ghaill, 1996, p. 22). The same prescription about class-reproduction is also to be found, but to a lesser extent, in relation to young women. While the studies which traced this connectedness in respect of young working-class women suggested that they recognized the domestic and labour market oppressions which their mothers, aunts and older sisters were tied up in, never-theless, they also experienced early adulthood as an expression of a clearly gendered cultural and labour market-reproduction (McRobbie and Nava, 1984; Griffin 1985).

In an attempt to move beyond this approach, there was a shift towards focusing on youth culture as a 'struggle for cultural space' – as a form of resistance. However, what this frequently resulted in was a further demonstration of connectedness. 'What youth cultures offered were 'imaginary' solutions to structural contra-dictions' (Brake, 1990, p. 216). Youth style and culture was read off as a signifier for particular classed tensions. Perhaps the classic study was the work carried out by Willis (1977), who made the compelling argument that earlier models of reproduction theory were problematic. Willis' 'lads' created a particular form of masculinity which stood against the values of their school, neither simply repro-ductive nor fully creative and resistant, but rather based on 'partial penetrations' of capitalist schooling. The difference now was that youth culture became a contradiction – what Brake (1990) calls a 'double articulation' where the style/ culture produced was both antagonistic to the status quo (school life and its claims of egalitarianism) while neatly 'fitting up' the lads for restricted life chance after schooling, rendering them 'perfect' for factory and shop-floor life. Thus, leisure and life-style were bound up in reproducing (a labour market) identity.

Because of this resolution, Brake (1990, p. 217) believes that since the late 1970s and early 1980s research into youth culture and life-style has been displaced by a material/structural analysis. He argues that 'British sociology is more concerned with youth policy, legislation, youth unemployment, and in the transition or "broken apprenticeship" (now elongated) from education to work' (p. 217). He continues that although there has been a concern with school sub-cultures, which concentrated on groups less evident in earlier youth culture studies (black youth and girls/young women), 'there is no large scale research centrally studying youth culture at present' (although see Fornas and Bolin, 1995 for work in Sweden).

In much of the current work which examines youth transitions there is a raft of 'silences' – and in particular, very few studies examine the status and role of leisure and pleasure in the lives of young people at the end of the twentieth century (but see Hendry et al., 1993; Roberts and Parsell, 1994; Hollands, 1995). The major thrust, work which centres on the 'learning society' or the movement towards 'life-long learning', has at its centre a concern with upskilling, reskilling and labour-market needs – policies of futurity, the work ethic and human capital theory which generate between them a very utilitarian version of what it is to be a young person in contemporary society (Rees et al., 1997). Furthermore, until recently, very few studies have examined the social context of relatively privileged adolescents in this (but see Du Bois-Reymond, 1998) or the impact for all young people of a growing common culture and youth life-style form (Willis, 1998).

One of the first studies in the UK to focus its attention on middle-class youth was undertaken by Aggleton (1987). In his work on post-school transitions he identified a range of what he called 'sub-cultural practices' – and 'a blurring of distinctions between work and leisure' (p. 98). The young people in Aggleton's study wanted to 'pursue educational opportunities which allowed for individual creativity and personal autonomy' but they did not just want to pursue education (p. 134). Aggleton noted that the middle class students in his sample were caught up in a culture of 'effortless achievement' where they:

> displayed apathy towards elements of self-denial, ritualized training, and prior effort in the attainment of qualifications. . . . Instead they acted as if their own innate talents and cultural capital would, *of themselves*, provide sufficient basis for entry into, and success within, fields of practice associated with creative art forms (pp. 134–5).

Many of the middle-class young people in our study exhibited similar attitudes. Their social lives are not just sub-cultural practices, they are pivotal elements of their identities and are equal to, if not more important than, their educational selves. For Aaron, Lucy and Anne, whose narratives are reported in this chapter, their identities are firmly (for now) centred in their leisure and social life (see Figure 11.1 below). As Wyn and Dwyer (1999, p. 5) have argued: 'established linear models of transitions, adulthood and future careers are increasingly inappropriate for the changed economic and social conditions of the late twentieth century'. For middle-class youth, becoming an adult, or at least a 'post-adolescent', is bound up with short-term choices and discontinuities, such as the 'gap year' and 'running wild before I commit myself' (Du Bois-Reymond, 1998, p. 73), as against the older linear transition from school, through college, into work. These discontinuities may even have something to do with 'running out' of motivation, interest or concern about education and training, at least for now – a form of 'learning fatigue'.

Aaron, Lucy and Anne

All three of these young people come from relatively 'new middle-class' backgrounds (see Appendix 2, Table 2.1). Clearly, it is more possible for them (financially) to have a positive 'imagined future' (a 'normal biography' of work, family and obligations) than is the case for others. Materially, it is also possible for them to have life-styles now where leisure and pleasure are intrinsically linked into an identity which encompasses a work/study dimension. Lucy and Anne did participate in post-compulsory education. Aaron had a year out at this stage. They are also all allowed 'considerable personal autonomy with respect to what they did within the home and when they were absent from it' (Aggleton, 1987, p. 59). They also have sufficient incomes from various employment and from their families to sustain an expensive social life.

Aaron: A Case of Learning Fatigue?

Aaron's parents divorced when he was 15. When he was first being interviewed for the project he was living with his mother and her new partner in their terraced house in South London. His mother was just moving into a new position – UK representative for an international company. His father, who is a graduate, works for an oil company and is based in Africa. Aaron has always kept in regular touch with his father and his step-brothers and sisters.

Aaron's life has been characterized by change and movement. He left the UK at six months of age with his family and has lived in Australia, Papua New Guinea, South Africa and Zambia. He has also travelled extensively; Canada, Hong Kong, Japan and Indonesia. For this reason he may not have been as 'tied into' the UK discourses of the learning society and the pressures to succeed at 16 which typified the narratives of nearly all our cohort – even those who were unlikely to do well (Macrae et al., 1997).

He registered as a student at Northwark Park in Year 10. He was not impressed with his UK school experience and was 'bored'; he thought it was too small with 'not enough people'. He also thought the work was too easy:

> I came over and I found the maths really easy. I had done it all before in Africa and the English, we did the same thing now that I did two years ago. . . . If I moved from here to Africa it would be a lot harder for me to do because it is harder work there . . . I could probably start my O-levels over there and come back and do University here. I would have caught up and got ahead from being in Africa.

In his interviews Aaron appeared to be very mature and very composed. He enjoyed 'skateboarding, rollerblading and raves.' He is a very attractive and personable young man. He has longish blonde hair which is very carefully cut. He wears very expensive casual designer clothing and clearly takes a great deal of time, trouble and money over his appearance. While he was still at Northwark Park he would go out to clubs and raves with his mates at the weekend. He mixed regularly with people in their mid-to-late twenties:

> Like, down Armitage they are all twenty seven and thirty down the pubs there. I know some people down there. You just go in and play cards and things. I know a few adults in Lydgate but I don't really go and visit them that much, they are just good mates. It is nice to have older mates . . . I mean, with older people it is all right, you don't really get up to that much mischief.

Aaron has a very adult life-style which seemed almost 'interrupted' by his school-child life. He attended school on and off (58 per cent in Years 10 and 11) and although he fully realized the importance of qualifications and wanted to earn good money, he was always reasonably sure that he could postpone things for a bit and take it easy. Aaron's mother organized him and managed to hold things together for him but admitted that he had an absorbing social life. She was 'staggered' by his knowledge of fashion, labels and his expensive clothing needs. He kept in touch with her through his mobile telephone. While he was still at school he said:

> I was thinking that I would like a little rest from this summer coming until the next one. I am quite young. I am 16 in July this year and then a month later I start college. So I was thinking I could have a year's rest and start when I was 17 and that would have been just on time. But no, I will just go for it – two years over and done with.

He spent much of his time 'bunking off' from school and did very badly in his exams. He spent time with his mother in her small house in Lydgate and then went back for a break to stay with his father. While he was overseas his mother obtained a place for him at a local college to do a GNVQ in Leisure and Tourism; an area he had always been attracted to. When he came back, he started the course but eventually returned to live with his father. Currently his mother reports that he is thinking of doing A-levels and going on to University in Africa sometime in the future. 'He has come good at last'.

The point to stress in this somewhat 'intermittent' narrative is that Aaron has always taken an independent stance towards his life: 'I really do what I want now really because my parents trust me. I can go out when I want and come back when I want'. His position is less space/time-bound than any of the others in his peer group. His socioscape is global rather than local. He believes that he can always catch up, or do courses at a later stage of his life and in a different place. His family has the material and social capital to support his life of postponed 'choice' – the rhetoric and persuasiveness of the learning society have less immediacy for Aaron. This is not to say that Aaron does not recognize the longer-term advantages of formal education and, in particular, the currency of a degree – he does. But not for now and certainly not yet (Du Bois-Reymond, 1998).

While other young people in our study 'dropped out' from education and training, 'choosing' to look for employment and rejecting the thoughts of any more schooling, Aaron and Lucy were the only young people to make the decision to have a 'gap year' after GCSEs. Kidd (1992, p. 129) argues that: 'young people will only remain in an education system if it is attractive, if it is accessible, if it caters for a wide range of abilities, if it is flexible and if success is the reality for the majority'. In other words, the students must perceive staying on as in some way helpful. Aaron had run out of steam and, temporarily at least, was experiencing learning fatigue: 'I think I will take a year off . . . I just need a break'. The 'need' to move on and progress from course to course in a linear fashion clearly was not an imperative and was not a central part of Aaron's identity or perspective at this moment of his life.

Lucy: A Mixed Model of 'Choice Biography'?

Lucy is a white middle-class young woman who has always intended to do media studies at university. (She also figures in Chapter 6.) Her mother is a deputy-head in a school and her father worked until recently as a Senior Administrator in a local Senior Citizens Home. He has just been made redundant. The family own a house in South London. In some ways Lucy is a bit like Aaron in that she is currently having a 'gap year' – a more conventional one between A-levels and University. She also inhabits a world where education, work, social life and domesticity are currently interwoven. However, she is different from Aaron – she has not disengaged from that part of her identity which is bound up with learning. She has actively chosen to have a gap between school and university, a well-earned break before proceeding onto what she calls 'the next stage'.

In her interviews over time she has emerged as someone who recognized the persuasiveness of the need for qualifications as well as the attractiveness and desirability of a good social life. Lucy has carefully 'balanced' these sometimes oppositional demands throughout her immediate post-compulsory trajectory – at least from 16 to 18. In many ways she has constructed a 'choice biography' which mixes work, leisure and study and can involve 'interruption and deferral of courses' (Wyn and Dwyer, 1999, p. 8).

While at Northwark Park Lucy had been 'freaked out' by the experience of careers advice when she was 16. While this is now an 'out-of date' experience which she may not recall, it is worth citing here as it underscores the inevitability of transition 'for people like her' and it accents the need for independence and self-reliance at a difficult and pressured time of life change in a 'risky' society.

> We had a careers interview which was meant to help but it freaked me out a bit more than it helped. The lady didn't help me much. Well she didn't tell me much. I have to go and find out about colleges myself and you just have to do it yourself really I think. Well I did . . . She made me a bit scared as

well because she made it sound like it was really close when it is not really (finishing education and obtaining work). Not for me anyway hopefully. She, I came away almost in tears . . . I got quite upset and I was kind of shaking and scared because she made it sound like tomorrow.

She became extremely stressed while she was working for her GCSEs and had needed to take some time out of school in order to cope – she had actually been sent home on a couple of occasions when she had broken down in tears. It is sometimes forgotten that even those who are 'more successful' are under considerable stress in the highly hyped period of public examinations which excite a growing amount of media attention each year (see Luke in Chapter 7 and Lucey, 1996).

Nevertheless, Lucy proceeded unproblematically to undertake three A-levels at Riverway College with an excellent reputation for academic success (see Chapter 6). In common with nearly all of our cohort who did stay on, she also worked to earn extra spending money. She had a number of committed relationships – serial monogamy – and, until recently, was going out with Josh, whose family lives nearby in South London.

Lucy has always had a good social life. This is important to her well-being and sense of self. She did not defer pleasure until after her A-levels. She was an experienced club-goer and was allowed to stay out quite late in the sixth form as her family trusted her. Even then, she was quite clear about what was acceptable/unacceptable to her:

> I went to the Coliseum in Honeywood. It holds about 4,000 people. We queued up for two and a half hours to get in. It is just a nightmare. I didn't want to go but it was someone's birthday and they begged me to come. Then they, the girls had to go one side and the boys had to go the other. They literally searched you, like touched you everywhere, then, they search you for drugs. You go in and as soon as you walk through the door 'you want some speed love, want some E's love?' It is like, how did you get in with drugs when I've just had this horrible search of my body, and they keep on pestering you. I was there, I stayed in the club for half an hour. I couldn't bear it. I was like, I am going home. I don't care if I paid £10 to get in. I'm going home.

She would sometimes go out in the middle of the week but nearly always went out at the weekend to have a good time with her friends. She was able to set priorities – and here it is obvious that education is too important to jeopardize for short-term interests and fun – but fun has to figure regularly too.

Lucy: I do go to clubs and stuff in London. My favourite club, Bar Rumba, I think it closes at 3.30. Yes, it's good. . . . Well they don't search you to begin with and no-one pesters you. That is why I like it. Nobody pesters you. You can just dance and get drunk and have fun.

Int: So this is at weekends, you go to these clubs? Do you go during the week as well?

Lucy: Only if it is a special night at a club. Some clubs do the odd special event. I go along but not really. It is not worth it. I would be too tired the next day. . . . It is £10 sort of average to get into these places, after eleven, between £10 and £15 just to go in. Drinks are like £4 each time. So it adds up and then there might be a mini-cab home. So £30 doesn't go far.

Lucy has worked doing baby sitting as well as bar work in order to supplement the allowance her parents have always given her but entertainment is very expensive. She works long hours if needed. What she has learned is how to construct and manage a 'mixed but balanced' social, work and educational identity

Currently she is in a serious relationship with Josh. She stays with his family and he stays at her parents' house. Both sets of parents have met. Josh is in the first year of a university degree. Lucy is intending to study Media Studies at the same university. They have rented a flat and have set up home together with the support of both sets of parents. However, while these domestic commitments are serious, Lucy still appreciates the need for her own educational progression. She recognizes that the possession of a degree will give her additional access to life-chances which will not be there for non-graduates. 'Most people just do a degree in what they want, what they enjoy and then look for a job and most jobs haven't got anything to do with their degrees.' However, she also recognizes the need for a good social life which complements (not supplements or substitutes for) all the important parts of her life and identity:

> Well, I go to the pub every night, every single night . . . every Monday, once a month all my friends go out to dinner. . . . We go to Pizza Express. We love it there. We stay there all night eating and drinking and getting fat. Only girls, no boys are allowed.

She has more or less stopped going to clubs which she recognizes are only there for 'pulling'. In some ways too she has moved on from an earlier set of leisured experiences which are for her currently redundant, towards a more adult context:

> We would much rather go to a cocktail bar and have some fun than go to a place where the music is banging and you can't hear anything and you can't breathe because there is smoke everywhere and horrible men chatting you up. . . . My ex-boyfriend, is still going to clubs every night of the week except for maybe Monday because Sunday night he is too drugged up to move or something.

Lucy is looking forward to enjoying her gap year which she will spend with Josh, rather than in travelling to South America which had been her original intention. She had always intended having a break before the last stage in her education. For now, through a process of interrupted education, and a committed domestic context Lucy is enjoying her life. She has constructed a 'mixed pattern' of 'choice biography' which distances her 'from the ethos of a work ethic that placed success in the workplace above all else' (Wyn and Dwyer, 1999, p. 17) and which asserts the importance of relationships and quality of life right now. She believes that the world has changed for her generation:

> There is more emphasis now on leaving your childhood and being young. Long ago people had to grow up like really early and go to work and pay money into the house and whatever. But now you might as well have fun this age because you are going to get serious as you get older. I don't know. My Mum reckons that you might as well do what you want to do and have fun while you are young and you can enjoy yourself because when you settle down and have children and a job and all that, it becomes more serious and grown up and I'm not ready to be a grown up yet. I just want to enjoy myself.

And just 'wanting to enjoy myself' is another side of post-adolescence, an extended 'transition' which has its own economy, and life-style specific accoutrements.

Anne: A Leisure-led Identity?

Anne is similar to Aaron in many ways. Both wear extremely expensive clothing: £80 on a shirt or nearly £100 on a little top would not be exceptional for either of them. Like Aaron, Anne spends a great deal of time and money on her appearance, her hairstyles, nails and general grooming. Both Aaron and Anne's attention to these details illustrate the way in which, for the middle-class young people in our cohort, there is a: 'greater attention to self-presentation and to style over substance . . . fashion and personal appearance increase in importance as central means of creating the self' (Gecas and Burke, 1995, p. 7).

Anne is a high achieving British-Chinese young woman. Her parents manage a thriving business in South London. She did well in her GCSEs at Northwark Park School and went to the same prestigious tertiary college as Lucy. She registered for three A-levels and had good predicted grades. Her two older brothers are currently at university and continue to live at home. Her family are keen that all their children should get good jobs which are financially rewarding – income is a keener marker of status than level of formal certification. However, Anne herself (at the moment) has little desire to continue with any more education and intends to follow a career in fashion retailing after completing her A-levels. She has had enough of formal education and wants to have fun and enjoy herself while she can.

In this chapter we have described Lucy as having a 'mixed' form of 'choice biography' as opposed to the more traditional 'normal' and sequential type of development – Lucy's domestic, occupational and leisure identities are equally valued. However, Anne's narrative reflects what Dwyer and Wyn (1998) would call a 'contextual focus' – that is, one where life-style dominates the identity and biography being constructed. This 'trend' is perhaps not that unusual in young, 'flexible', post-adolescents from middle-class backgrounds. It is easier to postpone decision-making or thinking long-term (normal biography) because ultimately 'this flexible attitude among post-adolescents also demonstrates a certain non-chalance brought about by their social origin: they know that they are backed up by their parents' financial and cultural resources' (Du Bois-Reymond, 1998, p. 71).

Du Bois Reymond's work involved a nine-year longitudinal study of 120 adolescents (and their parents) in the Netherlands where the majority of the young people were busy constructing 'choice biographies' similar to those explored in this chapter. Social life and having fun were at least on a par with 'success' in the sphere of work for the overwhelming majority of these young Dutch people. Similar findings are emerging elsewhere (Dwyer and Wyn, 1998). A recent survey of over 1,200 graduates by Coopers and Lybrand reported that 'British students said that a rewarding life outside work was more important than pay and promotion' (Charter, 1997, p. 4). Further, a study based on the views of 150 Leeds under-graduates argued that 'instant gratification' and a degree of 'transience' typify a dominant version of contemporary lifestyle which is being constructed by another group of 'privileged' post-adolescents (Wainwright, 1999).

In the feminized social world of the late 1990s 'goin' out' involves having enough money to pay for cabs to and from clubs (safety), pay admission charges and to buy cigarettes and drinks – soft as well as alcoholic. 'Goin' out', even just to parties, can involve a great deal of expense which young women assume they will meet themselves (more or less in full). While they were at school, very few of the young women in our cohort stayed at home at weekends preparing for university or for their A-levels or GNVQs (other than Agesh and Rena) – to a great extent they exhibited traits of being 'effortless achievers' (Aggleton, 1987). They almost all did part-time work and stayed out at the weekends. The majority of the sample had mobile phones. Even for those planning to go on to higher education, London club life and parties are seductive and essential.

While at college, Anne came to feel that she had had enough of school. Like Aaron she talked as though she had almost exhausted her current capacity to benefit from formal education. However, unlike Aaron or Lucy who were open-minded about interrupting for a short time and then picking up the project, Anne could see little reward in continuing along the 'typical' path for people with her academic credentials. Her college tutors had predicted that she could achieve high grades; A, B, B. Nevertheless, she has decided not to go to university and instead is hoping to get into a paid management-training position with a national clothing retailer. She wants to become a fashion buyer eventually. From her perspective, going to university would make no difference to her prospects in the field where she wants to work. As she freely admits:

> Well, the only reason I was going to university because I know there is a social life there. I don't want to go and get a degree because basically I know I will be slacking and at the end of the day I will end up with nothing or probably drop out and waste a few years of my life. I just don't see the point . . . I can't be doing it. I have to honestly say that I do not work hard at school.

Anne does work very hard in other ways. She has worked for a well-known beauty retail chain for some time for two and a half days a week, so successfully that they had offered her the opportunity of management training. She also helps in the family business with the paper work and the accounts. However the experience of seeing her brothers manage their university work at the expense of any social life has put her off:

> Because what has changed me from wanting to go to uni. to not going. It is basically, I see my brothers. Two of them are at uni. now and my oldest one, that is all he does. . . . He is just too caught up in . . . he is committed to it. That is fine for him. I can't be so committed to the work. At the moment I am not committed. I do what I have to do.

Anne currently invests a great deal of her time, energies and emotional and financial resources in her social life. She finds her academic world unrewarding. But she did not drop out – she kept up with her course work and attendance. She has invested in herself long-term: with A-levels she can always go back to higher education if she ever wants to.

Every weekend she gets a cab to her friend Judy's house where she meets up with Tracey and Shireen. They get ready to go out, make sure they have enough cigarettes because 'at the weekend on a Saturday night I will smoke over twenty between twenty and forty' and then they get a cab to their favourite club, Goodwill, which charges £15 per person to get in.

> My favourite drink is something like Malibu and pineapple and Martini and lemonade that sort of thing . . . not straight brandy or anything. Shireen drinks that. She likes that and she doesn't get drunk on it. I think she has like Bacardi and stuff to get drunk. She drinks brandy. . . . Nowadays we don't even get drunk basically. Before, when we first started going out I had fallen down a couple of times.

Anne and her three friends keep in touch by phone during the week. Judy, Tracey, and Shireen are all working. Anne is the only one still in full-time education. The others are doing low-paid office work. For all of them, their London-based club life seems to be their real life, the social world the 'real' them. She says:

> I have always liked London. I have lived in London all my life and I mean, I am even reluctant to go on holiday. I mean, last year, my whole family went to Singapore and I said, I can't go because I love London . . . I said, I don't want to go . . . I said, look, I want to spend it with my mates and that is why I didn't go.

Anne is involved in club life and is sexually active. Her mother has discussed this with her: 'What she says to me is, Anne, if you are going to, you know, whatever . . . make sure you use protection and I do. So, it's okay. So, and she knows me'. In the interview which focused on her social life-style and 'choosing' Anne became animated and was obviously bound into her friendships, possible relationships and fun. She believes that 'clubbing' has helped her confidence and personal style. 'I think I have got more now. Because it is like basically, if I like someone in a club I would go up to them now, whereas before, I would never, ever, ever, have done that'.

Anne completed her A-levels but was not successful at obtaining a trainee-management position in retail and fashion. She did not get her predicted grades and is currently working as a trainee manager/bar staff for a large chain of London-based wine bars, a setting which capitalizes on her youth, energy, personal style, familiarity and involvement with leisure activities. She is part of the 'new economies' available in a 'global city' (see Ball et al., 1999 for more on this point). Aaron and Anne are interested in these 'new economies' of tourism, fashion retailing, bar management – they embody new style workers (see Chapter 3), working on and for themselves. For both of them there is a blurring between work self and leisure self.

Learning Fatigue, 'Choice Biographies' and Leisure

Aaron, Lucy and Anne all come from relatively privileged 'new middle-class' backgrounds. Because of this, they are able to take more risks, to postpone and interrupt traditional or 'normal biographies' without necessarily experiencing any great penalty. Indeed, if they are able to 'present' their flexible decisions in a positive manner – a 'good' gap year, an interesting sojourn in a unique environment – so they may well be able to extract additional capital from what might have seemed to be a disadvantage. None of the three has cut themselves off from future participation in education and training. This is starkly different from those who exit at 16 with few or no qualifications (see Chapters 4 and 10). All three recognize and value the advantages which certification, particularly a degree, can bestow. Higher education is within their reach whenever they want it. In the main, they do not want it – yet, if at all.

What is evident from these three narratives is that middle-class transitions may well be more extended than in previous times – particularly in comparison with their parents' more traditional transitions (Aggleton, 1987). If, as certain theorists suggest, social reproduction is not currently always a straightforward matter, then 'processes which appear stable and predictable on an objective level may involve greater subjective risk and uncertainty' (Furlong and Cartmel, 1997, p. 37). Young people may well invest less of themselves in a work and educational identity and more in their social/leisure selves. Identities become 'strategic and positional' (cf. Aggleton, 1987) rather than constructed once and for all through schooling–(un)employment (Hall, 1996, p. 3). Young people may be involved in circumstances which (for now) circumscribe their identities in ways which seem more rewarding, challenging and desirable than alternative/educative ways of being or becoming. 'There are contradictions and coalescences between the cultural and the social, identity and difference' (Westwood, 1990, p. 57).

As Hurrelmann (1994, p. 11) has argued, a 'reshuffling' of the 'patterns, internal logic and social significance of youth transitions' has ensued. Being an adult may be differently constituted nowadays, being in post compulsory (pre-higher) education and training may also be shifting and changing as well. For some of the young people in our study, (full) autonomy and independence will be deferred as they make their way through an extended period of adolescence. Others like Anne want to shorten their education and training in order to get into aspects of adulthood and its 'freedoms' more quickly. All of this points up the need, as Aggleton also argued, to avoid essentializing the middle classes.

Identities constructed round lifestyle and 'leisure' may be as, or more, important than work/career and autonomy. They may also 'fit together' too – the DJs in Chapter 10 are perhaps an example of an attempt to coalesce work/leisure roles and identities, making their interests into a 'career'. This identity-shift may be on the increase in the 'risk society' where 'good' qualifications, working hard and 'not causing trouble' might not be a guarantor of a straightforward and unproblematic transition to adulthood and financial independence. Interestingly, the sorts of leisure activities in which our cohort were interested were not strongly differentiated by class – as Roberts and Parsell (1994) claim, 'the experiences of young people on all class trajectories have been subject to individualization . . . and one likely consequence will have been a blurring of class-related leisure patterns' (p. 47). As Roberts and Parsell (1994) also say, 'middle class dominance [has] spread from education, the labour market and politics into everyday teenage culture' (p. 43). The capacity to participate and consume will certainly be different for different social classes. Middle-class young people possess greater capacity – a combination of time and money as well as skills of time management – to do a lot more than their working-class peers (Roberts and Parsell, 1991). For those who are able to do so, living for today and having a good social life may be a sound tactic in uncertain economic times.

6 In a Class of Their Own
Classifying and Classified – Identity and the Science of Infinite Distinctions

One of the key features of the careership of almost all of the young people in our study cohort is the instability and unpredictability of their education and work transitions (see Chapter 2). The accounts presented in the other chapters demonstrate various false-starts, detours and hiatuses. At first sight the significant exception to this was those students following, or expecting (and expected) to follow, the path from GCSEs to A-levels to university to a professional career. Such young people often had this pathway well established in advance of the key 'choice' point at 16 and most gave little or no consideration to other possibilities. In one sense these young people had a wide range of choices available to them at 16 by virtue of their relatively successful educational experiences and attainments up to that point. However, in practice they had little choice in that they and/or their families assumed/expected/hoped that a university degree would provide them with the social advantages and insurance of a later point of entry into the professional labour market. Nonetheless, as we shall see, not all of these apparently settled and predictable trajectories turn out to be that way in practice (witness Anne in Chapter 5). Furthermore, these young people, these 'A-levellers', were not of a piece. The numbers of students taking A-levels has expanded markedly over the past ten years. As one would expect, many young people who now take A-levels are the first, or part of the first, generation in their family to do so. We found significant differences between what might be called 'traditional' and 'new' A-levellers (see Chapter 7 – Luke and Jordan). (GNVQ qualifications now offer another but distinct route into higher education.) The A-level experience is also very different in different places – small or large sixth forms, crammers, FE or tertiary colleges. The A-level route has been and to a great extent remains strongly 'classed' and certainly social class participation rates in higher education have changed only marginally despite the increase in overall age participation rates in the past 20 years. Indeed, the participation rate of children of the professional middle class increased from 73 per cent in 1993/4 to 80 per cent in 1997/8, the intermediate middle class from 42 per cent to 49 per cent, the skilled non-manual group from 29 to 32, skilled manual from 17 to 19, partly-skilled from 16 to 18, and unskilled, working-class from 11 to 14 (from Table 3.13, *Social Trends 29*, HMSO, 1999). Over this period the class differentials have actually increased.

In this chapter we examine the similarities but also explore the many differences between four middle-class female students as they complete their compulsory education and move towards higher education. They can all be described as 'traditional A-levellers' and can be treated in this respect as a single group. Their perceptions and appreciations of classifications, and their perceptions and appreciations of the ways in which they are classified by others. 'One's relationship to the world and one's proper place in it' (Bourdieu, 1986, p. 474) provides a recurring theme for the chapter.

Two points should be made clear. The first is that the term 'middle-class' was used by the young people to describe themselves; the second is that the school, Northwark Park, attracted a rather narrow and specific band of middle-class students, namely those from Labour-voting families, with professional parents employed in the public sector. Other traditional and aspiring middle-class parents largely favoured the selective Grant-Maintained schools in the area rather than Northwark Park. Therefore, although we had a number of middle-class students in our cohort, the sample was both small and skewed towards a particular class fraction (see Perkin, 1989; Savage et al., 1992; and Power et al., 1998 on divisions within the middle class). We try to say something about the specifics of this fraction later. As we shall see in Rachel's story, she meets a very different kind of middle-class student when she moves from Northwark Park school to Riverway College, and again later when she is interviewed for a place at Cambridge.

In examining the choices and pathways taken by these young women we want to emphasize that their choices do not take place in a social vacuum but are contingent upon other events in their lives. In other words, the decisions made are not necessarily technically rational, as much government policy (e.g. DfEE, 1998) would suggest, but are pragmatically rational and based on balancing various options at the time of choosing. In the space available, we can offer only a very fleeting glimpse into their rather complex leisure, social and emotional lives. Again more is said about Rachel in this respect than the others. We show that each stage of the choice process involves negotiating a set of contingencies. These can be structural/academic (as in the passing or failing of public examinations) or personal (relating to family, social or sexual relationships). The ways in which these contingencies are dealt with are clearly related to the cultural, emotional (Reay, 1998) and economic capital (Bourdieu, 1977) of those involved. It is important to reiterate that the pathways 'chosen' by the young women are typically culturally scripted and although all four spoke of making their own decisions, what Allatt (1993, p. 151) refers to as the 'transfer of responsibility', they were clearly following well understood and familially acceptable routes.

> [My mum] wants me to go on to higher education and everything, so does my dad. I have never really considered dropping out of school and getting a job so they haven't actually put that much pressure on me to go to higher education because I have always wanted to.
>
> (Agesh, January 1996)

Indeed personal and family hopes and aspirations are tightly inter-twined. These young people carry the hopes and aspirations of their family with them and these are thoroughly invested in their thinking and decision-making. Again, what Allatt (1993) refers to as 'normative expectations about obligations and reciprocities' (p. 147) operate:

> My mum doesn't pressure me, but I feel like if I don't do well my mum will be, you know, she will feel she has failed in some sort of way with her children . . . she always says to me I know you will do well, I know you will do well and I say okay I hope I will. . . . It's a bit of a responsibility . . . I would like her to be proud of me.
>
> (Lucy, April 1996)

The young women represented here are Rachel, Lucy, Kirsty and Agesh. All four described themselves, and were described by others in the sample, as 'middle class'. All came from two-parent, 'professional (mothers)/managerial (fathers)' families where both parents worked, although Lucy's father had recently been made redundant. He was the only parent without A-levels. Agesh described herself as Indo-Caribbean, the others as White. Rachel was spoken about by several students as the 'golden girl' of Northwark Park, admired and encouraged by the teachers who saw her as the 'bright star' most likely to enhance the school's reputation with good GCSE results. She was a vivacious, extremely attractive, out-going student not only academically able but also a gifted sportswoman and dancer. Both her parents were university educated. Her older brother was studying history at Liverpool University.

Lucy was the second of four children. She was regarded by the school as above average intelligence but was not described as a high-flyer. Her interests were broad and included theatre, dance, music and outdoor sports such as canoeing, in which she was encouraged by her mother, a keen sportswoman. As with the other young women written about here, the staff at Northwark Park would have liked Lucy to remain at school for the sixth form but Lucy had other plans. Her older brother, in Lucy's words, 'still has to find himself' and had done a series of unskilled jobs since doing rather badly in his A-levels which he took at Northwark Park. There was some parental pressure on Lucy to do well in order to atone for her brother's lack of academic success and this responsibility weighed rather heavily on her.

Kirsty, along with Rachel, was considered to be the brightest student in the Year and, like Rachel, was highly ambitious. She sang in the school's gospel choir. Kirsty's mother was a school teacher involved with a project on gender in the LEA. She was also studying for a Masters degree. Her older brother, under pressure from his parents, had started university but had subsequently dropped out after one year, much to his mother's dismay. He had then begun work in a branch of *The Dôme* where he moved, in a relatively short time, from making sandwiches to managing a café bar.

Agesh was a quiet, serious student who kept a low profile in school. She had a brother of the same age and he attended an 11–16 boys' school in a neighbouring

Table 6.1 Rachel, Lucy, Kirsty and Agesh

Project name	'Race'	GCSE A*–C	A-levels	Current pathway	Mother's occupation	Father's occupation	Older siblings
Rachel	White	10	A, B, C	Gap year	Lawyer	Architect	Brother in HE
Lucy	White	6	C, E, E	Gap year	Deputy head, primary	Manager nursing home*	Brother unskilled work
Kirsty	White	10	A, A, B	University	Primary school teacher	Software manager	Brother sandwich bar manager
Agesh	Indo-Caribbean	9	A, A, B	University	Nurse†	Customer services in bank†	Brother in HE

* Did not do A-levels.
† Born overseas.

LEA before moving to the same denominational Sixth Form College as Agesh. Both of her parents were born overseas and consequently Agesh was unable to draw upon the sort of 'educational inheritance' (Edwards et al., 1989) available to the other young women. We have no space to discuss it here but it is worth noting that in two cases the expectations and strategies of parents were inflected by the 'failures' of older siblings. Allatt (1993) notes a similar phenomenon.

Unlike the other young people we represent in this book all of these young women, perhaps Agesh less than the others, have aspects of their identities and self which are heavily invested in 'school'. As Wexler (1992) eloquently puts it, 'the self does not shape itself in response to a lack, absence, or emptying of some aspect of social relations' (p. 132). The investments in self made by these young women embedded them thoroughly within the expressive as well as instrumental aspects of their school and colleges. Their 'joining behaviour', participation in clubs, teams and societies, may be seen as part of the 'development of the cultural capital of social competence' (Allatt, 1993, p. 155) and the 'skills of exchange (sociability)' (p. 154). Agesh did not take part in extra-curricular activities.

Post-16 'Choices'

In all their interviews, Rachel and Kirsty in particular showed themselves to be highly ambitious and well-organized concerning their post-16 choices. In common with many other students they would have welcomed more help and guidance from the teachers about the various options but recognized and accepted that it was not in the school's interests to promote other institutions:

> They [school] implied that you should find out for yourself. But they are so into wanting you to stay here, that no one really says, 'Go and find out about

other colleges'. So they implied that is what you do, but no-one says it out loud. It is like, no one comes to you with any advice, so unless you do it yourself you don't get anything.

(Rachel, February 1996)

But like some of the teachers, they want everybody to stay. If you want information about the colleges you have to get it yourself and everything and we are saying, and what about the stuff they send you, the colleges send you, and they say, if you want that I suppose I will let you see it and that. Why do you want to go to other colleges and they really start to get a bit angry with you about it. What's wrong with here, what's wrong with here and you are like, don't take it personally, it is just like. . . . They make you feel guilty, like you're letting them down or something and you really have to find it all out by yourself. It would be better if you could discuss it with them, but.

(Kirsty, January 1996)

I think if you could like have more information of other things instead of just like keeping it from us, to try and keep us to stay here. And maybe assemblies where you could have other people from other College to talk to you. . . .

(Agesh, 1996)

While the teachers were understandably reluctant to promote other institutions, none, it appeared, had pressed the students to stay. However, two of their parents, both teachers, had been approached by the head teacher at the Year 11 Parents' Evening and pressure was put on them to persuade their daughters to stay. Both parents understood the head teacher's position, that the school needed 'good' students to enhance its reputation, and that the school had done the groundwork for their daughters' academic successes. Nonetheless the students themselves, in their own best interests, had opted to move on. This decision had the full support of the parents. It is at this point that the 'practical principles of division' (Bourdieu, 1986, p. 471) and in particular 'the distances that need to be kept' (p. 472) begin to come into play – GNVQ as against A-level, early leavers and stayers-on, 'doss' colleges as against those that are 'difficult to get into'. This is what Bourdieu calls 'the objectivity of "second order" ' – symbolic templates for practical activities (Bourdieu and Wacquant, 1992, p. 7).

As with the other middle-class students in the sample, these young women had done their own research for post-16 education and sent off for prospectuses from a range of colleges. These were then examined with particular criteria in mind reflecting the broad social interests and self-investments noted above.

I read them [brochures] seeing if they did the science subjects that I want in straight science, not modular, because that is important to get in [to the course of her choice]. And I had a look to see if they did the other subjects that I was interested in like, English literature and theatre studies. If I don't get my science grades that is what I want to do. And then I had a look at what after school clubs they offered and I am really sporty so I looked at what leisure facilities they had. I suppose I tried to make sure that they did everything that interested me, and if they didn't, I rejected them.

(Rachel, February 1996)

These young women attended college Open Evenings together, their mothers taking turns to drive the group to these events. A mother's presence on these occasions was welcome because of the advice she had to offer. Mothers are key figures throughout and both their emotional resources and, for Lucy and Kirsty, their professional 'insider' knowledge was important. Such knowledge was shared:

She said that it seemed all right and that is good coming from Lucy's mum because she is a teacher. She is a deputy head in a primary school so she knows all the right questions to ask so it was good having her there. And she said that she thought that it [Riverway] was all right but she wanted to have a look at St Faith's because she said that their results are on a par with Riverway and St Faith's is just down the road.

(Rachel, February 1996)

Kirsty's parents, and her mother in particular played a key role in her choice of St Faith's:

My mum's definitely the best, because my dad is helpful as well, but my mum is better at those sort of things and she is willing to come along with me, and when you get there and start talking to other people you forget the sort of questions to ask, she knows the right questions to ask, what about this and that, you think, oh I forgot about that, she knows the right things and because she is a teacher herself she is pretty good about most things, but she doesn't really pressure me into it.

This is very much Foskett and Hesketh's (1996) notion of the 'composite chooser' or what Allatt (1993) describes as 'a family project'. Kirsty's mother attended the Open Evening at St Faith's, and several other Colleges:

It was just for one evening so of course they were nice because they want you to go there so they were putting it on but I did feel, I thought it was nice there and so did my mum. We didn't say anything for ages we just walked round and that and then we both agreed it was nice and I was pleased my mum liked it as well.

As Quicke (1993) notes of his sample of A-level students 'for nearly all these students, parents still constituted significant others in their lives . . . they were principal agents in maintaining the students' sense of self and identity in the world' (p. 111) – although we suggest this is true of many other young people as well. The families of these young women are 'knowing' choosers, which have been described elsewhere as 'skilled–privileged choosers' (Ball, 1996). Despite changes in post-16 courses and procedures which they find confusing, these young women and their parents are able to 'decode and decipher' (Bourdieu, 1986, p. 2) the complexities of post-16 provision. At the heart of this choice-making the A-level remains a familiar touch stone. 'A-levels are the best thing for me and I can talk about it with my friends, my mum and dad' (Kirsty). In the terms of Bourdieu and Passeron, these families are not so much engaged in rational calculation as able to attain the goals that best suit their interests by following their dispositions and employing 'natural distinctions' (Reay 1995, p. 354).

A crucial part of Kirsty's choice of St Faith's and dismissal of other colleges rested on the different A-level syllabuses offered in the courses she wanted to take. She was also 'put off' some Colleges by their poor reputation and particularly by accounts of 'trouble'. Despite her interest in finding a College with a degree of social mix she was also keen to find a 'learning environment' in which she feels comfortable, to be with people 'like me'. As Lucy expressed it in relation to Riverway: 'If I feel comfortable and at ease with the atmosphere and the situation'. Or as Bourdieu puts it: 'The agents only have to follow the leanings of their habitus in order to take over, unwittingly, the intention immanent in the corresponding practices, to find an activity which is entirely "them" and with it, kindred spirits' (Bourdieu, 1986, p. 223). Other places are wrong, alien, uncomfortable, 'not for the likes of us'.

> I know it seems that I made up my mind really quickly like, that is what every-body says to me, but at Burbley I know this girl who has gone as well and she was saying that there are lots of fights there as well, it is all right if you get in with a certain crowd but sometimes it is not that nice to have other people who make trouble.
>
> (Kirsty, February 1996)

> [Mersley] they said that there wasn't so good 'A' level courses and it was lots of people going there who were doing more GNVQs and things, and it was a lot of people who just went and mucked about there so. . . .
>
> (Kirsty, February 1996)

The conclusion is *obvious* – these are not places for a student like Kirsty. They would not be 'rational' or natural choices. Once settled at St Faith's Kirsty's impressions are quickly validated:

> It's been really good because everybody wants to learn and the teacher doesn't have to keep stopping and going over it again and again. But he will stop and help people, which is good. So I'm really enjoying it and we're moving much quicker than we did at Northwark Park because the teacher can get on.
>
> (Kirsty, October 1996)

Kirsty's choice places her in a learning environment which confirms and reinforces her well established and very positive 'learner identity'.

> We are doing *Measure for Measure* now and everyone understands what is going on, not 100 per cent obviously but they get the idea and can understand certain things and you can move so much more quickly. It is much more interesting and I think, oh god, I am not the only one who understands it now. What a difference that makes.
>
> (Kirsty, October 1996)

The 'choice-making' of these young women is information-rich. With their parents, their mothers in particular, they collect and sort a variety of 'hot' and 'cold' knowledge about various possible destinations – brochures, visits, telephone calls on the one hand, friends' experiences, rumours and reputations, personal responses on the other. In all this Agesh relied heavily on Kirsty and her mother for information and advice. This was an effective tactic. She ended up choosing the same college and university as Kirsty.

> I looked at St Faith's, that is where I think I would like to go. I looked at Burbley, I looked at Riverway a bit. My brother went there and he didn't like it, and he didn't get a lot of support and so I didn't really consider that a lot. I haven't really looked at that many school sixth forms because I would like to go to, like, a proper college and I looked at Churchill and I can't remember where else. . . . My mum and me we went through the list and picked out the ones that looked interesting. Some I didn't get through to so mum tried later for me. I suppose you could say we did it between us. I rang some others as well, like I rang Streetley College as well but they weren't having a Open Day. They seemed really disorganised. I rang like loads of times and nobody answered and at Churchill they said they weren't having an Open Day but they said, do you want me to send you a brochure straightaway so I said that was nice.
>
> (Kirsty, February 1996)

In addition to reading about prospective courses, Lucy was interested in the range of extra-curricular activities on offer at the different colleges. Interestingly, only these young women within our whole cohort expressed any interest in such things. They work both as areas of self-development and as symbolic investments and markers.

> Well the prospectus was brilliant. I really, really liked it. It has got loads of after school activities and extra things that you can do and plays and stuff and musicals. I love that kind of stuff. I don't know, I just fancy going there. I really liked the prospectus and the way it was. I want to do all sorts of things not just lessons and Riverway really seemed like my sort of College.
>
> (Lucy, April 1996)

All the colleges visited by the middle-class students were those which had the best A-level results. Rachel spoke of wanting to study at a 'good' college, one that is difficult to get into. Here a schema of classification and system of perception and appreciation are at work in what Bourdieu calls 'an alchemy' of distinction:

> You want a challenge, something to aim for. I need some sort of aim like a good college that is difficult to get into. That's why I have been looking at the sort of best colleges round this way.
>
> (Rachel, February 1996)

'Good' colleges specialized in A-levels as against those which concentrate 'on GNVQs and that' – the young women work within a framework of 'semi-codified oppositions' which as Bourdieu (1986, p. 470) suggests can be traced back to class divisions. The results of these 'good' colleges could be recited by these young women and some of their mothers, like a litany. Of less importance but nevertheless of significance were the destinations of a college's 'high-flyers'. At the same time as considering post-16 colleges, Rachel was also checking university entry points as her brother was in the process of applying to university. Current choices are stepping stones in longer term planning – 'great emphasis being placed on the task at hand' (Allatt, 1993, p. 153):

> I have been looking at universities. I have looked at lots and I want to go somewhere where it is difficult, that only takes the best, where the grades are highest. I am ambitious and I want to do well. That is another reason I don't really want to stay here [Northwark Park] because it is not really a sixth form for the ambitious.
>
> (Rachel, February 1996)

GCSE Results and Choice of College and University

Here, initially, we concentrate in particular on Rachel's story (we have written further about Rachel elsewhere; see Ball et al., 1999). We do not do this because Rachel is typical in any way; she is not. Nevertheless her experiences illuminate several of the essential points of our overall analysis: the complexity of the social, personal and academic lives of our young people; the complexities and limitations of the concept of choice; the almost infinite processes and structures of 'self-evident' distinctions and differentiations that are invested in educational career-ship; the ever-present possibility of setback or deflection, even for the most 'successful' young people – that is, the role of contingency and epiphany (Hodkinson et al., 1996); the recurrence of the facticity of social class, in different ways, in the lives and opportunities of these young people; and the relativity of social advantage.

Rachel chose Riverway College at which to study A-levels in Biology, Chemistry and English. She had found the final decision difficult and as she explained:

I really couldn't make up my mind and we decided that I was going to be really arrogant about it and I knew that I would get marks which meant that I had pretty much the ability to pick and choose. So she [the drama teacher] said, 'Well don't, just don't decide until you get your marks through, because no one is really going to turn you down', and it was like, OK, fair enough.

(Rachel, November 1996).

Rachel's value in 'the economy of student worth' was made clear to her. As predicted, she had no problem gaining a place at the college of her choice:

I didn't have any problems at all. I just walked in and on enrolment day I went with Sheila and she was in there for like forty minutes longer than I was. I just walked in they saw my results and they just went like, blonk, blonk, and put me in the tutor group, and there you go, you are in. And I walked out within 10 minutes and other people were in there for like an hour, an hour and a half. I just walked in and out. It was that quick. I didn't have any problems at all.

(Rachel, November 1996)

Kirsty had opted to go to St Faith's Sixth Form College to study A-level English, German and Film Studies. Agesh joined her at St Faith's to study English, History and Film Studies. Lucy also moved to her first choice, Riverway College, to study English, Performing Arts and History. As with several other students, Lucy had decided on two of her A-levels (English and Performing Arts) whilst still at school but was undecided about the third. The choice of the third A-level, History, which she had not taken at GCSE, was more or less left to the tutor who interviewed her. This turned out to be a mistake.

As we note elsewhere several young people spoke of moving to college in order to make a fresh start. These were largely students who had negative experiences at school or at the PRU but as we see, Rachel too, had her reasons for wanting to wipe the slate clean:

I wanted to get away from the pressure that I was under at Northwark Park. I wanted to get away from how people perceived me to be, even though they didn't know me. And people like judge you at Northwark Park, 'Oh, you are Rachel Brown, you get good marks' . . . and I just wanted to go somewhere where nobody knew me and everybody had to take me for who I was rather than judging me already, which is what was happening around here. . . . I just wanted to get away from it all.

(Rachel, November 1996)

Rachel soon settled in at Riverway college although she found it rather daunting to begin with. Several students had previously attended private schools and 'were just so confident'. She had, however, been voted 'student counsellor' for her tutor group which meant that she 'was a bit chuffed. It is flattering when people vote for you'. Such an achievement would also stand her in good stead when applying to universities:

> It will look good on my UCAS form. I got in the netball first team, so I am doing all right; I am doing all right. I'm in the drama club and the netball team and met loads of like really friendly people there too. I really like it at Riverway and I'm glad I've gone there. I know I've made the right decision.
>
> (Rachel, November 1996)

That she had been able to have a wide choice of options was not lost on Rachel, who clearly recognized and understood the hierarchy of choice. Throughout Rachel's final year at Northwark Park and first year of A-levels it had remained her ambition to study medicine at university. However, as a result of visits to some hospitals and a spell of work experience at a teaching hospital (undertaken because 'It would look good on my UCAS form and show that I was serious about my choices') she had changed her mind:

> You're not addressing the problem in the first place and I feel that if I do human science first I have a much more broader understanding of that when if I do go on to do medicine, which I hope to do, if I can afford to do it, I hope I'll be a better doctor for it.
>
> (Rachel, December 1997)

Having decided not to study medicine immediately, Rachel had found, by serendipity it would appear, a course in human science at the University of Cambridge. 'I read the thing [course description] and I was like, wow, hallelujah, just tell me what to do! So that's what I've applied to do'. She had also applied to study psychology and neuroscience at Manchester and had already had an interview there 'which went very well. I was very pleased. . . . They gave me an offer on the spot. I was very chuffed'. The first part of the interview Rachel described as 'the hard sell to try and get you to go there . . . but there was no guarantee that you were going to get a place but that's what they were trying to do'.

 Just as Rachel had recognized that she could pick and choose among colleges to study for A-levels, so she was aware how wide her choice of universities was – although she had already limited her range to what she called the 'top' universities. This situation, however, had its downside in that Rachel felt she could not discuss her options with her old school friends.

> When you're applying to the top universities you don't want to sound as if you're bragging and that when your friends don't have these choices, you know. . . . Because there are lots of people like that. They scraped through their GCSEs and are scraping through their A-levels so they are tied down in their choices and some of them will just have to go where they can get in. They don't have a proper choice.
>
> (Rachel, December 1997)

The need to evaluate and position different universities was important to Rachel and she used both official publications and alternative guides to obtain a fuller picture of what was on offer in the institutions she was considering. She was well aware of the distinction between information and promotion which is thoroughly blurred in the practices of post-16 and Higher Education markets.

> My grandad sent me a NatWest sponsored one [guide]. I read that to help me choose which college I wanted to go to at Cambridge. . . . They're better because they're, it's all hard sell in a prospectus and you don't know what's true and what's not, really. They all sound like the best places in the world, like the world's best university but obviously they are not all good. So you have to look at other things before you make up your mind.
>
> (Rachel, December 1997)

Rachel chose her universities in the June of her first year of A-levels and was adamant that her first choice was Cambridge. However, in many of her conversations about 'choices' she spoke of the different contingency plans she had drawn up:

> I really, really want Imperial to give me a low offer, which I don't know if they will or, I mean, if I get in, I want them to give me a low offer then if I don't get into Cambridge, that'll be my first choice because that's the course I want to do. . . . I've got problems with the Sussex one, and they're the three universities that do this course. . . . If I do get into Cambridge then I need an insurance place and I want that [Imperial] to be it . . . realistically they're going to ask for A, A, B and I don't think it's wise to put A, B, B as my insurance place. I don't think it's sensible because one muck-up and that's it . . . if I get three Bs I'm good enough to go to a good university and I don't want to go to some second-rate university.
>
> (Rachel, December 1997)

Rachel went on to talk about universities giving reasons for her different 'choices' and again is very aware of the role of the deployment and acquisition of what are often referred to as social and cultural capital. Describing one she said:

> I know you have an interview as well and they must have some way of deciding who they think will be suitable. . . . I like the universities that are hard to get into. I don't want to go somewhere that takes anyone with the basic A-levels because like I say, I like a challenge and I want the best so I can improve myself all the time and be with people who want to improve themselves as well. I don't mean I want to work all the time because I want to do additional activities and take part in all sorts of things at college and then at university and meet new people who share my interests and that.
>
> (Rachel, February 1996)

Also looming large in this particular 'choice' equation was the matter of Rachel's current boyfriend, whom she had met during her recent hospital work experience.

> After spending a week in a hospital I'm now going out with a solicitor and it's a big coup because he's very, very old . . . he's 30 . . . and he's a senior partner.
>
> (Rachel, December 1997)

Although Paul's opinion counted for a great deal, Rachel was adamant that her first choice was Cambridge: 'I actually chose my universities in about June and that was it. I'd made my mind up. I wasn't going to budge. And I met Paul at the beginning of July, on July the fourth it was' (Rachel, December 1997). From this point, Paul became the focus of Rachel's social life, much to her parents' concern. To escape family squabbles on this matter she began spending more and more time at his house. He was unlike any of her other boyfriends, she explained:

> I was always known as the one to go out with the rugby player or the model. They always have to be like typically beautiful and stereotypically . . . whatever, and he's [Paul] not like that at all. And when all my friends met him they were like, 'Oh, no he's really not your type!' But it's like, all my other boyfriends . . . I was going out with them because they looked nice and we looked nice together. I started going out with Paul because I found him fascinating and I like his mind.
>
> (Rachel, December 1997)

But social relationships were not the only distraction from College and A-levels. Of the four young women, two had part-time jobs. Rachel worked in Tesco's and Lucy described herself as a nanny who also did some bar work. She had been nannying for some years, had built up a good reputation locally and was in high demand by several, local, middle-class families. She worked for several hours a day, five days a week and earned 'lots of money', most of which she spent on entertainment (see Chapter 5). Neither Kirsty nor Agesh worked and Kirsty's mother had explained that Kirsty did not 'need' to work as she was given a monthly allowance which provided for her needs and encouraged her to budget (cf. Allatt, 1993, p. 151). Her family wanted her to concentrate on her studies and considered that a part-time job would be both distracting and tiring. Agesh's mother was also against the idea of her working.

Rachel's parents paid for her travel every month but apart from that she was financially independent. In common with many other students Rachel considered her part-time job essential in order to meet her financial commitments:

> I spend about £150 a term on books and the *New Scientist* and things like that which I need for class. . . . I buy clothes but, I don't know how much I spend. I eat at college quite a lot of the time. Sometimes I skip food if I really haven't got any money, and then I'll go out on Friday and Saturday in the pub or to

the cinema or out to dinner . . . and then all your friends that you make, live out there [Riverway]. . . . And if you go out there and you like go to the pub, you can't get a train home. You end up having to pay £12 for a cab home or something stupid like that. But you have to do it because it's part of being 18!

(Rachel, December 1997)

Rachel had worked on a part-time basis at Tescos for 12 hours a week during her GCSEs and for 16 hours during her A-levels.

I got promoted [co-incidentally, after GCSEs] and because I'd got a better job I was supposed to work longer shifts. I was then contracted to do 2 to 11 at night on a Saturday and 5 hours on a Sunday. And it killed me because I just had no time to myself. But I carried on doing it, and I would have carried on but they underpaid me. . . . They changed my hours so I'm now working from 8 to 5 on a Saturday and 1 to 6 on a Sunday, which still kills me.

(Rachel, December 1996)

In common with many young people in our cohort, regardless of social class or academic attainment, Rachel occasionally smoked both nicotine and cannabis and enjoyed alcohol:

It's about being young and grown up and experimenting. I do smoke occasionally and I do drink. I smoke because it's a social thing, it's relaxing or whatever. I drink because it's a laugh, it's a social thing, it's about relaxing. Yeah, I don't think there's anything to worry about. Sure I would never smoke for the rest of my life.

(Rachel, December 1997)

When Rachel was interviewed just after finishing her A-levels she reported that she had been accepted by all six universities on her UCAS application. Her first choice was Cambridge with Imperial as her insurance place.

They [University of Cambridge] wrote to my college and said that they thought that I needed a challenge, I think that is more due to the fact that I go to state school, than the fact that they felt I needed a challenge. Because I think that they think, if we go to state school we need to be a bit more motivated than if we don't, which is silly . . . most people [in private schools] are motivated, because that is how it is and their parents are pushing them too and helping them. But it is more of a challenge in a state school because it is easier to drop out because lots of people are not working and so I think it is a bigger challenge in a state school. I think they don't know what it is like to do well in a state school. I think it is easier to do well in a private school, that is what I think. . . . Well at my interview for Cambridge I was the only person there who went to state school, the only one.

(Rachel, July 1998)

Rachel described how the interview took place over two days and how the first day had been 'a total disaster'. She thought she had not got in and was determined to 'show' them: 'and I think that was why I got in. I had that private school bit of arrogance the second time because I didn't care' (Rachel, July 1998). When asked to enlarge on what she meant by 'private school arrogance', she explained:

> I've seen it at Riverway. It's just the way people behave who have been to private school. They've got that extra bit of confidence and they can speak as if they really know what they are talking about, even when they don't. And when I first went to Riverway I found it off-putting because nobody at Northwark Park was like that, but then I just listened and learned how to be like that too and it's a bit of an act, really. I know that you need to be like that at Cambridge, it's how it works, you have to be able to like, fight with words and that is what I learned at Riverway. You have to come back at people with words, and show how you won't be beaten and that and that is what I did and I got offered a place.
>
> (Rachel, July 1998)

Rachel was in little doubt that she had coped well with the interview because of what she had learned from being at Riverway.

> I don't think I would have got into Cambridge if I had stayed at Northwark Park because it's not really a Cambridge kind of school. I don't mean that nastily, you know but at Riverway it was different because, well people had different backgrounds and that. . . .
>
> (Rachel, July 1998)

Rachel went on to talk about the strong sense of competition she sensed among the candidates at Cambridge. This was something alien to Rachel before going to Riverway.

> You have got people who are really, really competitive and I have never had that, really. Not at Northwark Park because no-one actually cared that much, because it was not that many people were that clever, then people would ask you for advice and it didn't become a competition, whereas at Riverway it is like, see who can get the best mark kind of thing. Nobody really pushed themselves at Northwark Park, nobody really pushed you. They wanted you to do well and all that, but nobody really pushed you. But people at Riverway have been pushed. More expect to do well and are expected to pass with good grades and compare themselves with other people in the class and all that was new to me.
>
> (Rachel, July 1998)

The summer stretched ahead of Rachel after completing her A-levels and she was busy working, more or less full-time, in Tescos and in her leisure time she was still with Paul. The plan was to earn as much money as possible in readiness for the new academic year but before that Rachel and Paul had booked to go to California on holiday. She hoped it would be as enjoyable as their holiday in Jordan the previous year.

When Rachel was interviewed after the summer she reported that she had failed to secure good enough grades to gain entry to Cambridge: Biology A, Chemistry B and English C. Cambridge had wanted A, A, B but would have accepted A, B, B. Rachel spent much of the results day ringing various other universities in which she was interested but with no success. She had sufficient points (twenty four) to get into Imperial but as they had over-offered they were being very fussy. Rachel spoke about the panic and stress of the whole procedure.

> I phoned them back and said if anyone drops out of the course can I be first on the list to get on the course, and they were like, well if anyone drops out of the course, to be honest it will be a god send because we are going to get capped because we have got too many people so there is no way that you will get on. . . . They weren't interested in equivalent points because they were doing all they could to drop people. But you know, you're all in a state, I couldn't think straight, I was in a panic and you've got to move fast if you're going to get something good and it's not fair in a way, it's such a scramble, but you can't think straight and people tell you things on the phone and you're just, oh right, and you just accept it and I know I couldn't get in where I wanted but I wasn't like thinking, because I was so gutted. They had already offered me a place for next year when they turned me down for this year, they said I had got a place next year, that was definite.
>
> (Rachel, October 1998)

Although Rachel had set her heart on going to Cambridge she was prepared to accept the deferred place at Imperial. She realized that she would not now be able to go to Cambridge.

> If I did re-takes and got three As and applied again Cambridge wouldn't take me. They just wouldn't. They wouldn't take people who have got re-takes, realistically. They don't need second-chancers, they have enough clever people to choose from first time round, I wouldn't take second-chancers, if I was Cambridge. It's the best and it doesn't want people who need two goes to get their A-levels. I am not prepared to do re-takes because I did well enough. It won't make me any better at doing that course. That course is to do with human biology and I can do it. I know I can do it and I don't need to prove myself to anyone. I want to do it and I can do it.
>
> (Rachel, October 1998)

Here again we see Rachel engaged in what Bourdieu calls 'the practical mastery of classification' (Bourdieu, 1986, p. 472). And we see Rachel, the 'golden girl', re-classifying herself – as a 'second-chancer' or some one who did 'well enough'.

As Bourdieu also points out, 'people's image of the classification is a function of their position within it' (p. 473). There was little sympathy from friends for her disappointment. Despite the setback Rachel remained optimistic and retained a strong belief in her ability to do well. Like the other young women in this group she retains and displays what Allatt (1993) calls 'the elements of agency – independence, responsibility, self-motivation and individualism' (p. 149). Perhaps however her cultural capital is over-extended here. There are ways and means and tactics, things she does not know about:

> I know I can do it, it's just not gone as I planned at the moment but, yes, I've done well, I know I have and I'll be all right because I know where I want to go and I can't see any reason not to. I'll work hard and I'm learning all the time.
>
> (Rachel, October 1998)

Rachel decided to have a gap year, although she frequently repeated that she had not planned for this; that it was not what she wanted. In this year she intended to work full-time in Tescos as assistant manager of customer services. Additionally, she was entering the world of modelling and had appeared several times on television advertisements. There was also the possibility of going abroad to do some modelling work (see Ball et al., 1999). Her main aim was to earn money to help her in her bid for independence. She intended to leave the family home altogether and move in permanently with Paul who, along with his parents, was putting gentle pressure on Rachel to start a family. At the time of writing she was determined that she would not consider having children until she had finished her first degree. Rachel considered that she had learned from the experience of not getting into the university of her choice:

> Just how to pick myself up again, because it won't stop me aiming for the highest goals. You have got to, otherwise what is the point. So I will always aim that high you have just got to learn to get up again. I don't want to be mediocre. When I found out I thought that was it, what is the point. It got really bad, and, you know, I couldn't really tell people because I had done not as well as I wanted but I'd done better than lots of other people. I suppose I just wanted a bit of sympathy but how could they give me sympathy when they got Cs and Ds and Es. They hadn't aimed as high as me and some of them got what they needed and that but I hadn't got anything at the end of the day. It's difficult because in a way I felt like I'd got nothing but people were saying how well I'd done. But now, I guess I am a stronger person than I was before.
>
> (Rachel, July 1998)

Rachel's setback perhaps exemplifies Chisholm's (1995) point that 'Taking one's fate into one's own hands in this individualised way also entails high risks because not only success, but also failure rests with oneself' (p. 47).

Lucy's post-16 experience bears some similarities to Rachel's but is also very different. Similar in that she was also moving from her family home to live with her boyfriend.[1] Similar in the sense that her A-level grades were a disappointment and that, on the advice of her mother, she chose to take a gap year. But very different in the sorts of universities that she was able to consider and in her conception of and relation to choice. Lucy's decision to start history at A-level did not turn out well and after one year she switched to sociology, in which she got her highest grade. However, her anticipated and actual, C, E, E grades put many of the 'old' universities out of reach. Her choices were for 'new' universities – ex-polytechnics or Colleges of Higher Education – and she wanted a combined English and Sociology degree. Nonetheless she had six offers, including Plymouth, Middlesex, Roehampton, Worcester and Northampton. Lucy was the sort of student that these Universities wanted:

> Bournemouth asked for two Cs, but my predicted grades they were like Ds, and they wrote to me after getting my application form saying, well whatever you get, I have decided to give you an offer of six points, which is three Es. I thought, crikey, if you want. . . . So I got in.

In contrast to Rachel's sense of disappointment and the blow to her self-esteem, Lucy was just pleased to get a place in Higher Education to do the sort of course she wanted without the worry of striving for grades she might not make. Also in contrast to Rachel, Lucy found the mechanics of offers, loans, grants, results etc. confusing: 'I don't understand how most people do it'. Nonetheless, Lucy was still aware that going to university was significant in itself, marking her off from others in the eyes of potential employers:

> Maybe people are more convinced that you are a hard worker if you have been to college and stuff. . . . I would have thought that anyway. Things like, 'oh yes, you're going to go to university, you have some kind of drive, some kind of motivation' . . . instead of, 'I will do this job because I have to do it', you know. Instead of motivated.

Lucy is also like Kirsty and Agesh in that she will be moving away from London to attend university. This was an important part of being at university – 'going to university properly' – for these young women; a further distinction. 'My mum always says you shouldn't stay in London' (Kirsty);

> But like talking to different people who stayed in London like, they just say they don't get into university properly, and I can see that happening, you just end up going with your friends and you just don't throw yourself into it fully, you just end up going home and that. I want to go somewhere outside of London but not too far.
>
> (Agesh)

Going out of London is an option unavailable or unthinkable for many of the other black and working-class students in our study. Their relations to space are very different from those described in Chapter 8. There are no fears or doubts. Indeed going to university 'properly' means being away from home, from the familiar. Their 'horizons' are broad – indeed, as we shall see, they display what Robertson (1992) calls 'globality': a specific world-view built on an image of the globe itself as an arena for social action. The financial aspects of going to university were not an issue for any of these young women. Their families were clear that the costs would be met.

> Yes I think both our parents [Kirsty and Agesh] are like prepared to pay for it, they want us to have the best one. I think my mum is going to try and per- suade me to not get a job, because like we can afford if I don't, and she is scared that I will get distracted and that, but I don't know, I might need to get a job, it might be more expensive than we thought. My brother went to uni- versity for a year and he took out a student loan, and they didn't know, they were upset because he could have asked them if they could have given him more money and everything, so they are like, when you go away, just tell us. . . .
>
> (Kirsty)

But like Rachel, and unlike Lucy, whose parents were enthusiastic about her boyfriend (an ex-public school boy), Kirsty (her boyfriend is a labourer) finds herself in conflict with her parents over the balance between her social life and her college work. Complex obligations and dependencies operate within these families. Kirsty's parents remain 'vigilant', as Allatt (1993, p. 151) puts it, 'taking steps to sustain effort':

> My mum and dad have still got the same power over me, because they are paying for me and because, I am living their house, I have to go by their rules whether I like it or not, and they tell me that and I know that. Whatever I want to do in the end, it is up to them. Well it is up to me and them, but as long as I want to stay and study, I have got to go by their rules, the thing that annoys me is that mum's like I've let you make your own decisions about when you come in and when you do this and that but when you make the wrong decisions, we have to help you, she says. It is like I am not making the wrong decisions, but you are trying to do too much. She says I am trying to do too much. We are having lots of these rows at the moment because I am getting more work but I am trying to do that and, of course I want to see my friends. I want to see my boyfriend. I want to go out. It is difficult at the moment. I am doing more than I have ever done before, and I am seeing so many people, and I have got more work than I have ever had before.
>
> (Kirsty, June 1998)

Kirsty, Agesh and Lucy were uncertain about the courses they might follow at university and the jobs they might be interested in afterwards. They saw a 'landscape of possibilities' (Allatt, 1993, p. 153). Their horizons and time-spans are extensive. It might be fanciful but perhaps their uncertainties reflect their class-fraction positions and their family ideologies and politics (see Langouët and Léger, 2000). Their parents are low-ranking managers or public professionals of some kind. Their interest in 'social' subjects and integrated courses and their ambivalence about private and public sector jobs hint at particular kinds of loose/loosening ideological attachments within the families. The young women talk of 'caring' and 'helping' but also about public-sector jobs that they do not want and the attractions of the private sector:

I am combining, I am definitely doing English but I am combining it with something. The thing that I am most willing to combine it with is Development Studies. The Careers teacher said I could ask to do a contrasting culture like African studies is a contrasting culture and I find that interesting as well but I would prefer to do development studies.

(Kirsty)

I think more in the caring area maybe. But then again I think, no I don't want to be a Social Worker or something like that, I don't know, I am still not positive what I want to do but I don't really want to be a Film Director any more.

(Kirsty)

I am thinking of doing American Studies with something, maybe English or I looked at Law as well, but they only do that at a few universities, I think North American Studies, Law and North American is both at Sussex and there was comparative American Studies at Warwick which seemed really interesting, it wasn't just American, it was like the Caribbean, Canada so that seemed quite interesting.

(Agesh)

I don't know, there is quite a range of things. I have done work experience. I worked in a Swiss bank in the City this summer [a job found through her father's social network] and I enjoyed that in a way, but in another way it was horrible. . . . we got all the Traders there and they were horrible, they are all sexist and nasty. I enjoyed working in the office though, I liked working with people . . . again work like that I would find interesting. I don't want to end up being a teacher, you know. Maybe something in the media, but then again I don't know if I would like it there. . . . [Mum] says I would be a very good teacher, but she is not going, she thinks I will get too ground down, and there are lots of teachers that are ground down already, and they are just in their early twenties.

(Kirsty)

I don't know about careers, I can't see a job, I would like to work in, I would like to work in a company, but I would still like to do something like helping,

> maybe on the side or something, because I thought it was really worthwhile.
> A good thing to do.
>
> (Agesh)

There is a subtle difference here between Rachel, and Kirsty and Agesh; a marker of class fractions perhaps. While Rachel is choosing a course related to a specific area of professional activity, Kirsty and Rachel see their degree as more like a general labour-market qualification. Like Rachel, Kirsty, and 'following' her lead, Agesh, were aiming towards what they saw as the 'better' universities. Such distinctions were well ingrained in the young people by their families and reinforced by their colleges and became part of their 'thinking as usual' about university choice. Thus, they were able to 'sense or intuit what is likely (or unlikely) to befall' (Bourdieu, 1986, p. 466) – a 'practical anticipation'. And such distinctions were also being related to the perceptions of potential employers. All this is as much about how others will see them as how they see themselves: 'they classify themselves in the eyes of other classifying (but also classifiable) subjects' (p. 482). They are involved in making themselves up within these complex schemes of evaluation – classifying and classified.

> Universities that ask for high grades, like mainly the lowest you have got to get, the lowest I could have to get would be B, C, C or B, B, C. We have applied to good ones, like we have been looking at places like they want twelve points, we are applying to the better ones. I think the Careers Department have encouraged us to do that, they said that there are going to be courses that you are going to find more interesting, and that push you harder. I don't know, people are taking it more seriously.
>
> (Agesh)

> Lots of jobs look at where your degrees are from. Like if you got a degree from Oxford and Cambridge, I know that where my dad works they look at degrees, if sometimes they can't decide, oh right they have got a degree from Cambridge and they will get it automatically because it is more prestigious. I think if you go to red-brick universities they recognise it more than like the old polys, but not as much as the old type colleges, they are bit snobby about that.
>
> (Kirsty)

While they certainly did not talk in terms of the social reproduction of their families and their class position these young women clearly articulate a sense of striving for a certain positioning in relation to A-levels, university access and the labour market. They place themselves in relation to others and see going to university and particular kinds of university as realizing or achieving a destiny, the occupancy of a social space, 'a sense of one's place' (Bourdieu, 1986). Exactly as Bourdieu describes they are 'producers of classifiable acts but also of acts of classification' (p. 467).

I am going for like B, B, C and I am predicted like A, A/B and B and so if I got them, but I don't know whether I will get them, I should be all right but that is why I am worrying about universities. After that then it is going to be all right once I am in to university I won't care about it but it is just getting there that is the problem. It only matters really for getting into the university you want, it doesn't matter at all after that.

(Kirsty)

They saw themselves creating the opportunity for jobs which were not accessible to friends who did not achieve or attempt the A-level/university route.

Yes Tracey [Anne's friend from Chapter 5] is like, you can get loads of jobs, there are lots of jobs out there, but they are not necessarily good jobs. They are both doing receptionist, secretarial and that is as far as they are going to go, and, like, if they had just got A-levels, they could have gone, like, one step further. They are sort of stuck in these jobs. They hate their jobs.

(Agesh)

Agesh, Lucy, Rachel and Kirsty are purposeful and agentic young women. In many respects they are 'ideal students'. They are the beneficiaries of those 'commonplaces and classificatory systems' which dominate the socio-logics of the education system. These 'advantageous attributions' (and opportunities) – self-knowledge and social power – are key to their identities.

But their stories and their identities are not as simple as all that. Their social lives, of which we could have written at much greater length, are complex, often hectic, sometimes adventuresome and full of other possible ways of 'making up' an identity. They live in and through but also beyond their families. Rachel and Lucy have 'escaped' their families and their vigilance. They and to a lesser extent Kirsty have strained against their 'circumscribed freedoms'. They belie and embody, at the same time, the stereotype of academic single-mindedness some-times associated with academically successful young women. They carry their social advantages lightly but their academic careers are clearly defined by these advantages as a whole variety of familial resources and skills are marshalled to support them through key moments of 'choice' and deployed in 'the minutiae of daily family life' (Allatt, 1993, p. 156). While, as we have tried to show, their transitions and epiphanies are not always smooth or as anticipated, their personal narratives remain coherent, future-oriented, full of 'real' possibilities and oppor-tunities. The have a rich and affirming narrative vocabulary available to them. They have little need to 'reconsider who they are' (Bloomer and Hodkinson, 1997) – although Rachel does this to some extent in response to her 'failure'. They display a relative fearlessness. Their 'opportunity structures' transcend geography and are not constrained by personal perceptions of risk. In part at least their confidence and competence rests on the material and emotional support of their families. Rachel's narrative in particular is a good example of the 'partial rupture' which now characterizes some forms of class-reproduction in global cities. In a society where more and more, higher education is a mass rather than an elite experience, some fractions of the middle class seek to achieve their certification at 'better' universities in order to assure the reproduction of their class advantages. In a risk society class-reproduction may be increasingly less inevitable. Rachel is aware of this and she takes 'risks' to attain distinction, to gain a place at the 'best' university. But she misses her mark.

These young women are classified and are classifiers – very clearly as they negotiate their educational careers, 'they comprehend the social world which comprehends them' (Bourdieu, 1986, p. 482). They are active in implementing a practical, class knowledge of the world of education – perceptions and appreciations about college, course and university statuses. Out of which a set of 'reasonable' actions emerge. They share a set of basic perceptual schemes, a network of oppositions, which guide their choices, and reinforce their identities – who they are and are not – through various 'exclusions and inclusions' (Bourdieu, 1986, p. 470). They are what they know. The social order and social divisions of the education system are, through these acts of cognition, conserved and reproduced.

Notes

1   Neither Rachel's nor Lucy's relationship lasted and in the summer of 1999 both were working for Tescos in junior management positions and both were considering postponing further going to university.

7 Just 'Ordinary' Young Men
Luke and Jordan

Speaking of Luke and Jordan

In this chapter we want to consider the choices which have been navigated by two of the 'ordinary' young men in our study: Luke and Jordan. In many ways they are very similar. Both are very strongly rooted in their family. Both have highly organized social lives – they belong to organizations which dominate their spare time: football/little league and Air Cadets. In many ways Jordan and Luke can be regarded as compliant and conformist young men who want to do well. As MacDonald (1997, p. 191) has indicated, 'young people in the 1990s tend to share quite conventional aspirations'. Luke and Jordan are interested in fitness, their families, their relationships (hetero) and in 'getting on' (Bynner et al., 1997). Both are motivated towards work and achievement and are positive about the need for and benefits of education. They are both kind-hearted and loving towards their families – both want to do well and not let their families down. Again, there are 'reciprocities' (Allatt, 1993) in play here.

We have chosen to write about Luke and Jordan (although we could have included other young men like such as Earl or Kenneth) because in this chapter we want to attempt two matters simultaneously. First, we want to attend to a substantive concern, a narrative of choice-making and transition which is less frequently heard – that of the 'ordinary', less visible male; and secondly, using their stories, we want to start to excavate some theoretical concerns which will be returned to in the final chapter of this book.

Luke and Jordan are the sort of young men who are usually 'absent' from much of the work in youth studies and in classic sociology. They are not immediately at risk of exclusion. Both are law-abiding and ambitious. Both live lives which (for now) fall between the cracks of sociological theorizing and categorizing. Their narratives are not represented in the 'masculinity' literature and they are certainly not in the sub-cultural youth studies. In their interviews with us they have produced cultural scripts which illustrate that their choices are bound up with and into 'multiple commitments' (Wyn and Dwyer, 1999, p. 10). That is, both young men place equal emphasis on a range of activities and occupations, as opposed to giving priority either to occupation, education, life-style or vocation. Even when they experience some 'mishaps' in their plans and projects, both generally take a positive view towards their post-compulsory transition-making and life choices.

Descriptions

Luke lives in Armitage in a small ex-council house on a small estate where the family has always lived. His Dad is a Pest Control Surveyor and his Mum is a teacher in the local secondary school. Luke is very quiet and seems shy on initial contact. His main interests are sport related – his family and all his friends are connected with his football world. His Dad organizes and manages the local little league. Luke plays for the first team and coaches the third team. All the members train in the middle of the week, play at the weekend and socialize in the club-house. Luke is a goalkeeper, his brother is a striker. His mother works in the club house every weekend and sometimes on the mid-week session too. Luke has always dreamed of playing football at a professional level but is also aware of the need for good qualifications and perhaps sport-related qualifications. He would like to work in the sports-leisure industry and combine this with football in some way. He also participates in athletics and cricket. When the project started Luke did not have a steady girlfriend although this has now changed. His girlfriend Mary loves football and is also drawn into the little league.

Luke is tall and slim with short, blonde hair. He generally wears casual sporting clothes. He is polite and softly spoken. His closest friends at school are Jordan, Kingsley and Harry who all play football. Luke knew he had to remain in education post-16; GCSEs were never going to be enough. His family had always hoped that he would stay on and had wanted him to go on to higher education. Even before his GCSEs, he had driven past some colleges of higher education with his Dad. His Mum had been to Teacher Training College but his Dad has no post-compulsory education. The family were hoping that Luke would be the first to go to university proper.

Jordan lives in Bertram in a maisonette on a 'difficult' council estate with his Indo-Caribbean Dad who is a driver and works at night and his African-Caribbean Mum who is having a one year break from her college course. Jordan has a younger brother, Gary and a much younger sister, Jessica, who is still at primary school. Jordan is best friends with Luke and is also involved in the little league where he trains and plays on a regular basis. He is an active member of the Air Cadets where he has attained the rank of corporal. (Air Cadets is a youth organization which prepares adolescents for entry to the Royal Air Force.)

Jordan is an extremely neat, well-presented young man. He dresses carefully in neat sports tops and well pressed trousers. He is a slim, medium height, attractive mixed-race/dual-heritage young man. He, like Luke, is softly spoken and very polite. Jordan has always wanted to join either the armed services or become a fire fighter. Like Luke, he seems drawn to well organized, hierarchical settings which involve commitment, persistence and respect for authority – organizations which almost seem to provide a safe 'world within a world'. Luke and Jordan both call themselves working-class and are not comfortable with the label middle-class, although they had originally been identified as such by Mr Jones, the head of Year 11 at their school, who knew both boys and their families well.

Here, as elsewhere, there are distinctions which need to be drawn between aspirations, economic status, and cultural/material capital. Both families are 'respectable' working-class/lower middle-class and middle-class aspirant for their children – thus Luke and Jordan are both 'ordinary' boys 'with working-class origins who have adopted a socially mobile trajectory within education' (Mac An Ghaill, 1996, p. 298) and within their local setting. In both families the mothers aspire to be or are 'new middle-class' public-sector workers (Crompton, 1998), which influences aspirations within both families.

Post-16 'Choosing'

When both boys were in their final year of compulsory schooling they were faced with a big decision. Should they leave their familiar school and go to another institution? Jordan was keen to leave school and move to a local sixth form college which enjoys an excellent academic reputation. He applied to St Faith's and was given a place. However St Faith's has 'high' standards and students who fail to obtain five GCSE passes from A* to C are not permitted to start A-level courses. St Faith's insisted that Jordan did some GCSE resits. He felt this was a form of 'going backwards' and wanted to press on. A few weeks into the term he returned to Northwark Park where he was able to go straight on to A-levels. What is interesting here is that Jordan did not do well at 16 (he gained only three GCSEs, grades A*–C) and it might have been in his long-term interests to do resits (or a GNVQ course). It was however, in the school's (financial) interests to re-admit him and let him progress onto the A-level courses he had selected. His parents were not involved. They wanted him to remain in education and 'knew' that A-levels were better than resits, and probably knew little or nothing about GNVQs. They did not intervene at all in his choice-making. At this time his long-standing girlfriend was taking her A-levels prior to applying for university, which might have been a significant factor in Jordan's choice-making.

Luke had never contemplated leaving school. He had always intended to stay on to the school's sixth form. What he says indicates a certain lack of confidence , a fragile 'learner identity.' In Rees et al.'s (1997) terms, Luke could be seen as a 'dependent' learner. He is reliant on teachers to direct, support and cajole him into coping with school work. As we will see later in this chapter, he is strongly reliant on the 'personal' care he has always had from school.

Int: Did you go and have a look at any of those colleges?

Luke: No.

Int: Not at all?

Luke: No . . . because I am going to do art and the art here, I think, is probably like the best there is and I didn't think much of what I heard of college and I think the sixth form (at Northwark Park) would suit me better. It is more personal.

Int: What have you heard about colleges then?

Luke: No, it is just like, my Mum's a teacher. She told me about college and a few of my friends, they say it is really good but they say you have to make sure you keep up with your work by yourself because you don't get chased up and I know here they will chase me up and make sure I keep on doing the work.

Jordan's story of choice-rationalization shows the same signs of doubt and dependency. Both young men were easily swayed by the advice they were given from the school. They were both entering new territory and had undertaken little or no forward planning. As learners they are perhaps more involved in coping and managing with what they know and understand rather than exploring different options or embarking on a risky unknown type of provision. 'Staying on' was easier to achieve by remaining at Northwark Park which was itself desperate to retain 'steady' students like Luke and Jordan.

> I don't know if I want to start all over again, a big change. I know all the teachers and I had an interview with Miss Nightingale. She advised me to stay on because you get more attention at school than you would at college. I am not quite sure yet.
>
> (Jordan)

Neither Jordan nor Luke had spent much time considering their post-16 options. They could be described as 'inert choosers'. They both accepted that the school 'knew best' about them and their educational needs. And while they did not invest time in collecting brochures, attending open nights and visiting possible colleges as did the 'active-choosers' in our cohort who were, in the main, more typically middle-class in origin (Macrae et al., 1997), both Jordan and Luke did pay attention to particular adults.

Critical Adult Advice-givers

Luke and Jordan have always spoken with key adults and thought carefully about the advice they have been given – unlike many others in our sample. They are 'respectable' boys who are polite and perhaps a bit deferential towards authority. They talk with their parents, careers advisors and key teachers. All these people play a part in their decisions although ultimately both Luke and Jordan recognize that 'it's up to me in the end'. Both recognize that their families are 'willing' them to stay on. In the extract which follows the way in which choice is socially embedded in family and families becomes evident:

Luke: Well my Dad is football mad, he never went to school because he just used to do football. He said to me that I have got to have my education but he obviously wants me to do well in football.

Int: Whose advice do you respect?

Luke: Oh, I listened, I obviously went to the sixth-form things [at Northwark Park school]. I have spoken to Mr Jones and he is quite helpful and that because he is a PE teacher and that, and he is quite sporty and he understands what I want to do. And my form tutor, because, I think it was her sister that is, like, did the same kind of thing that I did, so she told me that there are universities and that afterwards. . . . Obviously I had to speak to my parents and that, but they just, they gave me advice and that but they know that the final decision is down to me.

Luke moved into the school sixth form where Mr Price took responsibility for career and pastoral support. Luke developed an excellent relationship with this tutor for whom he has a great deal of respect:

> I wanted to check it out [university] . . . and I had a long conversation with Mr Price so in the end it worked out.
>
> Jack [Price] sat down and talked me through very carefully about going on to Higher Education. My Mum supported me, my Dad supported me. . . . Jack and Dick [teachers at school] gave me lots of advice and helped me fill in the UCAS forms.

Jordan (unusually) found the careers service helpful. He gathered advice and acted on it. However, and perhaps critically, he did not seem to have developed a close relationship with any teachers in the way that Luke had. The careers service provided a 'one-off' point of contact – the sort of support which Luke received was long term and based on relationships developed over a long period of time. Thus, even with 'good students' there is a degree of serendipity involved. Some get a lot of support while others get much less.

> We did have a Careers woman come in and advised us what to, sort of to do, what sort of job I wanted in the future. . . . It was good. The woman asked what our future plans were, what I wanted to do when I left school. She advised me what to do, to stay on or go on training. For what I wanted to do, I needed to stay on and get two A-levels . . . she sent stuff to my house . . . because I want to join the RAF when I leave school.

As with Luke, the final decision was left to Jordan, 'it's up to me', but also like Luke, it was evident that his family had played a part in this (Brannen, 1996).

Reay and Ball (1998) have discussed the complex ways in which middle-class and working-class families 'work' the choice-making process in respect of primary/secondary transfer. They suggest that the majority of middle-class families (in their sample) 'guide' and 'channel' choice-making, ruling some options out and gently positioning other choices as real alternatives. Working-class families and indeed, recently arrived immigrant families may ascribe a greater degree of educational expertise to their children who know more than they do about the educational system and who, after all, have to live with any decision.

This democratic stance may simultaneously be connected with parental perceptions of powerlessness and 'not knowing best'. There is no reason not to suppose that the same is true of post-compulsory choice-making and indeed, perhaps too of Higher Education choice-making.

Reay and Ball (1998, p. 431) drawing on Bernstein (1996), found that (in the primary/secondary transition) there were different types of families: those who interacted in a 'personal' manner within the family, locating choice in relation to the individual characteristics of the child, and those where choice related to the position of expertise within the family. However, 'there was no simple correspondence between social class across family types' (Reay and Ball, 1998, p. 431); that is, both middle and working-class families sometimes exhibited the same styles of interaction in relation to choice. Jordan and Luke talked about their role in choice-making in a similar way; their families had given clear messages about what was culturally acceptable and expected (Aggleton, 1987) within the family (college and post-18 education) but emphasized the key place of individual choice and responsibility.

> Mum said I should go to college but she still said that I have to choose what I want to do. My Dad don't mind as long as I stay in school and do something. . . . Sometimes we talk about it, but it still comes back to the same thing, that it is up to me to choose which one. I am not really forced to do one or the other.
>
> (Jordan)

In the 'new middle-classes' or in recently embourgoised families such as Luke's, there may be uncertainties and ambivalences about how to proceed – particularly in relation to post-compulsory schooling and university entrance. And as we have already said, neither of Luke's parents had been to university. Luke however had an additional 'critical friend' in Jack, the head of sixth form at Northwark Park. Jordan lacked this kind of support.

Pragmatic Choice of Courses and Subjects for A-level

Luke signed up for Northwark Park's sixth form not knowing if the subjects he wanted would be available. He had wanted to do Biology but this clashed with Sociology and as a result he had to make subject changes to fit in with the timetable but declared himself 'happy' with the outcome. Jordan also had a pragmatic subject decision to make from the small range of what was available. Both accommodated to the institution and fitted in. It was apparent that in both cases, their families were not concerned at all about subject choice and did not see this as an issue. The awareness of subtle distinctions in evidence in Chapter 6 are absent here. The only issue was to ensure that A-level status was maintained in what was being pursued. What this signifies is that for 'respectable' working-class/ lower middle-class students, A-level carries the cachet of high status as well as constituting a non-negotiable factor in accessing a desirable future.

Luke and Jordan were involved in a very different type of choosing – or not choosing at all – from the careful sifting and sorting which the 'informed and embedded choosers' in our study (Macrae et al., 1997) were deploying. For the privileged young people, choice at the post-compulsory point was merely another step along a well-known pathway where subjects were carefully selected in relation to content and university entrance requirements (cf. Chapter 6). For Luke and Jordan the post-compulsory transition was unplanned and 'almost happened to them' rather than their taking active control or asserting themselves. Perhaps they simply wanted to avoid making choices altogether. From what Jordan says, it is evident that he is partly 'aware' of having missed an opportunity:

> My parents wanted me to do A-levels and I myself wanted to do A-levels because I didn't want to do another year again, do all the same work I have done before. I suppose if I had been advised better I would have got things . . . [information, brochures].

Unlike Luke, Jordan had a perception that St Faith's was 'better' than Northwark Park in some ways:

Jordan: The classes seem more organised. They had a bit of trouble with the timetable here (at school) . . . [St Faith's] is a nice college. It is more free than in here. In the sixth form there is nothing to do. You either sit in the [sixth form] house or sit somewhere. In St Faith's it's much bigger and more people to mix with.

Int: Why are you so keen on doing an A-level?

Jordan: Because I need two A-levels to join the RAF when I leave school and it doesn't matter what the A-levels are in anyway. In St Faith's I was going to choose the ones I liked, but any ones would do, frankly.

In fact Jordan was doing English A-level and was clearly going to have some difficulties as it was not a subject he had enjoyed in the past and he had not been outstandingly successful in his GCSE work, achieving grade C. He had to change his A-levels four months into the course. Luke's choice of A-levels was also a bit haphazard/pragmatic but not as clearly so as Jordan's.

Jordan: Well my English teacher said that media studies was easier than sociology to get to grips with, so that is the only other choice because there were like Art subjects left. I can't draw . . . English is getting a bit tedious going over the same stuff. Reading takes a long time, going into it all the time.

Int: Do you like reading?

Jordan: Not really. . . . It depends what you are reading but I can't really sit down and read books.

Luke and Jordan had very instrumentalist approaches towards their subject choice of A-level. One of the other 'problems' which Luke and Jordan faced was that they signed up for A-levels where there were few students. Indeed, they were the only sociology students and there were only two others doing history. Both young men saw this as an advantage; they thought they would get individual attention. The families of both young men also seemed to take the same view. (This perception may not have been shared by more 'traditional' middle-class parents who may have been concerned about the lack of dialogue in such small groups.) Thus, there are different meanings and interpretations in play where doing A-levels means different things in different class contexts.

Both young men are ambivalent about their subjects – as long as they do a certain number, the discipline and the content are much less important and, indeed, in Jordan's case, of no importance whatsoever. (All this contrasts strongly with the choice-making of Rachel, discussed in Chapter 6.) This marks the way in which the 'premier A-level route' (Banks et al., 1992, p. 49) is itself becoming more and more internally divided and stratified.

Attitudes Towards School/Studying/Learning

Luke and Jordan recognized the need to do well and spoke frequently about the need for qualifications in their attempt to 'make something of themselves'. While they were studying for their GCSEs, both seemed to be trying to keep up with their work but did not show the motivation and positive attitude displayed by the female students in the cohort (Macrae and Maguire, 1999). This gender-difference was recognized in the school itself. Typically, both were sometimes behind with course work and were less well organized than the girls in their year group. Luke said at his GCSE stage:

> I am a last minute person but I have always been. I mean, I tend to get the basics done, I don't leave it to midnight but it tends to be a couple of nights before.
>
> I just think girls, there are boys who want to learn but I mean, overall, I think boys, some of them do want to work, but once their friends start mucking around, they do. And I think boys probably don't realise that if they don't knuckle down and do it, they think, 'I will do it later'. Most of my friends they say, 'I will do my course work on the Sunday night, the Monday before'. And the girls, they say they have, like, done it.

Post-16 Luke worked really hard but said that he 'just lost it' before the exams. He had a panic attack and had to be taken home by Mr Price. On the day of his exams, the teachers met him early in the school to see that he was calm and ready to take the exams, further evidence of the great deal of support and care given to Luke. He got extremely good grades (two As) but at the end of it all he said, 'I was actually relieved, I didn't feel pleased, just relieved that it was all over and I'd got there'.

Jordan had a harder time getting down to work in the sixth form. He realized the importance of qualifications and recognized that he 'is a bit slack.' However, essentially he takes a 'human capital' view of this process in which education and training enhance social capital independent of family origins and structure (Becker, 1964).

Jordan: I think there is more pressure on us to do better at college and universities now, to stay on and do things. It is easy to get part-time jobs like Sainsbury's and stuff, but if you want something that you can get a career in you have to do really well in college and that. So it is a bit. . . . If you are not very clever, not bright, clever, if you won't do well in school, you haven't got much chance of going up, you will stay like a do-what all the time.

Int: Like what?

Jordan: Like a person who is a labourer.

He recognizes that he has problems sticking to the work and recognizes that his girlfriend is a good influence in this respect; another example of the way in which his 'learner identity' is invested and embedded in his family. Unlike Luke, who has really changed in the sixth form, Jordan is still unfocused and easily distracted from his studies:

> The sixth-form house is really nice but it is a bad influence. You are always going to go off to the side and play pool. . . . Yes, there is pool over there. There is one working side and the pool side. I just keep drifting off to the pool side so I need a break to work really hard.

After School and After A-levels

Luke accepted a place at a local university. He had always wanted to stay in London and live at home. Greenwich university was 'really bubbly and lively' and it made him feel welcome and as if the university wanted him, which was the reason he eventually went there. But he wasn't 100 per cent convinced that it was what he really wanted. Within his family there had always been this expectation that he was going to do a degree. It was strongly assumed that without a degree he would have no chance in life. He himself just wanted what he called 'hands-on experience' doing some coaching or something like that. He gave the strong impression that he had had enough of formal education – he had almost 'exhausted' his learner identity.

Jordan, however, failed all his A-levels and did not know what to do. He had thought about doing resits but at the end of the summer, by chance, he saw an advertisement for a trainee-manager's job with Burger King, linked to a graduate training scheme. Burger King employ a small number of people as trainee-managers and pay £16,000 a year. After a highly competitive selection procedure, the trainee has to undertake to attend an FE college (Middleton) to do an HND and 'top-up' afterwards with more study in order to gain a degree. Burger King give their trainees two days a week off and pay for them to do the course.

In exchange, the trainee works flexi-time and can be called in at short notice. Jordan thinks this is excellent. Basically he is getting very good money which he is spending quickly. He has upgraded his computer and has bought lots of clothes. In his view he is at university and he is working – the best of all worlds.

Feelings, Family and Relationships

Luke and Jordan are 'ordinary' young men who have a small circle of strong friendships. Both live highly organized social lives which function round time-heavy commitments to community-based groups. These activities are set within the family; other siblings and parents encourage, support and are also committed to these community centred activities. Both Luke and Jordan are well organized and disciplined in their social lives, as demonstrated by their long-standing commitments to these practices. These are 'respectable' conformist young men who 'play safe', don't over-indulge (either in drinking alcohol or drugs) and take no part in deviant behaviour. They are the 'ordinary boys' who, by virtue of their very ordinariness, seldom feature in youth studies. They are not 'rebels without a cause' (Aggleton, 1987); neither are they the 'macho-boys' nor 'reet lads' of contemporary studies (Mac An Ghaill, 1994; Dixon, 1996). Yet, they feel troubled by the pressures in their lives and by the risks and demands which they see all around them.

They want continuity and predictability in a time of high levels of economic and cultural/familial uncertainty. In some senses they are 'out of tune'. Their sensibilities, attitudes and various capitals are adjusted to a different cultural-economic milieu. Perhaps their psychic 'defence' in times of high risk and uncertainty is to reach back to a myth of certainty, 'ordinariness' and 'fixity' which they attempt to re-institute in the identities which they are busy constructing for themselves.

Luke: I'm very shy, I'm very shy. I don't like change. I like normal things. I don't like change. I hate change. I hate change, change is hard, I don't like change.

Int: You want a professional job, why is that?

Luke: Because it is the security, your life is set for you, you know that you are not going to switch and change.

Jordan: I don't mind changing but I am not very . . . I don't mix easily so. It just takes me a bit of time to get used to the change.

At the centre of Luke and Jordan's worlds are their families and their girlfriends. Luke is currently not enjoying university life. In some ways he would not mind leaving and getting a job, but, at the back of it all he is aware of what his family wants and expects for him. So while both Jordan and Luke reiterate that 'it's up to you' in both cases they are 'driven by' and hedged in with family-centred pressures, obligations and expectations that are hard to escape.

[about leaving] I mean, I know I wouldn't, but if I did, I would say it wouldn't happen. Because my Dad didn't go, he is even more determined than Mum to make sure that I get an education. My Mum is a teacher, she knows. . . . Mum just says, 'Don't worry, the first year is always hard. It'll be all right'. Dad doesn't understand the sorts of feelings and concerns I've got.

(Luke)

In both cases, their front rooms/sitting rooms resonate with ideals of 'family,' aspiration and success. While one front room is in a small ex-council house and the other is located in a 'difficult' housing estate, both curiously share certain features. There are many school photographs of Luke and Jordan with their siblings, taken over time. There are also photographs of parents and other relatives and these are the main ornaments in both houses. In addition, both families are bound up with community experiences. In Luke's front room there are many footballing awards. Luke laughed and said that his Mum had moved most of them upstairs because there were too many. But (like Jordan's family) there is a clear impression of a united family, sharing interests and being involved in organized/time-heavy competitive sporting activities.

In Jordan's home, the front room is filled with the computer which is shared and lots of photographs of the three children. There are also lots of awards, badges, cups. Gary, Jordan's younger brother, has won a coveted place at Mansfield Park (a local performing arts CTC) and Jessica, their younger sister, is involved in gymnastics at national level (British Junior Squad). All the children are involved in organized activities and are competitive and successful/high-achievers in their social lives. As with Luke's family, Jordan's celebrate one another's achievements and support one another strongly.

Both Jordan and Luke have committed sexual relationships which are known about and supported by their respective parents. In this respect there has been a 'weakening of the distinction between adult and child practices' (Aggleton, 1987, p. 58). Luke and Jordan were keen to talk about the importance of these relationships. They loved and respected their partners and appreciated the relationships they were in.

Jordan: I have had my girlfriend for a year and a half now. She is in Bedford and Royal Holloway College doing a History degree, so she is more of a good influence than a bad influence because when I am at her house she studies and I have to do my homework as well, or I get bored. When you were ringing me, I wasn't in. I was at my girlfriend's house. She lives quite close. I am always there.

Luke: If I don't see her every day I have to phone her to check that she's okay. I feel unhappy when I don't see her. I like to see her every day.

They sleep over at one another's house and spend a great deal of time together:

I tell her things I would never tell my Mum and Dad. She's critical. I don't know how I could cope if she wasn't in my life. Mary is exactly like me and Mum says, 'you two are so alike I can't believe it'. I think she's going to be my life companion.

While these committed relationships indicate that Luke and Jordan are loving and caring young men, they also indicate a fair degree of 'closure'. Both have already committed themselves to extended relationships at a fairly early age. Both are looking to reproduce a degree of security and continuity in their emotional lives. Both are perhaps seeking to reduce risk and are investing (inwardly) as much in their domestic worlds and identities as in their external vocational/occupational selves.

Reinstating the Family/Reasserting the 'Ordinary'

To return to the start of this chapter, we said that we wanted to do two things: first, to consider the choice and transition narratives of two 'ordinary' males; and second, to use these stories to begin to excavate some theoretical concerns. In some ways these aims have overlapped. Luke's and Jordan's stories demonstrate that 'choice' and transition are heavily bounded by contingency and lack of predictability, as well as the desire to manage the wide range of multiple commitments that pattern the lives of young people in this period of late-modernity. What is also evident is the role of 'the household domain . . . a key arena in which transition to adulthood takes place' (Brannen, 1996, p. 115) and one which has, like 'ordinary' male lives, been sidelined in many youth studies. Luke and Jordan are for now, playing safe; minimizing their risks in order to maximize their security. They are 'ordinary' men steering an erratic course through the post-compulsory education and training market underpinned by a set of somewhat 'fragile' and haphazard 'learning-identities.'

8   Lost in Time and Space? 'Drafting' a Life – 'Just' and 'Not Yet'
Fiona and Jolene, Daryl and Warren

One of the sub-themes which runs through our analysis of the local market in post-16 education and training in Northwark is that of space (Ball et al., 1998). Spatial issues underpin both the 'choice' behaviours of young people and the market behaviours and tactics of providers (Ball et al., 1997). In relation to the young people the 'use' of space is a key differentiator. Space and scale (Skelton and Valentine 1998) can constrain or open up new opportunities. As Harvey (1973, p. 82) argues, those with the capacity to 'transcend space . . . command it as a resource. Those who lack such a skill are likely to be trapped by space' (Harvey, 1973, p. 82). Spatial practices and meanings are 'raced' and classed and gendered. Spatial meanings 'get "used up" or "worked over" in the course of social action' (Harvey, 1989, p. 223). The 'friction of distance' and personal space are both mentally and materially constructed as a social physics of possibilities, limitations and worth. What de Certeau (1984) calls the 'space of enunciation', literally 'footsteps in the city', is a collection of 'innumerable singularities' which 'weave places together' and keeps other places apart. For some of the young people in our study, their footsteps are set within tightly defined spatial horizons and imaginary spaces (locals); others range more widely in both respects (cosmopolitans). These are the different 'socioscapes'.

The four young people discussed in this chapter are very much home-based 'locals'. They are all currently unemployed or in some kind of 'subemployment', as Roberts (1982) calls it. They are Jolene (black – seven D–G grade GCSEs), Fiona (white – three D–G grade GCSEs), Daryl (white – no GCSEs) and Warren (white – 'left' school early, no GCSEs). Daryl and Warren are friends (and also friends of Wayne, see Chapter 10) and all three share an interest in music and DJ-ing. Jolene and Fiona are technically unemployed but both are involved in the informal economy of child-care. As noted, all four have narrow circumscribed socioscapes. Their 'horizons of action' are set within the Northwark–Westing locality. Their employment opportunities are framed within the possibilities offered by the local high streets and their neighbourhood 'estates'. In this respect and others, the lives of these young people are shaped in the relationship between a set of structural and material limits and possibilities (the local youth labour market in particular) and various individual factors. Their 'opportunity structures' are in part self-made, constructed out of perceptions and assessments of risk and need and personal efficacy but are also framed by 'real geographies of social action' (Harvey, 1989, p. 355). The daily routines of these young people are focused within 'a [highly] localised kind of situatedness' (Durrschmidt, 1997, p. 64) – long-established spatial barriers remain firm. And there are clearly both personal and class-cultural dimensions to their 'localism' (O'Bryne 1997). As regards the former, (Durrschmidt 1997) suggests, capacities in handling space vary and such capacities are 'a crucial attempt to create and maintain spatial and social order' (p. 70); (see also Ball et al., 1995).

None of these young people had a positive or successful school career, although Jolene did have expectations of getting good GCSE grades but had already expressed ambivalence about continuing her education. Her ambivalence was reinforced by her relatively poor performance at GCSE and she did not return to school. Daryl initially chose to 'stay on' in the sixth form but 'just for music' and was soon asked to leave. Fiona developed what could be described as school phobia early in her time at secondary school, was out of school for a year and finished her compulsory education in the PRU, where she was a sporadic attender. Warren was a chronic truant in his last two years and stopped attending Northwark Park entirely after his mock GCSEs. For Fiona and Warren their aversions to school are non-specific and could be said to reflect the beginnings of a more general marginal life-course, as well as, in Warren's case, having a relationship to a disrupted and sometimes very difficult family life. Neither found positive opportunities in school to 'become somebody'. In their different ways they retreated, to attempt a positive sense of self elsewhere. Schooling does not have enough to offer these vulnerable young people (see also Chapter 10).

> I know that most people like think it is bullying or something like that, but it was nothing like that, I don't know, the teachers were all right, I never got in trouble with them. I don't know, there was no problem really. I was really bored going all the way to Westing to school. I didn't like it.
>
> (Fiona)

> First of all I just started truanting with my friends. It just went on from there really. It got worse and worse. Eventually I was out of school more than I was in school. . . . I kind of liked school, I liked being with my friends and that. . . . I look back on it now and I wish I never did it. . . .
>
> (Warren)

> It is not over yet because I just want my grades to be good so that when I go to college and get that stuff then I will be able to do something. I am happy that I am leaving school. . . . I wanted to go to work for a year so I got some money. Then after a year I go to college so that I could do business adminis-tration. I wanted to go to work because basically I wanted to take a year off from school and everything and get some money so that I don't have to keep depending upon anybody so that when I go to college I will have enough

money for everything that I want . . . I think it will be quite the same really, I don't want the same thing . . . I want to change for a bit and then go back to it.

(Jolene)

Daryl: I would prefer to come back here [Northwark Park].
Int: You would. Why?
Daryl: It is easier for me to get to. Like I know some of the people that are staying here so I wouldn't have to make new friends.

In these extracts there are various indications of both their tightly defined localism and a sense of drift and fatalism.

While there are some elements of future planning and deferred gratification in each of these narratives, they are very different from the kind of purposeful 'strategies' of the middle-class/A-level young people. These often harness the resources of a whole family to achieving progression towards a later point of labour-market entry (see Chapter 6) or blend individual enterprise and future planning in FE and work (see Chapter 3). The middle class/A-levellers would be represented by what McCrone (1994) calls 'making out'; although, crucially, 'getting by' does not indicate incompetence or hedonism and there is a 'very fine line' (p. 80) between the two. We will see this particularly in relation to Fiona and Jolene. The young women are home-based, even home-bound in Fiona's case. Daryl also spends most of his 'leisure time' 'round my mate's house'.

Mum and me wouldn't go out at night because it's not really safe. Usually take the dog out that was about it really. That and watch videos, we all like videos . . . I still don't go out at all.

(Fiona)

I have got loads and loads of friends but I don't know how I met them. Sometimes I go out to parties, but most of the time I just feel like staying in and doing nothing. . . . I don't know what my interests are, I don't know . . . I am boring you know, I just stay at home and do nothing, I have got a boyfriend.

(Jolene)

They live, at present at least, within relatively narrow social and spatial horizons – very narrow indeed in Fiona's case. Their self-selected opportunities for work are set within these horizons and the immediate, local job market. This is different from many other young people in our sample who will range widely across the city to find work, or a particular kind of work. The locality is familiar and 'safe'; it provides ontological security. 'Localities can give a sense of identity to parts of the landscape. They can help people to build a feeling of belonging and security – people know where they are' (Smith, 1994, p. 11) and 'who they are'. Jolene, Warren and Daryl talk about visits to local shops in search of work – their view that there are no jobs derives from this (see below). 'I've tried most record shops.

Table 8.1 Warren, Fiona, Jolene and Daryl

	Warren	*Fiona*	*Jolene*	*Daryl*
Family	Mother suffered nervous breakdown and 'used to drink', time in hospital, father 'mentally-ill'. Brother works in factory, has been in court for drug dealing, sister is nanny. Warren spent time in care	Mother and father both long-term unemployed. Sister is home-worker, has two children. Parents rarely go out	Has single parent mother who is unemployed, brother works occasionally as painter and decorator	Parents separated, mother recovering alcoholic. Brother in prison for drug offences and is drug user. Sister is assistant manager of betting shop
Year 11 1995	Truanting from school	Attending PRU – no ideas about post-16 'apart from getting into the army'	High expectation of 'good' GCSEs	Intends to stay in sixth form for music course, wants to be DJ and music producer
1996	Sitting at home, out with mates, smoking, looking for work, retail or music. Does occasional DJ work at parties	Unemployed, interested in child-care, looking after 'mum's friend's child	Working in shoe-shop and doing NVQ as part of Network training	Began sixth form GNVQ business studies, asked to leave. Unemployed, spends time recording own 'tunes' in studio. Benefit £30 pw
1997	Unemployed, in independent living scheme, living in hostel. Benefit £40 pw	Still looking after child three mornings a week	Shop closed after eight months, unemployed	Unemployed
1998	Unemployed – 'just going out – night life'. Has one DJ-ing slot on Internet radio station. Hopes to open record shop with Daryl. Expects to start on New Deal	Caring for two children, one on two mornings and one in afternoons, £100 pw cash-in-hand	Baby-sitting every morning for friend of family, £30 pw cash-in-hand	Looking for shopwork

I've tried all the music shops. Like *Our Price*. They haven't got anything' (Warren). As elsewhere, friends and relatives are key in accessing what local possibilities there are – both Fiona and Jolene found their child-care sub-employment through relatives and neighbours, by word-of-mouth recommendations. 'The lady I used to baby-sit for . . . she knew somebody that needed help in the morning' (Fiona). These are perhaps extensions or re-workings of older working class 'strategies'. But all four have also visited the local Careers Office, with little reported success. In this sense being local, using the locality and local social relations has a logic and a consistency. The inability of state services to provide 'proper' alternatives throws them back on their local networks.

> I spoke to the Careers . . . I was going on a training course but they were fully booked up. I have looked in Job Centre's stuff like that really. I gave up on that idea.
>
> (Warren)

> [At the Dole Office] they look at my Job Search and that's it really. . . . You have to write down what jobs you have applied for and what has happened and all that.
>
> Int.:   What are you looking for, when you're looking for work?
> The local papers, I just go about in shops, go to Careers.

Fiona and Jolene spend most of their time at home or in the homes of the children they care for. Fiona likes to 'come home and relax'. Her social life revolves around her local estate with friends: 'just sort of hang around and that, go to their place, meet in the park and that'. Saturday shopping in the local shopping centre with her mother or sister and an occasional afternoon film with the children are her only 'outings'. Fiona and her family do not eat out, preferring to order take-aways.

Warren, Daryl and Jolene do go to clubs and raves. It is the only time, it would appear, that they venture out of their immediate locality but even then, they do not go far. For Warren and Daryl this is a part of their attempt at creating a 'music' lifestyle. Wayne (see Chapter 10) can sometimes get them onto the 'guest list' at local venues which means free entry. For Warren and Daryl most of their time is divided between their slots on the Internet station (run by Wayne's father), their 'night life' and visits to a local music studio, when they can afford it. 'I either go around to my mate's house, it's all to do with music really, or we go down the studio a couple of nights a week, or we go down to the clubs' (Warren).

Reading through the interviews it is difficult not to pick up a sense of lethargy and fearfulness, of things put-off, of passivity and reactivity. There are plans, ideas, possibilities but they mostly remain as 'not yet'. The young people talk about 'just' doing something, for the time being. A kind of social minimalism. As Fiona puts it: 'I am just really waiting to see what happens'. There is an avoidance of planning, of commitment, of long-term perspectives.

> I didn't really want to move schools and all that. I feel more comfortable, even if it is not a music course, I feel more comfortable staying here [Northwark Park]. . . . It all depends on how far I get on and all that how I get on.
>
> (Daryl)

Int.:   So what sort of work are you planning to do?

Jolene: I don't know, something that pays money . . . When I went to work experience I did office work but that was a bit tiring. I liked it there, but I will probably do shop work, probably shop work. Supermarket or something like that.

Even for Daryl and Warren, underlying their commitment to music is a sense that nothing is likely to come of it, although their persistence should not be underestimated. Both exist on a sense of unrealized possibilities:

> I'm hopefully going to play at a club. . . . I've done a demo tape for that and now I'm on a station they like, they just think I'm good enough.

Int.:   So when do you think that'll be coming up?

> In a couple of months hopefully.

> Daryl and me went over to Northwark Enterprise Scheme [with a view to setting up their own record business] . . . all the other people there were like thirty-ish so we just felt out of place, so we didn't really carry on with it.
>
> (Warren)

Futures are vague, postponed – difficult to think about. Fiona displays a more general resistance to a future orientation and adulthood (see below), feeling safer in the here and now, in 'getting by'. In a slightly different way, Jolene is clearer about the things she does not like and want, rather than what she does like and want. She finds work 'tiring' – but does have a 'fantasy' job (see later).

> I don't want to go to a college where everybody knows me. . . . I don't really want to go to college, not now, straight away. . . . I don't want to be a big business woman. . . . I don't think I would do resits . . . I don't want to do A-levels . . . I had a Saturday job at a hairdressers and everything. I wouldn't want to go to hairdressing again though, because I don't really know, it is a bit tiring and that, but every job is tiring really anyway. . . . I don't know what my interests are, I don't know. . . . .

Int.:   What can you see yourself doing this time next year?

Fiona: Hopefully I would have a job but what, I don't know.

Int.:   Perhaps you are not thinking that far ahead?

Fiona: Not really. I am just taking it as it comes, like day after day and just, well, I don't want to rush things.

When asked to imagine their lives two years ahead both young women struggled to respond with anything specific. The young men envisaged or 'hoped for' the realization of their dreams of music careers. 'Hope' is a powerful recurring motif. There is a sense among all four of waiting for something to happen, something to change. All very different from the explorations and risks undertaken by Amma, Michael, Rena and Delisha (see Chapter 3). In Chapter 3 we emphasized 'improbable' opportunities and attempts at escape. Here it is tempting to point up 'impossible' barriers and a relative lack of agency, and almost an avoidance of reflexivity – although occasionally in interviews, Daryl and Warren did begin to talk about themselves as 'not working toward anything' (see below).

Int.: Can you think further ahead? What do you imagine yourself doing?

I don't know. I don't really know.

(Jolene)

A proper job, like something that will always be there . . . something on a permanent basis [working with children] hopefully.

(Fiona)

I think I'll have a job hopefully . . . in music or a course to do with music . . . sound engineering, something like that, a proper studio. Doing my regular set at a club hopefully. . . .

(Warren)

Hopefully a professional DJ, hopefully . . . in a big rave hopefully.

(Daryl)

Interestingly, when asked 'what about in five years?', Daryl replied 'I'll be old then'. It was only Jolene who saw herself entering FE, at some point, as a way of getting the qualifications which were so often referred to as the key to employment. However, she became less certain of the value of college over time: 'I don't think it will make me get a job quicker'. For now, for her, any job would do.

Jolene: I just want a job so badly, that I will just walk into anywhere and say, 'have you got any job vacancies?'
Int.: Right. So when you say walk in anywhere, where would you walk into?
Jolene: Like a supermarket or something.
Int.: What, like, Sainsburys?
Jolene: Yes, and there is a new one opening up in Northwark. I heard they want some people in June, I think it is. I want a job before that. I want one straightaway.

Significantly, 'anywhere' is not 'anywhere'; it is again the local shopping centre. While she continues to refer to the possibilities of 'going to college',

I am not really looking forward to it then I will do it. I didn't really like school so I am not really looking forward to going to College really. . . . I will just go there and do my work, go home, I can't be bothered with it all.

Perhaps Jolene's fatalism is a recognition of the real constraints and improbabilities that confront her – a polarized labour market. She is caught between being over- and under-qualified. She has no real sense of what difference qualifications might mean to her and whether the effort would be worth it. Within her 'horizons for action' and based upon her experience so far there is little encouragement for action. Jolene has made no moves to explore or arrange a college course; she also says:

> I am not into those who go to college for years and years, and then after that you have to go out of the college and look for a job and maybe you can't get one, you are over-qualified, you are under-qualified. That is why I haven't rushed into college, I don't think it will make me get a job quicker.

Possibilities and 'maybes' are common in Jolene's talk. Her impatience is set against inaction. She commented that:

> I am thinking of going on to New Deal [and] . . . I have been twice to the Careers Office . . . they try to give me training all the time, which is like £45 a week and things like that. I was on that before and it weren't no good.

As with Warren, Daryl and Fiona, there is a strong theme of postponement in Jolene's accounts. In Jolene's case this might, in part, be a reaction to her dis- appointment with her GCSE results but it seems more than that. The 'space' of commitment, perhaps for the purpose of assembling a response in the interview, is filled with 'fantasies'. Du Bois-Reymond (1998, p. 69) makes the point that 'the eventual choice of training and profession amongst the "undecided" is partly the result of intense reflection, but also has a temporary or even arbitrary character'. As with Rees (in Chapter 10), her fantasy is opened up and closed down in a single paragraph:

> I've always wanted to be an air hostess or something like that or working in an airport, something like that. It has never really changed over the years . . . something in the travel business . . . but if I couldn't get into it, I wouldn't really be upset or anything.
>
> (Jolene)

There is also a more pervasive 'fearfulness' in her responses in interview. When asked about drug use, she responded: 'No way! I wouldn't take an E. I am frightened of them things'. And asked about pregnancies among her friends replied: 'I see it, I think, oh! I couldn't handle that'. And about her boyfriend: 'I don't really know, he doesn't know what he wants to do really'.

The premises of the research and the interviewing is an issue here. In some respects, the questions asked assume a 'making out' rather than 'getting by' (see below) perspective. While not intended by the researchers, young people like Jolene tend to be inscribed in the interviews as in some way deficient, as 'not-planning', as not having a future orientation, as not pro-active. Hodkinson et al. (1996, p. 141) talk about this: 'the sometimes implicit assumption that . . . the future career trajectory is knowable and often known – that, once the transition to work is complete, adult working life is firmly set into predictable patterns'. We may be in danger here of doing violence to those we seek to represent. As Lather puts it: 'telling stories always involves misrepresentation' (Lather 1999). The political and educational normativities of the 'learning society' discourse are pervasive and seductive. The 'learning society' is predominantly articulated in terms of futurity, of the investment in and production of 'future workers', whose skills will enhance the nation's international economic competitiveness. There is no attention to, or valuing of the present of these young people. Prout (1999) makes this point about policies and discourses about children. So while in our account we are seeking to 'get away from familiar categories' we are always in danger of slipping back into those familiarities and pathologizing Fiona and the others. Nonetheless!

Fiona also displays a marked fearfulness about her engagements with the world of work and is clearly embedded in a 'getting by' perspective: 'I just want to try and find what I am going to do for the rest of my life and I am taking each day as it comes . . .'. The future is on hold: 'I'm not rushing into anything, because I don't like trouble and that, and I don't want it to go wrong, so I am just taking my time'. This stance is a way of 'coping' for Fiona. 'Once this is all over, what I am going to do, I don't know'. Like Jolene, she 'does not know'. She simply does not fit neatly into the norms of and normalization of 'career planning' and a 'future orientation'. Fiona does not feel ready to assume the responsibilities and roles of adulthood (see also Wyn and Dwyer, 1999):

> I still feel as if I am a little girl . . . I feel very young and not sure of myself. . . . I feel I should be making all these decisions I am not ready for . . . other people are making these decisions like jobs and College and I just don't want to have to . . . I just like what I am doing. . . . I just feel like I am a little girl and I shouldn't have to go though all that.

When asked to describe herself, Fiona summed herself up in one word: 'shy'. Jolene commented about herself 'sometimes I am a bit boring'. For both young women their identities are very much 'home-based', and socially rather fragile – constructed by avoidance, postponement and fearfulness. Somewhat differently, Warren and Daryl almost seem to live their lives on two planes: an optimistic fantasy life of future possibilities and a more dour 'real' life of limited immediate opportunities.

> I have got some application forms for Safeway and stuff like that, been giving them in . . . there ain't more jobs. . . . I suppose if you have got the GCSEs and all that and you have got the grades, but it is kind of hard to get a job nowadays. . . . I have been in the recording studio about three or four times now, making my own tunes and that. I've tried sending tapes to big raves.

Int.:   What kind of thing would you like to be doing?

To be quite honest anything at the moment, anything that brings in the money . . . anything in retail, a record shop . . . I've asked about in a couple.

I think I'll stick with it. In a few months things will start putting themselves together and I'll start seeing what's going to happen in the future. That's why I want to get a part-time job as well, just in case it doesn't work out, so I've got a little back-up. . . . I wouldn't like a food shop. Anything else would be all right.

(Warren)

I haven't got around to phoning them back yet.

(Daryl)

Again there is a sense of things standing still, of hope and uncertainty:

Int.:   How have you changed in the last two years?

Nothing really, nothing really.

I don't think I'll be DJ-ing for the rest of my life . . . I think I might switch completely and do something completely different, working towards something different. I'm not too sure.

(Warren)

However, Daryl did express some shock when he met old school friends who had jobs, money and good clothes. He did not like the comparison. For once he saw something beyond his immediate 'horizon for action':

I want to look towards the future . . . I've seen some old school friends and what they're doing, what they're working towards, before I wasn't really working towards anything. . . .

In a sense, Daryl and Warren are 'drafting' lives and identities for themselves, part-realized 'imaginaries', as DJs and music producers. While they save money to spend time in the music studio and make demo tapes in their bedrooms, they are living lives of 'risk' and 'hope' – static and marginal lives based on postponed commitments and evasion of the 'normal biographies' they see some of their friends leading. In the interviews they construct fragmented and frequently interrupted narratives of their lives as DJs, as part of 'the music business'. These narratives are punctuated by many 'not yets' and 'justs' – 'just doing this'. Their giro-cheques and financial support from their families allow for only pale shadows of the 'work' and leisure lives they would want to lead. Their 'drafted' lives as DJs, as part of the music business, remain very fragile. It could be argued that in

McCrone's sense Daryl and Warren are acting strategically; they have a goal and plans, they are not just 'getting by' but Daryl's own view would seem firmly to contradict this. Furthermore, as Du Bois-Reymond (1998, p. 75) suggests we might see Daryl and Warren as positioned, or as attempting to position themselves, between adulthood and adolescence, and a lifestyle that blurs leisure and work – 'a life-concept with a double professional-personal identity'.

At least to some extent these young people are individualists, expressing a sense of individual responsibility for their lives, even if that responsibility seems burdensome. In this sense, perhaps perversely, they reflect the perspectives reported in Roberts et al.'s (1994) study of 'not feeling that there were rigid boundaries to their opportunities' (p. 51). This may be a discursive effect of 'responsibilitisation'. In this sense they are very much Thatcher's children. When speaking abstractly in response to a general question, as opposed to talking about their own possibilities for work, they used a familiar political voice and produced self-recrimination – they have no one to blame but themselves.

> People say that there isn't any work out there, I think they're lying. There is work out there if you look hard enough, it's just getting motivated. Even myself I sometimes feel there's no work out there but really and truly I know there is. I'm just not looking hard enough.
>
> (Daryl)

Int.:   Do you think it is any harder for black people than white people?
Jolene: I don't really think it is any more harder. No, I don't really think it is any more harder. It's up to yourself really, that is what I think.

More accurately we can identify here a tension or confusion between responsibility and refusal. To the extent that they 'accept' or confront responsibility for their own lives and decisions – acting as adults – they are also made aware of risks and demands that they feel unable to cope with – not wanting to grow up.

They are also children of the welfare state. Warren, in particular, sees crucial areas of his life being organized for him by representatives of a vague and anonymous state. His parents will be moving into sheltered accommodation: 'so hopefully they're [social services] going to find me a place and, hopefully, I'll get housing benefit'. And: 'I'm on the New Deal . . . so they've got to find me a job either in music, something to do with music, which is what I first put down when I started signing on, or retail'. His move into a hostel 'wasn't really my choice, it was the social worker'.

Money and dependence are other recurring issues in the young people's narratives. All four live at home, although Warren has spent time with foster parents and in a hostel, in an Independent Living Scheme. He spent time in a Council flat but did not like living alone and moved back home. Daryl is not in any rush to leave home: 'I'm happy here for the time being, I wouldn't mind getting a place in a year or two'. Out of work, Jolene, Daryl and Warren are constantly short of money. Fiona in contrast has money enough for her needs and to contribute to the household finances. Getting a job is about having 'money in my pocket to go out and have a good time' (Daryl). In the meantime parents continue to subsidize the young people – directly and indirectly (see Irwin 1995):

> Yes. I just want to get some money in my bank so that when I do go to a college I don't have to be dependent upon my mum, you know.
>
> (Jolene)

> My mum gives me £20 every Monday. . . . I used to take a lot of money from my Mum and Dad and we've had a few problems over that so I just kind of learnt that's not the thing to do. . . . [my parents] don't mind what I'm doing, they'd like me to do something different like a proper job, earn some money but I'm looking to stick with it at the moment.
>
> (Warren)

Int.:   What about dad? What has he said?

> He doesn't really say anything. He does say, you are going to have to get a job, and I say, yes I know, but I want to do a job that I know that I am going to be able to do. And he says, fair enough just, you know, but hurry it along and that is it. Finished.
>
> (Fiona)

> [I give my Dad] about £20 out of my giro for housekeeping. . . . Sometimes my Dad lets me off, if it has been a good week for him, he lets me off most of the time.
>
> (Daryl)

The perspectives and 'decisions' of these young people identify patterns and points of significance similar in many respects to those outlined by Hodkinson et al. (1996). As they put it: 'Young people make career decisions within their horizons for action, which incorporate externally located opportunities in the labour market as well as the dispositions of habitus' (p. 149). Those horizons are social/perceptual but also spatial and temporal. For some young people all three aspects – the social, spatial and temporal – are narrowly set. They are locked into a set of limited possibilities which are local and short-term. Their knowledge about and confidence in the education, training and labour market are framed by what is familiar and necessary and are often beset by multiple contingencies. Their personal narratives are tentative and often fragmented, punctuated with 'not yets', but are typically aimed at the achievement of a 'normal biography', an 'ordinary life' even if their attempts sometimes seem fragile. Others, as noted above, envisage long-term career development, move with confidence around the city and experiment with different sorts of lives and identities. Their narratives stress possibility and opportunity. There is nothing in their previous education or experience in the education and training market to suggest that they might not achieve a 'glossy' life or high ambition. Thus, as regards space in particular, Jolene, Fiona, Daryl and Warren's local 'spaces of enunciation' can be compared with Michael's urban (see Chapter 3) or Aaron's or Rachel's (see Chapters 5 and 6) global spaces. Our sample of young people is stretched across a local, urban, global continuum. The labour market opportunities and lifestyles at the extremes are very different. 'These people inhabit co-existing social spheres, coeval and overlapping in space, but with fundamentally different horizons and time-spans' (Albrow, 1997, p. 47).

Clearly some young people change position on this continuum over time as they encounter set backs or (less often in our sample) 'break aways'. Therefore, it is important to bear in mind again that these are 'unfinished' stories and that many of these young people are continuing to struggle to 'find' themselves and to make a life for themselves often in difficult or discouraging social, familial and material circumstances. Jolene, Fiona, Daryl and Warren, like Rees and Wayne (Chapter 10), are outside of the 'learning society' and the 'high-skills economy'. They have been for a long time discursively invisible in terms of educational and economic policy. They are part of a sizeable minority, maybe 20 per cent of their age-cohort, who are neither in work nor in education or training. In recent policy they are the new 'others' – the excluded (Pearce and Hillman, 1998). They are certainly now being 'targeted' by policy initiatives like the New Deal, New Start and the re-orientation of the careers service (see Pearce and Hillman (1998) for details), which is no bad thing, but their 'learning identities' and their personal negotiations of opportunity and risk remain only vaguely understood by either policy makers or researchers. The central tenet of this chapter is that 'opportunity structures' are complexly constructed within particular locations in relation to both objective possibilities and individual identities and dispositions.

9   Futures on 'Hold'
Gabrielle, Gillian, Carlene and Mehalet

In this chapter we consider what choice and change mean for the lives and identities of another group of young people in our cohort. Here, we draw upon the narratives of four of the young women who are now mothers: Gillian, Carlene, Gabrielle and Mehalet. So far, only these four young women from our sample have had children. One young man became a father at 15.

Gillian lives in a council flat with her partner Terry; they are both aged 18 and together they are caring for Ellie, their one-year-old baby. Betty, Gillian's mother, is herself a lone parent and is very supportive of her daughter, daughter's partner and grand-daughter. Carlene, also aged 18, is busy bringing up her son Tyrone who was born when she was 15. She lives on her own in a council flat with Tyrone and his sister Talisha who is now seventeen months old. Carlene is supported by her mother, sister and aunts as well as the father of her two children. Both these young working-class mothers had done well at Northwark Park in their GCSEs (each gained four GCSEs, grades A*–C) and might have gained some A-levels if they had enrolled and completed the courses. Gillian is white and Carlene is African-Caribbean.

Mehalet also attended Northwark Park. She had come to the UK from Somalia as a refugee and eventually, after a number of moves, had been placed in a South London children's home. When she was no longer eligible to stay, her ILS worker arranged for re-housing in a local Housing Association, one-bedroom flat. Mehalet has a long-standing relationship with Meles, another refugee from Somalia. When Mehalet found out that she was pregnant she 'was quite shocked actually . . . when I found out and that, I didn't know what to do and then it was too late'. Currently she is living with her partner Meles (who has moved into her flat) and their daughter, Victoria. They have decided to focus on their daughter's upbringing for the first few months and their learning and vocational plans are 'on hold' for now. Mehalet has three brothers and a younger sister in the country. When the family was in Somalia, both parents went missing. Their father is now presumed to be dead and their mother recently 'turned up' in Australia where she has remarried and started another family. Mehalet relies on Meles, a small number of friends (also refugees), and family for support.

Gabrielle has a young daughter Chelsea and is currently housed in a hostel while waiting for permanent accommodation. Chelsea's father, Robert, visits (on an *ad hoc* basis) and sometimes stays over. Gabrielle's parents are alcohol-dependent and have related disabilities. Her seven siblings are all currently being looked after by the local authority. Gabrielle has spent most of her life parenting 'the kids' and placed herself in voluntary care when she could no longer cope with all the pressures. She had enjoyed primary school but had not managed well in secondary school and had attended the local PRU, which had been more supportive. Gabrielle is white. (For more on Gabrielle, see Ball et al., 1999.)

For now, all the young mothers in our study have 'chosen' to stay at home looking after their young children. Thus, their identities and horizons for action are powerfully circumscribed by motherhood. All four women are currently in situations where, it might be argued, they have conformed to 'typical' patterns of gendered and classed socialization which may well constrain their long-term life chances and opportunities. The sorts of contemporary normalizing educational discourses, to which they have all been exposed, of accessing as much education as possible for as long as possible, gaining credentials and participating in post-compulsory education and training have all had to be sidelined or positively rejected (for now). These young women have all made choices which might well attract a degree of moral censure or at the very least be read as a 'waste' by educationalists. Research on the 'learning society' and school–work transitions typically fail to represent these aspects of youth (female) transitions.

In much of the related literature and in policy-making around teenage mothers, there has been a tendency to regard early motherhood as a 'problem' and as a point of closure, constitutive of a 'fixing' of a domesticated identity. In this chapter we want to examine the ways in which one aspect of identity (motherhood) has indeed become a major turning point, a time of 'biographical discontinuity' (Alheit, 1994). Our point is that all life stories are frequently characterized by turning points which have implications for identity formation and which frequently involve a significant reappraisal of decisions and choices about life, family and work. Becoming a mother is obviously one of these major turning points.

Certainly, young mothers face difficulties, mainly economic and material, but early maternity is not an end in itself; it is another dimension in identity-construction. In the stories which follow it is apparent that for the young mothers in our sample motherhood extends their identities, but this is not at the price of other earlier 'identities'. Being a mother is bound up with other aspects and is another part of identity as a 'mosaic or collage of elements in a contingent relationship with one another' (Lees, 1993, p. 14). Gillian, Carlene, Mehalet and Gabrielle are 'centred' differently at different points in time – exercising their 'choices' in a complex, unstable way (see Figure 11.1).

For Gillian, Carlene, Mehalet and Gabrielle, becoming a young mother is a point of rupture where those parts of their identity which centred on education and training, as well as on their social and leisured 'selves', are currently side-lined. For now, all these young women are heavily involved in their domestic and family roles – their work, education and training as well as their social life has to 'fit' with being a young mother.

Carlene, Mehalet and Gillian have a reasonable clutch of GCSEs and might have been expected to take A-levels. Gabrielle attended the PRU and although she has fewer academic credentials, has always recognized the value of training to enhance her work opportunities. Mehalet, a hard-working student, had done reasonably well in her GCSEs, despite struggling to learn English (gained six GCSEs, grades D–G) and had gone to Burbley College to do a GNVQ Intermediate in Business Studies. It was not that she did not like the college or the course, although she did not receive as much second-language support as she would have liked/needed – but towards the end of the first year she was offered a flat and she fell behind in work she was already struggling with. On the advice of another refugee, she decided to start again at Streetley College, which had better second-language support systems, to do another GNVQ in Science (Intermediate) with a view to moving on to a Nursing Course.

As young mothers they have been/will be housed by their local councils and currently are reliant on social welfare payments. All 'match' the typical research profile of young single mothers: they are working-class, unemployed and susceptible to the 'subdued moral panic' which surrounds teenage mothers (McRobbie, 1991, p. 220). Statistically, as working-class teenage mothers-to-be, they were less likely to contemplate a termination (Dunnell, 1979) and they are more likely to remain financially dependent on the state (McRobbie, 1991).

Managing Motherhood

All four women were generally coping well and caring well for their children, and were enjoying motherhood as well as running their homes effectively. Gillian, Carlene and Mehalet had decorated their own flats with help from their families and partners. Gabrielle was looking forward to being re-housed and making a permanent home for her daughter. Mehalet had no support from older women in her family and said that sometimes: 'It is frightening because we don't know what she [the baby] wants, like sometimes. She don't cry that much.'

Carlene was asked how she was coping with two small children under three years of age and said 'Just do it, innit! (laughs) I don't know how I coped . . . 'cos no-one thought I would actually'. Gillian and Carlene had contemplated terminations – but not for long. Carlene said the pressure was very strong when she was pregnant for the second time but that she just decided that she wanted her second child and that, in any case, it was not unusual to have children at a young age in her family and in her community.

> Yeah! They all had their children young, as well. My mum, she had us, she had me when she was eighteen. And, I mean, me and Jade are fifteen months apart, same as Tyrone and Talisha.

When Mehalet discussed her pregnancy with Meles 'he said, have an abortion, to me, and then it was too late, so I have it.' Mehalet was concerned about her early motherhood:

I would have been much more careful to have a baby. I wouldn't have a baby now. No I wait . . . because it's not good to have a baby so soon before you are ready. It's better to wait until you have finished your course and done your training and that . . . having a baby, like, it was a mistake, like, it was too young.

Gabrielle had also found out at a late stage that she was pregnant.

Because I was four months pregnant it was too late for me. If I had wanted an abortion it was too late. So at the end of the day I had to have her anyway. But me and her Dad spoke about it and we got used to the idea, you know. At the end of the day we are still young but . . . I wish I had been more careful though. I really wish I had been more careful because it's not the best way, is it? It wasn't planned or nothing, no, I wouldn't recommend this way to no-one.

Gabrielle was used to looking after her seven younger brothers and sisters and coping with difficulties. She had been involved in their parenting for all of her life and had even accompanied her mother through her last delivery: 'It was either that or she came home with no baby because she was planning to give him up for adoption'.

I'm like their [siblings] Mum really and I'm too young to be a Mum to them and to Chelsea. It's not right that I have to do it all, but I suppose I've done it for ages now and the social workers just ask me the things that Mum and Dad should be answering . . . like when they [siblings] first walked and what schools they have been to.

But since having her own baby her priorities have had to change: 'Since I have had Chelsea I have had to think more of Chelsea'. For Gabrielle, who had experienced being looked after by the local authority, getting her own place with her own front door and her own key was of paramount importance. When asked what she would like for herself, she replied, 'to have my own little home and just being settled'.

Support – Formal and Informal

Because of their age as well as recent pregnancy and delivery, all the young women have been involved with different forms of professional intervention. They have negotiated loans, visited the Citizens Advice Bureau and have become aware of their rights to welfare support. In many ways they inhabit a distinct and specialized identity and social world – the world of the young mother. They have also had a wide range of informal support as well, from family, friends and partners.

Diana she used to be at school, she has got a baby and she is only about six months older than her so I go around to Diana a lot. Tonight is the first time

> I am actually leaving her [baby] alone, I am giving her to Terry's sister and we are going out to bingo. . . . It took me a while, but I have had loads of help. My mum has been there for me.
>
> (Gillian)

> I think she will be a bit like me, a survivor, but I didn't want her to have a life like mine. I wanted her to have it a bit easier, you know. She's a fighter. She'll succeed but I think she is going to get a bit hurt on the way. . . . As far as setting them up, I went out and got them everything they needed, microwave, kettles, toasters.
>
> (Gillian's mother)

Carlene had initially stayed with her mum while she was still at school. When she was pregnant for the second time she was housed in a mother and baby unit some distance from her family and friends before getting suitable accommodation near her home.

> And it's right near my mum. The other block . . . I said, I can't live there. 'Cos my mum appealed for me, she wrote them a letter for me saying that. 'Cos I was 17 at the time and I was carrying Talisha and I had Tyrone and I, I can't be left away from my family 'cos I need help!

Carlene lives much nearer to her mother than Gillian who has been housed in a 'good' estate some distance away. Nevertheless both young women are in regular contact with their mothers, who support them through child-minding, helping with shopping and accessing professional external support. Carlene's mother helped her get a good flat near herself.

However, with two children Carlene has been more susceptible to professional intervention, which she was unable to turn to her advantage:

> I had an interview with social services, like, to have, erm, a social worker 'cos I was so young – and I had two babies, living by myself. But, when they interviewed me, 'cos I had my family and everything, they said I don't need a social worker and I weren't allowed one. . . . 'Cos if I did have a social worker, then I would be able to get them two into child care, early, then I would have been able to go back but because I'm not . . . 'cos I cope and I'm not going mad [laughs] or nothing like that, I'm not allowed.

Gabrielle's support situation is different from the other young mothers. Her family has always been surrounded by professionals who have worked with them. 'We've had social workers in and out of our life all the time since I was little and that and I know a lot more than some of the social workers. You know, I can tell them things they don't know.' This intervention and support is on-going. At an earlier stage Gabrielle had realized that she couldn't cope with the pressures in her life. She put herself into care but still feels guilty about this because, in consequence, the other children were eventually placed with foster parents. 'It's like I am responsible for them and I'm not really, that's my Mum and Dad's job, but they never done it, did they.' She does have access to support for herself:

> Yes, I could still phone Gloria if I needed to. She is there for me if I needed her but the health visitor is round the corner as well. We haven't had any problems with Chelsea. All the problems we did have I was at Mary's [foster mother] or at Robert's Mum's, so there was always an adult there in case I got a bit funny. . . . No problems now.

Mehalet has had the least support. Initially she kept her pregnancy a secret so she did not get any support other than from Meles. 'First there was just me and him [Meles] because we didn't tell anybody. After six months my brother find out and just like after that, there was more support.' Now she gets some support from her ILS worker and sees the health visitor but other than that she spends much of her time in the flat with Meles and Victoria. 'It's all right but there's nowhere to go. I don't know where to go, so I just stay here. I don't mind. Meles wants to be here with our baby and so he go back to college later, when the little one is older.' Her mother sent her a pushchair from Australia for the baby. Mehalet does not have the day-to-day support of her mother but her sister baby-sits, her older brothers help a bit financially and she has other refugee friends who visit.

Educational Futures

Gabrielle, Carlene, Mehalet and Gillian do not regard early motherhood as an obstacle to their future progress. Obviously they have had to reconsider their options and revise their plans accordingly, but they all have plans for the future which involve moving back into formal education or training.

While at school Carlene and Gillian were, and still are, ambitious and intend to return to complete their post-GCSE studies. Independently, both say that they have identified teaching as a possible career. Carlene had already found out about a local college with good crèche provision and was considering which A-levels she wanted to follow. She had already started finding out about primary-school teaching. Gillian, who had held officer ranking in the Sea Scouts, believes that she has the organizational and leadership skills needed in teaching. Coupled with her love for children, she is sure she has a contribution to make to teaching. Both regarded teaching as a good career which would complement their roles as mothers of young children. They have always recognized the value of qualifications and have always wanted to obtain good well-paid 'careers' as opposed to 'jobs'. Gillian said that more training was going to be useful to her:

> It will give me more qualifications and actually helps me out, gives me more chance of actually doing what I want to do. I started my A-levels but I didn't actually finish them and I was actually capable of doing it.

Gabrielle had not been as successful academically. She had left the PRU and had found a job in the local dentist's surgery, which she had thoroughly enjoyed. She had had to leave this job as her mother had frequently caused trouble in the surgery, coming in drunk, shouting and asking Gabrielle for money. 'So I just left. I had to leave, it got so hard. I couldn't take the pressure.' Nevertheless, Gabrielle recognizes the importance of finishing her education and getting some qualifications. She is interested in pursuing a career in child-care or a related activity.

> Most jobs, you need to have been to college. You need to be able to say, 'Well I done this or I done that. I've got this qualification' and that. I'd like a good job like in a dentist or something and you need training. You need to be able to say 'I done this training'.

Gabrielle was 'hoping to go to college next year when the baby is a bit older. I don't think it is fair to put her in a crèche just now.' But, significantly, she knew which colleges had crèches and this would have to feature in any future plans. She was also now considering child-care training.

Mehalet was emphatic about the need for a degree. 'Everyone in my family has a degree . . . my brother has a degree. I would like to do the same thing, to go to university, to get a degree.' She has ambitions to become a graduate nurse and clearly subscribed to much of the 'learning society' rhetoric (see Chapter 1) as the following extract indicates:

> I don't want to do a job and then another job and that, all different. I want to get on and not be at the bottom. Like, if you don't have no qualifications, it's hard to get to the top. You have to move from job to job because you can't get anywhere and the job is not good and you get bored. But you can't get to the top because you have no qualifications. And so you leave from job to job. But all at the bottom. But, if I have qualifications, if I do a degree, I will be all right. I can stay in one job and move to the top.

Being Young Mothers

Gillian and Carlene strongly rejected any easy stereotyping of young mothers and early motherhood.

> It's stupid really, 'cos, just 'cos you're a single mum don't mean you can't cope, you still have people around . . . to help you. If you want help. It's when they're saying, like, oh, things like, oh, 'they only got pregnant to get a flat', or 'only got pregnant 'cos they wanted some money' and things like that. That's stupid, 'cos why would you have a child to just get a flat? You wouldn't bring a whole new life into the world and have that responsibility for the rest of your life just to have a flat. And saying things like, 'Oh, single parents, they don't

wanna work'. They do wanna work, it's just that there's no child care to go and do that, to get qualifications.

(Carlene)

Many people think if a woman has a baby that is it, their life is over she can't go out to work and it is wrong, I mean women are just as equal as men, to have their babies and the men could stay at home and look after the babies and do the housework.

(Gillian)

Gabrielle was far less optimistic. Because of her childhood and family experiences, she probably has a more realistic perception of the difficulties involved in raising children in complex circumstances. She is well aware of the pressures involved from her own childhood.

My life wasn't my own. It was like I couldn't do what I wanted because I always had to be there for the kids. If I didn't come in, the babies wouldn't get fed, you know. My Mum just didn't bother, she just wanted to go down the pub. And it wasn't right that I should be looking after the kids all the time and being a Mum to them, feeding them and that. Putting them to bed, sorting out their fights, getting them up, dressing them, feeding them when my Mum was out all the time or in bed.

Gabrielle has regrets and wishes that she had stayed in school rather than going to the PRU:

It would have been better if I'd stayed, so them two things, stay in school, finish school and not get pregnant. What I done, they're not the best ways to go on. . . . I wouldn't do it like this if I could like, turn the clock back. I wouldn't have her so I could have more time to get on and live my life, so. But I wouldn't change the fact that I have got her now. I want to wait until she is older before leaving her and going to college.

And Mehalet too, as we have already said, would have waited a little bit longer. However, she does not think that Victoria will make any difference in the long term: 'She will go to a crèche and that, and she will be all right there, and I do the course. I don't think it will matter, no. I will study as long as it takes to be a nurse.' All four see early motherhood as a detour rather than dead-end, one of many circuitous routes towards adulthood and 'being qualified'.

Social Lives

Gillian had only recently had her baby and was still in the process of settling into her flat. She was however thinking about her social life. She was involved with regular visits to Diana, another young mother and a friend from school. She was also just starting to go out in the evenings – a difficult arrangement as she was still breast feeding. Carlene on the other hand was an 'old hand' at balancing a busy social life with being a mother.

Int.: Yeah. And what about going out? 'Cos when we last spoke to you, your mum was really good and you, you were going out clubbing. And you were going out all night and your mum was having Tyrone.
Carlene: Yeah?
Int.: So, can you still do that?
Carlene: Yeah! I've been . . . it's just that, em, most of the time I come back a bit earlier because I will be too tired to look after the kids the next day. Unless someone's looking after them for the next day, then I'll stay out until early morning.

Carlene said that she had been 'too fussy' with the first child but that she was more experienced and relaxed second time around. She went out regularly and had fun. Her life was organized so that she could do this. She said, 'I breast-fed her for two months and that's it. I hate breast-feeding! . . . You don't want to keep breast-feeding when you wanna go places and that.'

Gabrielle's life is very bound up with her younger brothers and sisters who come to stay with her. She also has full family contact once a fortnight. She is still in (intermittent) contact with her foster mother. However her social life is still spent with her friends who live locally:

I go and see my friends down on the estate . . . most of them work now. Yes, Paulette, she works in McDonald's, Marlene works in a shop down the market. I only talk to them two really. Oh, Hayleigh, Paulette's sister, she has just had her baby. Once she is back on the mend, because she had quite a bad birth, once she is on the mend we will probably see more of each other being that we both have babies. We'll get together and sit and chat and that.

Mehalet's social life before having Victoria had been based around a Somalian club in North London where the community congregates. She was now very much house-bound.

Partners

All of the young mothers are in contact with the fathers of their children. Gillian, Mehalet and Carlene have good relationships with their partners. Gillian is living with Terry and says that he is very helpful with their child.

He does actually change her, he bathes her. If I need a bit of sleep in the morning, she actually likes to talk in the morning. At nine o clock she is very active and he will play with her and let me put my head down. . . . He actually helps out a lot. When I actually express the milk he will feed her. He has fed her twice in the night.

Gabrielle lived with Robert on and off, first at his mother's then at his father's home but Robert is unemployed and has learning difficulties. He is dependent on his parents. He was present when Gabrielle said:

> We're not together, together now, because we've been arguing a lot, so we have just called it a day for a little while. But he still comes up to see the baby and that and he stays occasionally because he knows that I don't like this area.

Robert is involved in caring for Chelsea and enjoys feeding her although 'No, I don't bath her. I ain't no good at bathing her'. But Gabrielle added that Robert is very good at getting her to eat: 'Sometimes she won't let me feed her but she will let Robert feed her'.

Carlene has a strong need for her independence. She seems strongly resistant to 'looking after a man' and while she welcomes one aspect of domesticity, motherhood, she is not prepared to become a 'housewife'. She maintains her relationship strictly on her terms.

> I don't live with him. He lives with his mum. He used – he wanted to live with us but I said no, don't want him. 'Cos I don't want, I've got children don't mean I'm a housewife or nothing like that [laughs] . . . I'm only 18! I don't want to have to be cooking dinner, washing clothes, and – I've got their clothes to wash and my own clothes to wash, and our own dinner to cook. If we lived together . . . 'cos when he comes here, he's so damn miserable [laughs]. He's miserable! And after a little while, I say, 'All right, go home now'.

Mehalet's partner Meles is currently a 'job-seeker' but has intentions of completing an engineering course. Mehalet says he is 'doing a better job than me' with Victoria. 'He was up all night yesterday. I was, like, sick in my stomach and he was up all night feeding her, changing her. I was asleep.'

Young Mothers: Difference and Diversity

> Mothers who are under 20 when they first give birth are generally discussed as if they constituted a unitary group. This is not the case. They differ with regard to colour and ethnicity, marital status, employment histories, reasons for becoming pregnant and having children, as well as with respect to how they and their children fare.
>
> (Phoenix, 1991, p. 250)

Carlene, Mehalet and Gillian, more than Gabrielle perhaps, are different from the young women in some of the earlier classic studies on teenage mothers. As with many contemporary young working-class women, they have completed their compulsory schooling and have some platform qualifications. However, all four want to work eventually and fully accept the need for more qualifications. All that appears to be holding them back is the age of their children/lack of child care for young babies and toddlers.

Carlene is a strong, independent young mother. Gillian is at an earlier stage of motherhood. While these young mothers are enjoying their babies they certainly want more in the near future. Both have extremely supportive families to whom they can turn for help. Gabrielle has been giving emotional support to Robert, Chelsea's father. She is probably the most experienced in terms of caring skills but is perhaps 'ground down' by the constant demands and pressures of coping; 'getting by' day-to-day. Understandably her long-term ambitions are to do with stability and security, for herself, Chelsea and her brothers and sisters.

> That's all I want. To be settled and not worry about the kids because they're all right. Having my own little home. . . . I'm busy looking after Chelsea and the kids and that and I just think, well, when she's older I'll go back to college and see what I want to do . . . I'll definitely go back to college.

Domesticity – But Only for Now

As with the four young mothers in our cohort, Phoenix's (1991) study on early motherhood revealed that many young mothers had friends or relatives who were having or had had children at a similar age. Many were supported by a network of family and friends. As with our four mothers, most of the women in Phoenix's study said they would have deferred motherhood: 'their preferred age was only a couple of years older than their current age' (p. 250). Early motherhood was commonly part of their mother's biographies and commonplace in their communities. Early motherhood was not subjected to moral scrutiny or censure within their family and friendship networks in the way it sometimes is in the popular media (Jacobson et al., 1995). The problems they face derive from their social circumstances rather than their age (Gillham, 1997).

Phoenix cites another earlier study (Boulton, 1983) which suggests an important reason why (some) young women find motherhood satisfying. Boulton found that young working-class women found motherhood far more rewarding than 'dull, unskilled and uncreative work' (Phoenix, 1991, p. 250). While all this suggests that early motherhood is not necessarily the 'tragedy' it is sometimes portrayed to be, McRobbie (1991) believes that there are still difficulties. She emphasizes that the problem of financial dependency still remains, as does the reality that not all extended families are supportive. Certainly there were moments of grimness, hard times and varying degrees of desperation, struggle and stress in the stories of these young women – particularly for Gabrielle and Mehalet.

In considering these four particular stories there is a lot of interpretive difficulty. Do we simply accept their commitments to the learning society – the mantra of qualifications – at face value, or accept the persuasions of the policies and stereotypes that see teenage motherhood as a life-course in its own right? Neither. Here we want to indicate the possibilities for these young women of various points of 're-entry' into education and training, their view from motherhood does not exclude a future orientation to 'imagined futures' which encompass other identities, other life courses.

> Women do not simply accept normative assumptions about motherhood, age, marriage and employment. Instead they subscribe to ideas that suit their particular circumstances and beliefs.
>
> (Phoenix, 1991, p. 100)

These young women are among the few in our cohort to have achieved some domestic independence, although they draw upon the support of their family and the welfare services. In some respects their transitions to adulthood have been fast-tracked; various other responsibilities and roles are attendant upon, attached to mothering and motherhood. Motherhood is a perspective from which they now envisage/'imagine' their futures. It feeds, refracts and deflects such imagining but it does not inhibit other imaginings or necessary action. It is also a powerful but not exclusive basis for reflexivity and identity. In a sense the currently held 'imagined' futures that these young women talk about reflect this: teaching, nursing and child-care.

10 Constructing New Futures in the 'New Economies'?
Rees and Wayne

Set against those young people for whom A-levels and university were either obvious or possible, or for whom further qualifications at college seemed like a necessity, is an equally decisive but again diverse group for whom it is 'obvious' that A-levels, university or college are 'not for them'. Indeed for a significant proportion of working-class young people in our cohort the end of compulsory schooling offered an 'escape from learning'. They had had enough; at least for the time being (see also Chapter 8). This is for many the key moment of class reproduction.

In this chapter we look in some detail at two young men who are seeking to make their ways, rather differently, in the world of work, in a youth job market with few 'real' jobs. They are outside of the 'learning society' and on the fringes of the new service economies. They might be described in terms used by Lash and Urry (1994) as 'reflexivity losers' in the wilder zones of the disorganized capitalist socioscape' (p. 143), but it is not easy to read their stories as simply pathologies of exclusion and desperation. There is much more to them than that, although there is equally no doubt that both are at risk of the sort of long-term unemployment and poverty reported by Bynner et al. (1997). Rees and Wayne are both white and working class.

We begin with Rees. In interviews, especially at school, he always came across as being older than his years. He was always well dressed and obviously spent time and money on his appearance. He had little interest in school work but avoided trouble with teachers.

> My brother always tells me to get an apprenticeship to learn something. I don't know, I would rather just stay myself, do what I want to do. I appreciate that they help but they tie you down. I just want to do what I want to do and change my mind if I want. I don't want people telling me what to do all the time. I've had enough of that at school. I know there have to be rules and that. I go along with that but I want to make up my own mind about things. I want to work and I'll work hard if I like it and that but that's about it, really.

Rees left Northwark Park with four D–G GCSEs; his mother does not work and his father has occasional jobs as a plumber. He began a Network Training placement as a Stock Control Assistant in an electrical wholesalers. His experiences closely parallel those of Helen, recounted by Hodkinson et al. (1996).

> Well I did do Network Training for about five months. Then I finished that and then I was out of work for four months. So I then did finally get a job at Thorpe Park but I got the sack from that. That is it really. I have been out of work for about two or three weeks. [The Network Training] was okay, but for the work I was doing, the money just weren't right really. I was doing the same work as everyone else there and getting so much less. It weren't right, really. I worked like nine to five. Monday to Friday. Once a week I went up to Mersley College and did a few bits of work and that and then I went to Burbley College like once a week. That was it as far as training was concerned. I just didn't like it at all. They were going on about equal opportunities and treating employees the same. But I was doing so much stuff compared to like the rest of the people there. They knew what they were doing but for someone like me who didn't know what they were doing, I was doing a bit too much, I reckon. I didn't think it were right. I was the youngest. And they didn't really want me to go. They tried to tell me to stay and that. They said I was like throwing away opportunities but, it was my choice really. And I knew what they was saying but it's my life, my choice.

It is not the case that Rees does not want to work but he is clear throughout his personal narratives that he is in control of his own destiny. He also knows what he does not want. In one sense his choice-making is open – but then certain options are closed-off or never contemplated. He sees himself as responsible for his life and what he makes of it, but his 'planning' is limited and his actions often lead to regrets. If he makes mistakes they are his mistakes. His personal logic puts him at odds with his parents and other adults and the discursive logic of the 'learning society'. What is important to Rees is 'real work' with 'working men'. What he and others in the study referred to as 'a proper job', with regular employment, a full wage and equal status with other workers. What you *do*, is maybe not quite so important. In this muted counter-discourse we can see some vestiges of the rejection of qualifications (p. 94) and commitment to 'generalised labour' (p. 100) (although labour of a different kind) captured by Willis (1977), in which 'particular job choice does not matter too much' (p. 99). As Willis puts it, 'one should not underestimate the degree to which "the lads" want to escape from school – the "transition" *to* work would be better termed the "tumble" *out* of school' (p. 100). Rees' decision to leave his Network Training job brought him into conflict with his parents.

> They weren't happy at all really. They weren't happy and they went on at me but what could they do. They all tried to make me see sense and I knew what they were saying but I'd had enough. I didn't want no more of that. It is my

own life, really. I make my own decisions and that. I should have stayed really. I suppose I could have. I suppose there are ups and downs in every job, but at the time it just felt like the right thing to do. I didn't really think ahead, you know. It just felt right at the time. But I could have stayed and tried a bit harder. And mum and dad went mad because they warned me. They said, 'you'll get the sack' and then I did. But that's life, I said to them. But then I didn't do nothing for a while and then I did a bit of agency work. But that was on and off so it weren't every day. It was just, it was a waste of time really, like odds and ends here and there. It's not real work and I didn't know if I would be working one day or not. I got like £3 an hour. But at the time anything helped, really. And it stopped my mum moaning.

Rees' parents – again his mother in particular (as is so often the case in our data) – remain significant, in their response to his leaving Network Training, his search for another job and later getting the sack significant but not decisive: 'They all tried to make me see sense . . . they went on at me'. They represent a kind of 'sense' – an attitude or disposition that Rees attempts to resist. His response is a combination of fatalism and self-determination. Significantly it was his brother, rather than any formal agency, who provided his next work opportunity:

Rees: I was looking for a job really, for months. Then my brother handed me a list of like phone numbers with jobs. Everything from like Leisure and stuff like that. So I saw Thorpe Park and thought I might as well have a look at that. I rang them and they come up, they sent me a form, I just got the job, basically.

Int.:   Yes. But then you got the sack. What for?

Rees: Smoking in the toilets. A silly mistake really. I enjoyed it. I was annoyed and disappointed. I wouldn't have minded but I weren't the only one. To make it worse, it was my day off as well. I was working on my day off and I got the sack. I was in the wrong place at the wrong time really. But that's life, I suppose. Yes, I felt really gutted about that. I felt really gutted, if I'm honest.

Int.:   I bet you did. And what did mum and dad say to that one?

Rees: Went mad again. They're fed up with me but life goes on. Everything happens for a reason.

Int.:   So what is your next move?

Rees: I don't have a clue yet. Retail really in the shops, I don't really want to work in any other thing but shops.

We might suggest that Rees' fatalism – 'that's life' – is vestigial; another manifestation of an historically located working-class habitus; although this is clearly a disposition not shared by his parents, and in other respects, as noted above, Rees displays a clear sense of personal responsibility. Rees is perhaps unusually aware of himself as making choices about his life while also being aware of the limits of those choices. To a great extent he also sees those limits as self-imposed. His 'learner identity' acquired and developed at school works as a mechanism of self-exclusion, education and training are not for 'people like him' (Bourdieu, 1990). Indeed in some ways he exemplifies Bourdieu's conception of the interplay between individual agency and inculcated disposition. Rees is very much making a virtue out of necessity. In knowing himself, he 'knows' his limitations.

> Because most of my friends that did go to college have dropped out anyway so I would have only been the same. The only difference is that I knew I wouldn't last at college and they fooled themselves. But I could have told them they wouldn't last. They didn't like school and none of us did much work so I knew they wouldn't work at college. But it was their choice. Anyway, I am more independent. I just do my own thing really. . . .

The same sense of choice and agency was noted by Bates (1993) in her study of a group of working-class girls. She suggests that 'The values of personal reflexivity and self-actualisation facilitated the reconstruction of "fate" as choice . . . ' (p. 30). Rees' freedom is conditioned by realms of impossibility. He is aware of what is not possible. His fantasy future is opened and closed in a single paragraph.

> For some reason I was watching a programme about the stock market. I was thinking about that. But there is no way I could ever do anything to do with that. It is quite interesting though, but I don't know nothing about it. It is just in the back of my mind, I will never put it into action.

But he also has a clear sense of a 'real'/imagined future, a set of possibilities, 'goals' set for himself, as he puts it – a 'normal biography' – 'like everybody else'. This is very conventionally conceived (see Pilcher and Wagg, 1996) and he is more future-oriented than the young people presented in Chapter 8. Nonetheless, these real goals remain abstract. The idea of 'a job' is a generalized category, a space to be occupied rather than a specific ambition or projection – 'Retail really, in the shops'. What is missing for Rees is the strategic link between now and then. He is heavily dependent upon the vicissitudes of the local labour market, local, social networks of information and chance encounters. His optimism and self-belief cannot over-ride the lack of job opportunities for unqualified 16–17 year olds in the immediate locality and Rees' horizons do not extend far beyond Northwark and Westing (see Chapter 8). But having found one job he continues to believe that he can find another and in two years time:

Rees: I will be sorted out, easily. I will be all right.
Int.:   What can you see for yourself?
Rees: Not anything in particular. But I will have a job and everything like that and a car. I will have my life sorted. Probably be out of my house as well. I have got to start making goals for myself. I can't say anything for sure but I reckon I will be all right. I just want the same as everybody else, a job, a car, a house or a flat even, a girlfriend. That's about it. But I have to get a job

first. That's my first goal because you ain't going to get the rest if you ain't got a job.

Life is hard. It's no good feeling sorry for yourself. You just have to get on with things. Something better will turn up. I'm hopeful, you know. But you have got to go by the rules sometimes. That is about it.

Two key aspects of Hodkinson et al.'s (1996) frame of analysis are particularly relevant here. First, we can perhaps see Rees' sacking as a *turning point*: 'these points in development occur when an individual has to take stock, to re-evaluate, revise, resee and rejudge' (Strauss, 1962, p. 71). It remains to be seen how much he, or his perceptions of work, are changed by the experience. Secondly, throughout this account we can see the limits of Rees' *horizons for action*. Limits which are both practical and perceptual, rooted in Rees' sense of the possible, his sense of what he wants and his fatalism. It could well be argued that Rees' early engagement with the labour market is about the repair of an identity and sense of self-esteem 'damaged' by his school experiences. As Wexler (1992, p. 132) expresses it: 'self-establishment has to be repeatedly accomplished before any other direction or shaping takes place'. Rees is developing or regaining a sense of personal efficacy but, in his own terms; he makes mistakes. His careership, at this time, is perhaps more than most as much about what he does not or cannot want, as it is about what he does. He would seem to fit almost perfectly what Evans and Heinz (1994) call a mode of '*passive* individualisation . . . in which goals are weakly defined and strategies to achieve them uncertain' (pp. xiv–xv). But it is important to keep reminding ourselves that Rees and Wayne, and the other young people in our study, are not fixed or finished people; their self-identities are unfolding temporally.

On the face of it, Wayne is very similar to Rees in terms of social class background, school career and learning identity, and future perspectives. But a comparison between them also illustrates Bourdieu's contention that the practical logic which defines habitus is not one of the predictable regularity of modes of behaviour.

Wayne is white, he wants to be a music engineer/producer, his father works as a free-lance DJ and van driver, his mother drives for Meals on Wheels. He gained five D–G grades at GCSE. At school he always seemed tentative, unsure of himself. Little that went on at school interested him, except music. His dress, baggy jeans, tee-shirt, trainers and baseball cap, worn backwards (ragamuffin, as it is called), remained the same over the four years of the research. In his first project interview, while still at school, he talked vaguely of 'going to college' but could not identify a course he wanted to do. His mum, he said: 'wants me to go to college'. However, Wayne did have a strong sense of what he would like to be, but this seemed to be a kind of fantasy. He saw little chance of getting from where he was to where he would like to be.

I want to be a studio engineer for music and she [Careers Officer] said that I would need to get quite high grades for that. That is when she said to me that I would need something else to back me up just in case. . . . Well, my back-up plans are, I'm not sure. If I had to stay on here then I would, but I wouldn't really want to. . . . I try not to think about it that much, not during school anyway. No, just like now and again I think I get worried.

Talking about his friends Wayne explained, again in a way reminiscent of Willis's (1977) 'lads' that:

> Most people, you know, they have been in school for so many years they just want to get on with their lives now. They've had enough of sitting in class-rooms. They're bored. They just want to get a job and some money . . . they want a fresh start, a job, a new life, not more writing and learning things that nobody cares about. . . .

Essentially, Wayne has had enough, his learner identity is exhausted, indeed his identity as a learner may be in Weil's (1982) sense 'inhibiting' even 'destructive' (p. 223). There are intimations here of a kind of identity formation that Wexler (1992) calls 'defensive compensation'. He is caught between ambition and experience. He sees no future for himself in education, at least for the time being. Evans and Heinz (1994, p. 10) suggest that:

> [I]n cases where individual decision-making about training and employment does not lead to a balance between personal preferences and job require-ments, identity development is precariously limited, because one's ambitions and orientations cannot be carried through in the work context.

However, this conception represents identity as developing within only one dimen-sion – the narrative of education, training and employment. The 'catch' for Wayne is that he is half-heartedly caught up in this but also has another emerging identity – based in music – which was not 'spoken' in the context of schooling. Within the former Wayne must contend with failure and inadequacy; within the latter, he is knowledgeable, focused and talented. In the early interviews Wayne's own narrative displays what Bettis calls the liminal state: 'If students perceive a lack of certainty or predictability in their lives . . . envisioning their future lives is a gamble' (Bettis, 1996, p. 13). Wayne did rather half-heartedly explore the possibility of a college course and had a vague sense of what was out there:

Wayne: I have rung up a few but I can't remember what ones, but they said you have to ring back at another time, because the time I get back from school it is a bit late, so I suppose I will probably have to take a day off school and do it.

Int.:   So you haven't got any information from the colleges yet? Have you seen any college brochures?

Wayne: Yes a couple but it is not really what I want to do.

Int.:   No, which college brochures have you read?

Wayne: St Faith's and I just had a look at Mersley?

Int.:   Where did you get those?

Wayne: Well it was from other people who had sent off for them and I lent them and had a look at them.

Int.:   Have you seen any other information about careers guidance or colleges maybe on the tube, or in the local newspapers. Do you get a local newspaper?

Wayne: Oh yes, but if I do look through that, I look through it quickly and I haven't seen anything.

Int.:   So you haven't seen anything. What about college Open Evenings?

Wayne: I haven't been to any yet.

Little of this information seemed relevant to Wayne. The substance of most careers teaching and advice at school had passed him by. It was in Willis' (1977) terms 'heavily filtered' (p. 92). 'If things are remembered, they are picked up by some highly selective living principle of the lads' culture' (p. 93). As was the case with many other students, he could remember little of the advice or guidance proffered. Nonetheless, he is aware of the landscape of possibilities in post-16 education and training. He knows where information is to be found:

Int.:   You have the City and Guilds lessons, don't you. What sorts of things go on there as far as Careers are concerned?

Wayne: He just gives us sheets and that, just things like that, and tells us to read the question, write about it, what do you think.

Int.:   So do you get any sort of information from him about what you might do next year?

Wayne: Yes I suppose a bit yes.

Int.:   Can you think about anything you have done?

Wayne: (Long pause). No not really.

Int.:   Did you get a copy of this little booklet called *Choices*.

Wayne: Yes.

Int.:   Have you read that?

Wayne: Yes it was in that lesson City and Guilds and we read through it.

Int.:   Was it any good, can you remember?

Wayne: I can't really remember.

Int.:   What can you tell me about Network Training?

Wayne: Yes I spoke to the Careers Officer about that and I know someone who went on it, it is like you go on a part-time course and it is like experience of working, a bit like work experience. Yes, I can't remember the name of the book but there was this big book in the library.

Int.:   *Occupations?*

Wayne: Yes, I had a look through there, about three times now, once with the Careers Officer, and on Open Evening she showed us a few, and just with a few friends and that we were looking through it.

Int.:   Can you remember what you were looking for?

Wayne: Just like courses that would help me for what I wanted to do.

Int.:   Courses in sound engineering do you mean. Did you learn anything from it, was it useful?

Wayne: Not really.

Int.:   OK fine, so let us just move on. You have told me what has happened so far; can you just tell me about the range of courses available to people at the end of this year?

Wayne: I know the Careers Officer told me there was a few that I could go on but I can't really remember. Some people might do A-levels and GVQs or something. We spoke about them in City and Guilds but I can't really remember that much about them.

Int.:   NVQs?

Wayne: I don't really know about them but I have heard, I just remember like the teacher saying something about them.

Int.:   Right OK, did you remember if any of them interested you at all?

Wayne: I can't really remember what it was about.

Int.:   Yes. Now if I said to you what colleges could you go to, what colleges could you name?

Wayne: I can't really remember.

Wayne's locus of interest lies elsewhere, outside of school, outside of formal training, outside of mainstream careers and job markets. This also points up the subtleties and difficulties of ethnographic interviewing (see Chapter 8). In concentrating upon Wayne's non-engagement with the formal sources of 'careers' information we could have been in danger of neglecting the alternative informal and familial and much more 'relevant' system of advice and guidance.

Int.:   So let us just think about this sound engineer business. How long have you been thinking about that?

Wayne: Years.

Int.:   What has attracted you to that?

Wayne: My dad is a DJ. He plays music, I am as well, I suppose that is why, and I know a few people who make records and things like that.

Int.:   Go on.

Wayne: I have been in there helping like and it is just something that I have always wanted to do.

Int.:   Right that makes sense, so your dad is a DJ, how did he get into that?

Wayne: When I was about eleven or something he just got the equipment and just started off. He goes to all different clubs and he gets paid for that.

Int.:   Are you working towards being a DJ as well?

Wayne: I am not quite that far yet.

Int.:   Oh not yet, but tell me what you do when you help your dad.

Wayne: I am too young.

Int.:   What have you done, tell me what you have done so far.

Wayne: I have played at a few clubs before, three times, that my dad has actually done with friends and I just wanted to go into sound engineering to do it, because that is what like most of the other people the bigger names, that is what most of them do, that is how they get well known. . . . DJ he just plays the music. I think I could do that because I've seen my dad do it and it looks easy.

By the time of his second interview his focus had shifted towards an interest in Network Training. Like the vast majority of our respondents despite all his ambivalences about further education and training Wayne still expressed a belief in the need for qualifications.

Int.:   Yes, I see, so if you could get a real job, you know a job straightaway would you rather do that?
Wayne: No.
Int.:   Why is that?
Wayne: You need qualifications and you wouldn't, you probably wouldn't get that if you just had a job.
Int.:   Why do you think qualifications are important?
Wayne: I'm not sure but I don't think, I think you will just get a rubbish job that won't go anywhere if you don't have qualifications.

Network Training seemed to offer the right balance between getting a qualification of some kind and gaining some 'experience' without the rigours of more 'writing and thinking and being bored'. In all this Wayne's school-based, academic, qualifications-oriented learner identity appears fragile, 'used up' rather than thoroughly alienated. However, Rees et al. (1997) make the important point that: 'Learning identities are not simply the product of formal education . . . they also emerge in relation to informal learning opportunities, with rather different implications for the evaluation of alternative courses of action' (p. 493). Wayne's parents are presented as supportive of his decisions rather than directive (cf. Chapter 6) but again it is his mother who is pro-active in finding and sorting options. They seem to be trying to establish a loose framework within which Wayne might make a choice they approve of.

I don't know, I think it [Network Training] gives you more experience than college, rather than sitting there being taught all over again you can actually go and do it and move about and do things not just writing and thinking and being bored. My mum sent off for a few things and that from colleges, but I think I told you about that before. Anyway it wasn't really what I wanted, and after I found out about Network, I just wanted to go and do Network. [My parents] think it is a good idea. My mum just says whatever I want then do it. [My dad] is the same, he doesn't say much.

However, the one constant in Wayne's general uncertainty about life after school remained, his interest in music production and DJ-ing. He saw Network Training as a possible 'way into the business', in part an investment in the development of social capital:

> I don't know, I suppose I could always try and get other work as being a producer or something like that, because like through my dad, my dad knows a few other people and that, that do all that professionally and make their own records so I could just go to them with what like I have done or whatever, Network Training or whatever and just see what they think.

For Wayne, his involvement in music and the 'club scene' was a way of beginning to develop traditional social networks and characteristic trajectories in place of those which had existed locally until the economic restructuring of the 1980s. His introduction into these social networks is through his family and a kind of apprenticeship into the 'family business'. These represent an 'opportunity to develop a different conception of [his] . . . abilities from that gained for formal education' (Rees et al., 1997, p. 493).

Eighteen months on from leaving school Wayne had begun a college Studio Engineering course but dropped out because the course 'was rubbish' and 'was more electronics than there was engineering' and 'I was only in the studio for about a month'. The course did not provide the kind of 'hands-on' practical training Wayne wanted and there was too much 'writing and thinking'. He then worked with 'an uncle's mate' installing fitted kitchens but found this interfering with his increasing involvement in DJ-ing. 'I was playing at the Lyceum on the Friday and a couple of stands on Saturday' and 'doing the Internet on a Saturday afternoon as well and I thought, sod it'. He now spends three days a week working for his father's Internet radio station, without pay. This involves 'on air' work but Wayne commented that 'when I was at school I wasn't too interested in computers and then like, as soon as I started doing this with my dad I have learnt a lot about computers. I can even type now'. The acquisition of computer skills is now located within a practical context of relevance. Wayne's father's interests and his lifestyle continue to be a key influence on Wayne; 'my dad has always inspirated [sic] me in the music and that, so soon as he got decks and showed me how to do it, I have watched him. Since then I was, like, right into it.' And in some senses he is recreating his father's rather 'chaotic' existence and becoming part of the 'family business'. Even Mum, who wants Wayne to get a 'proper job', is being drawn in; 'my mum is starting up a DJ agency'.

Wayne continues to live at home but does not contribute to the family finances, although his mother wants him to pay rent. 'I had an argument with my mum last night. She said I have got to. But I'll cross my fingers', and 'my mum was always saying to me, you should have a job but now she understands, now I am playing out a little bit more'. ('Playing out' refers to DJ-ing in public venues as opposed to in the home or among friends.) 'I told her that I would help around the house, but I don't.' Arguing with your Mum about money and work seems one of those 'normal' things of family life for our young people. Wayne's lifestyle and work habits rest upon a continued financial dependence upon his parents and are part of what Irwin (1995) calls 'the deferral in the timing of transitions' (p. 1) and more generally the 'changing circumstances with respect to the organisation of social claims and obligations' (p. 6).

Currently Wayne sees his future firmly in DJ-ing. 'I suppose I am quite happy where I am, for now. In two years I would like to be playing out somewhere bigger.' But 'when it comes to five years' he does not rule out the possibility of 'going back and doing a course.' Wayne appears to have developed or rebuilt a sense of personal self-esteem and efficacy which was undermined through his school career. He says 'I don't know how to describe myself, I don't think I am stupid'. He is making a career and an identity in what is literally a 'twilight world' of late-night 'stands', cash-in-hand activities; £60–70 for an hour's work; clubs that open and close, loose networks and fragile reputations – 'the DJ world is about who you know'. Beck (1992, p. 15) writes of 'a new twilight of opportunities and hazards'. But this is where he feels at ease, competent, engaged. 'I get bored with things really easy, music I never get bored, music changes all the time, do you know what I mean, especially drum and bass, it changes all the time'.

Wayne could perhaps be seen as an archetype of the Giddensian 'self-reflective identity'. He certainly illustrates Hodkinson et al.'s (1996) point that 'decision-making is part of a wider choice of lifestyle and is strongly influenced by the social context and culture of the person making the decision' (p. 139). Wayne mixes a strong 'commitment' to his music with at least some degree of 'questioning', strategy and reflexivity. He manages, and in some ways thrives, in a liminal world somewhere between work and unemployment, adolescence and adulthood, independence and living at home; it is 'too cushy at home'. He is self-employed but not paying tax. He does not 'sign on' and the Job Centre has nothing he is interested in. There is perhaps something here of Erikson's concept of youth as a moratorium, a period of experimentation. Or more sociologically, this is an example of that 'new institutionalised stage . . . which we might term post-adolescence' (Zinneker, 1990, p. 28) or what Baethge (1989) terms the 'destruc-turing of adolescence'. As Wayne puts it: 'I suppose at some point I am having to get some kind of job but not yet though'.

Despite their personal optimism and sense of 'individualised forms and conditions of existence' (Beck, 1992, p. 88) it is difficult to see Wayne and Rees simply as 'agent[s] of reflexive modernisation' (p. 93). 'Suitability for the labour market demands education. Anyone who is denied access to either of these faces social and material oblivion' (Beck, 1992, p. 133). Nonetheless, Wayne and Rees are trying to 'make out' on the periphery of the new urban economies. These new economies are pre-eminently risky enterprises. They are part of the process of restructuring and re-spatializing the urban landscape, offering 'a multitude of public places for experiences of excitement, pleasure, entertainment, recreation, dining, dreaming and consuming' (Falk and Campbell, 1997, p. 127). They depend upon and underpin forms of sub-employment and under-employment, 'flexibility' as it is called, and play their part in the development of a polarized 'dual-economy'. 'The new employment structure continues to offer job opportunities to the unqualified, but preponderantly within unstable sectors of employment, presenting recurring risks of unemployment and economic marginalization' (Gordon and Sassen, 1992, p. 127). And such employment is double-edged: 'Surplus or discontented workers find other jobs more readily within the metropolitan region than they would elsewhere, while employers have less need to hang on to these workers' (p. 107). Crucially, most accounts of urban economies appear to neglect these new forms of cultural production or personal service in their concentration upon either more traditional forms as the paradigm for economic analysis or their fascination with information technology as the basis of an alternative 'knowledge economy'. Rees and Wayne are struggling to make something of themselves within these new economies but without qualifications their opportunities for work and progress in work are extremely limited. They draw heavily on their own social and familial networks for information and support.

11 Themes and Issues and 'Overburdened Representations'

> This text . . . will not be written until I figure out how not to reduce this project to some network of themes, emergent or not, how to not inscribe some mechanism of identification and projection.
>
> (Lather, 1994, p. 26)

As the title of this chapter indicates, this text, by Lather's criteria, is a kind of failure, a collapse back into conventionality. The text generally and this chapter in particular are highly reductionist. It is about bits and pieces of young peoples' lives inscribed within the language and concepts of social science. This is an exercise in compromise – a betrayal if you like; but it is also the outcome of a struggle, a 'glorious struggle' (Ely et al., 1997, p. 159), with our data, our selves and our words. Our discussions and debates in project meetings have latterly been as much about how to write as about how to research, analyse and interpret our 'field' – an interplay between 'fieldwork, textwork and headwork' (Van Maanen 1995). What we end up with is a shadow play that is incomplete, still in the making, an unfinished project of writing, a set of 'overburdened representations'. We are also aware of being caught in 'tangles of implication' (Britzman, 1997) with these narratives as we 'respond' to them, personally and professionally, in complex ways. Nonetheless we have tried to write in such a way as to escape from closure and from determinism. Our closing is anticlimatic and down to earth (Hebdige, 1988). We have tried to make space, again in Lather's terms for 'returns, silences, interruptions, self-criticism' (1994, p. 26). We hope even so that the 'sets' of young people presented here capture a range and speak to a generality of youthful positions and perspectives. We also hope that they retain at least some sense of who these young people are.

This is certainly not the sort of study that generates a simple set of firm conclusions – except in one very particular respect: differences in social-class participation in post-16 routes and the confirmation of class reproduction for many. What we will do here is to rehearse and discuss some of the themes and issues identified in the substantive chapters. We are interested both in the experiences and perspectives of young people and in developing ways of understanding these experiences and perspectives theoretically. We are assembling a conceptual tool-kit, working with and adding to existing bodies of work (see Chapter 2).

Post-adolescence and the Family

One of the stark points of contrast between the young people in our study and the representations of youth in contemporary policy and some contemporary sociological theorizing rests upon the question or issue of individualism, more accurately, individualization. The work of theorists like Giddens (1991), Beck (1992), Alheit (1999) and the writers of recent policy on post-compulsory education and training for that matter, conjures up a vision of high or post-modern society in which key aspects of 'traditional' modernist society are 'eroding', 'breaking down' or 'disappearing' – 'have undergone drastic change' (Alheit, 1999, p. 74). We certainly do not want to argue that things have not changed but for empirical researchers seeking to make sense of 'the social' there are two problems. One is that of tense, and relatedly, the other is the deployment of stark, all-encompassing binaries. The language of these theories conveys the idea that the processes of change are complete and change itself is total. The possibility of continuities or the re-working or re-emergence of 'traditional' forms is eschewed by the grammar of such theorizing. The problem is perhaps too much of a concern with 'the exact essence of things' and too little with dissension, 'disparity' and 'minute deviations' (Foucault, 1970, p. 142).

Our work certainly draws attention to the importance and effects of change – for example our discussion of the 'new urban economies' – and we do not want to reject or ignore the work of the 'new' theorists; indeed we use their ideas through-out the study. However, we do want to draw attention to the significance of vestigial structures and values like family and locality (see remarks below on socioscapes) for the young people in our study. In our interviews, the family in particular emerged as a much more significant component of their social and educational lives than we had anticipated, although not necessarily in the form of 'the standard norm of domesticity' (Beck, 1992, p. 120). Their families certainly took a variety of forms but it is difficult to see support for Beck's contention that 'the basic figure of *fully developed* modernity is the *single person*' (p. 122). As other writers have suggested, the life-course period with which our study deals is best understood as 'post-adolescence'. A period which is denoted by complex patterns of support, dependence and obligation within the family (Irwin, 1995) and a set of mixed or conflicting statuses. To a considerable extent these ties and dependencies are themselves the product of economic and policy changes effecting young people. In the study sample, families played a role, greater or lesser, in the 'career' or 'life-planning' of almost all the young people we worked with, excepting those few without families or whose family life had totally broken down (see tables in Appendix 2). Families were clearly important for most of these young people in forming social perspectives and generating resources for identity formation, even if in some cases the young people were struggling (with themselves) against the force of these (e.g. Rena and Delisha). The family remains here a key source of belonging. As Brannen (1996) puts it: 'The household domain, which is a key arena in which transition to adulthood takes place, has been ignored' (p. 115) – although this is not the only arena of transition. In wanting to hold on to or recover these aspects of structure and values we want to take care not to produce casual ontologies – we need to think carefully about how individuals are constituted (Hodkinson et al., 1996) (see below on identities and leisure, pleasure and planning).

Very often parents seek to 'interpret the world' for their children and attempt to instil an attitude or disposition. These interpretations and dispositions are either concomitant with or set over and against those of friends. These 'categories of perception and assessment' and the possibilities and impossibilities which structure them are 'inscribed in objective conditions' (Bourdieu, 1990, p. 57) but are by no means inflexible. They form part of the construction of what Bourdieu calls 'a matrix of perceptions'.

Having attempted to reassert the family, it also has to be made clear that families and parents differ. Some parents (typically the middle-class) have clear aspirations for their children and are pro-active and interventionary in choice-making at 16 and beyond. Others (typically working-class) cede decision-making to their child while expressing concerns or giving their backing to the choices explored by their sons and daughters. For those parents who have no personal experience of further education (mostly the latter) purposeful intervention is difficult. Nonetheless, most of the young people operate within a 'framed field of reference' (Foskett and Hesketh, 1996), loose or tight, established by their parents. While some working-class parents do attempt to establish tighter 'frames of references' for their children's choices, among the middle-class respondents tightness of frame was the norm, although in either case this framing could be resisted or ignored (see Rees Chapter 10 and Kirsty's brother Chapter 6). This is similar to the class patterns found in previous work conducted on choice of secondary school (Reay and Ball 1997). Mothers are to the forefront in all of this – not much evidence here of Beck's (1992) 'negotiated family'.

Families (and friendships) also differ in their access to emotional capital (Reay 1996). That is, in their ability to mobilize and deploy emotional involvement and support. Reay argues, in particular, that class and economic factors affect mothers' ability to 'divert their emotional involvement into generating academic profits for their children' (p. 4). Clearly other aspects of the nature of the 'family' unit are also of importance here (see Gabrielle's story, in Ball et al., 1999 and Chapter 9 for an extreme case, and Macrae and Maguire (1999). Within all this, what we might call the choreography of decision-making within families is complicated. Different parents defined their participation and the autonomy of their children (looseness/tightness) in different ways. As a minimal position most parents had a clear view of unacceptable decisions and what was 'best' for their child. What is notable nonetheless is that the family is significant except for a small minority of young people.

Classing Youth

As signalled already, the other very modernist concept which we wish to defend empirically against the inroads of the 'new' theorists is that of social class. We are not aiming to defend class though in terms of a sense of collective identity or political consciousness – both were conspicuously absent from our data, as is the case in other recent research (e.g. Roberts, 1993; Wyn and Dwyer, 1999). Rather we want to reinforce Crompton's (1998) crucial point that: 'It is somewhat debatable, however, whether a relative absence or erosion of collective identity (even if it is occurring) indicates that a society is no longer class divided' (pp. 128–9). Beck (1992, p. 88) pushes this point a little further, further than we would want to go, in suggesting that 'we increasingly confront the phenomenon of capitalism *without* classes, but with individualized social inequality'. While we have used different methods and worked on a much smaller scale our conclusions parallel those of Roberts et al. (1994) from their comparative study of English and German youth: that despite the sense of individual choice and personal optimism displayed by the majority of young people in our sample, 'in practice their opportunities were stratified and access to different levels depended on the familiar predictors – family and educational background, sex and place of residence. . . . [T]he spread of flexibility, and the trend towards individualised transitional experiences, [have not] destructured young people's opportunities' (p. 48). (See Appendix 3, Table A3.1 on the relationships between routes, destinations and social class.) Conceptually and theoretically we need to avoid simplistic binaries and find a way between the 'dissolution' theorizing of Beck and Giddens and a re-assertion of a simple categorical structuralism. We need to recognize the development of new labour-market conditions and structures but not ignore the formation of new class hierarchies, inequalities and exclusions arising from these conditions and structures. Clearly though, in our work there was a tendency for crises and exclusions to be seen as personal failings rather than 'problems of the system' (Beck, 1992, p. 89). These young people see their lives as 'up to them', but the possibilities and probabilities of a 'future' are constituted differently within the different social-class contexts. However, as we point out later, the 'future' is not all that important to all these young people; a disposition towards the present, a sense of deferral, weave through the narratives. Many, but by no means all, of our study sample are pro-active and resilient; they are 'making out', hanging on to aspirations and possibilities. 'This positivity may be puzzling to us as researchers but it is not easily dismissed' (Wyn and Dwyer, 1999, p. 12). Roberts et al.'s (1994) concept of 'structured individualism' is very helpful here – as they explain: 'Even when individuals have moved consistently, towards pre-formulated goals, these aims themselves, and the individuals' ability to realise them, were products of their structural locations' (p. 51). Social-class differences in the modes, processes and points of engagement with the education and labour market permeate the study. In this sense inequality cannot be thought of as 'classless' (Beck, 1992, p. 88). Too much emphasis given to processes of individualization may obscure the continuation of common routes and fates. As far as working-class young people are concerned, our data suggest that while many of them are focused on the need for qualifications, on achieving the requirements for a later and different entry point into the labour market, they certainly do not display a totally reconstructed sense of possibilities and aspirations. Rather, 'a practical anticipation of objective limits acquired by experience of objective limits, "a sense of one's place"' (Bourdieu, 1986, p. 471). (Again see Appendix 3.) The young people 'choosing' post-16 routes bring with them a baggage of previous experiences, learning identities, self-esteem and possibilities of exchange. They are positioned differently in the 'economy of student worth' (Ball et al., 1998). Furthermore, and importantly, those young people within our study sample whom we have identified as 'socially excluded' are exclusively from working-class backgrounds (see Chapter 4).

Underpinning and valorising 'the economy of student worth' and the concomitant individual classifying practices there is a more general politics of classification, what Bourdieu (1986, p. 479) calls 'the classification struggle', the 'power over . . . classificatory schemes and systems'. The focus of this struggle in the field of post-16 education and training has two main inter-related aspects. One concerns the school/FE division and the other the academic/vocational division between A-levels and GNVQ/NVQs. A-levels and the 'sixth form' in particular stand as defensive bastions of educational elitism. Their continuation, in Bourdieu's (1986) words, 'reproduces, in a transfigured form, in the symbolic logic of differential gaps, i.e., of discontinuity, the general gradual and continuous differences which structure the established order' (p. 480). Class and racial advantages are maintained by the re-assertion of this symbolic logic.

Leisure and Pleasure and Planning

One of the generic 'problems' of policy and of social science indeed is that 'focus' or parsimony often leads to misunderstanding and misrepresentation. This study dances around misunderstandings in a number of ways. Most notably our focus upon education, training and work marginalizes or obscures other points of focus that may be 'really' much more important in the lives of the young people. Certainly, over a four-year period of interviewing, our 'control' over focus has deliberately weakened. The topics of the interviews conducted with the young people have become broader, the style more open. While the early interviews were mostly about education, training and work, in many instances the later ones are more about 'sex, drugs and rock and roll', because these topics were of more 'interest' and relevance to the young people. In other words, we are in danger of making these young people sound more serious, more organized and planned than they really are.

There is a clash of priorities and meanings here, a clash that is deeply embedded in education and training policies. These policies, so commonly expressed now in the reductionist terms of the requirements of international economic competitiveness, are almost exclusively concerned with the production of future workers with particular skills or dispositions. These policies rest on an unexamined premise, on what Prout (1999) refers to as 'futurity'. The present of and for young people, their 'self-realisation', is of little interest or value in these policies. In our research we increasingly felt it necessary to eschew the overly simplistic character-izations of young people evident in policy documents – as individual, rational calculators or human capitalists. While some instrumentalism and economic rationalism is strongly apparent, this is unevenly distributed across the sample. While some of these young people are clearly 'planners', others are stridently avoiding the future – either unwilling or feeling unable to contemplate the longer term. This is the idea that 'I don't want to commit myself yet', as Du Bois-Reymond (1998) puts it, reporting similar dispositions among a group of Dutch young people. One condensate of this clash of priorities is represented in the idea of 'living for the weekend' (Hollands, 1995). In other words, young people have multiple, 'other identities' (Marginson, 1997, p. 225).

Generally, in much of the current work which examines youth transitions there are 'silences' around the role of leisure and pleasure in the lives of young people at the end of the twentieth century. The major thrust, as in policy – a 'taking' rather than 'making' of problems – centres on the 'learning society' or the move-ment towards 'life-long learning' and has at its centre, a concern with upskilling, reskilling and labour market needs. The work ethic and human capital theory gen-erate between them a very utilitarian version of what it is to be a young person in contemporary society (Rees et al., 1997). Wyn and Dwyer (1999) argue that 'the focus on young people's passage to adult status has failed to take account of fundamental shifts in social and economic relations which affect *both* young people and older people' (p. 19).

A small number of recent studies, like that of Du Bois-Reymond (1998), have begun to suggest, or to recognize, a different kind of hedonistic youthfulness. Clarke (1999) describes a 'quick-fix' mentality and reports that even among young people with 'career jobs' time is precious and therefore life needs to be lived to the full. Those without career jobs lived life 'getting by' rather than 'getting on' but nevertheless for this group too 'the present rather than an uncertain future takes on greater importance' (p. 1). However, while trying to avoid the generalities about young people as rational calculators we do not want to homogenize them as 'risk managers' or 'biographical engineers'. As Alheit (1999) indicates, responses to social and economic change – the 'erosion of lifeworlds' – what he calls 'biographical coping patterns' differ between people and groups and, we would add, may differ for individuals over time. Even so Alheit's typology of coping patterns tends to essentialize its subjects. In contrast, one fairly simple way we have found useful in thinking about these issues, as young people 'negotiate and balance a range of personal, occupational and educational commitments in their lives' (Wyn and Dwyer, 1999 p. 7), is in terms of changing emphases between three primary 'arenas of action' or transition. This needs to be thought of in relation to 'horizons for action', to 'socioscapes' (see below) and to what we have called elsewhere 'imagined futures' (Ball et al., 1999). That is to say, these arenas have to be located in time and space.

Some of our young people, such as Rachel and Lucy (Chapter 6) and Michael (Chapter 3), manage to negotiate with great aplomb across and between all of

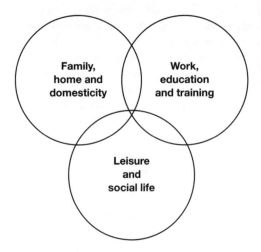

Figure 11.1 Arenas of action and centres of choice

these arenas. Others, such as our teenage mothers (Chapter 9), for obvious reasons are for the time being mostly locked into family and home. Others again, like Daryl and Warren (Chapter 8), are to a great extent excluded from work, education and training. Young people such as Delisha and Rena (Chapter 3) and Kirsty (Chapter 6) find the management of these arenas throw up tensions and dilemmas within their identities and social relationships. Anne (Chapter 5) is very much 'living for the weekend' and developing a lifestyle rooted in 'leisure and pleasure', although earlier in her educational career she appeared to be on route to higher education, while Fiona and Jolene (Chapter 8) are home-focused and as child-minders are 'homeworkers'. There are times when young people such as Debra and Ayesha (Chapter 4) find themselves unable to manage within any of these arenas and are in danger of disappearing from or between them. Clearly, the 'play' between these arenas of action can be seen as a product of choices, as young people negotiate 'their own way into adult life' (Wyn and Dwyer, 1999, p. 7), but they are also, for some, 'fixed' by constraints. As we have tried to emphasize above and earlier, 'opportunity structures' vary. Exposure to or insulation from 'risk' and contingency are unevenly distributed, as are personal, professional and familial 'coping' resources. As expressed by Furlong and Cartmel (1997): 'although the collective foundations of social life have become more obscure, they continue to provide powerful frameworks which constrain young people's experiences and life chances' (p. 109).

Space, Place and Socioscapes

In a way, somewhat like Los Angeles in the USA, London plays a key paradigmatic but largely unacknowledged, role in UK social theorizing. The particularities of London as a global city[1] are often taken to stand for trends or patterns that can be spoken of and applied generally to the whole UK. Local and regional idiosyncrasies are ignored. Here we want to recognize the specificity of London and the particular 'opportunities' it offers for new kinds of work for young people. London is a contradictory space in many senses. It consists of several inter-penetrating economies – old and new – varieties of ethnoscapes[2] and changing patterns of opportunity and constraint. The post-recession economy of the city is markedly polarized. As elsewhere in the UK the extremes of wealth and poverty have increased over the last twenty years.

As signalled above these young people operate across and within spaces in the city in different ways and display 'a variety of forms of social coping' (Buffoni, 1997, p. 125). The unfolding of time and space in their daily lives varies consider-ably. For some the relatively narrow confines of Northwark are the 'limits of possibility' in their representations of space. Other places are only vaguely comprehended and often regarded with some suspicion. As suggested in Chapter 8 this may be part of a more general fearfulness. The home and the bedroom are places of safety for these young people – 'affective space'. This is a particular kind of 'organisation of space' which defines the relationships between people, activities, things and concepts (Harvey, 1989, p. 216). It is a 'compression' of space that is typically linked with very foreshortened time perspectives and even a 'refusal of the future', of planning. Again we need to be careful here. This begins to sound remarkably like another 'casual pathology'. We also need to take account of the materiality of all this. The 'friction of distance' was a key factor for many when considering post-16 education and training options – costs, transport and, especially for young women, security were all factors. In contrast, at the other extreme, the 'spaces of enunciation' within London, and perceptions of space beyond, were for some young people relatively unfettered. Opportunity and imagination, rather than fearfulness, characterized their 'extended' horizons. They really were 'living the global city' (Eade, 1997). Their social, work and educational lives were marked by movement and boundary crossing. The 'frictions of distance' were overcome, at a cost (taxis home from clubs, foreign holidays, school trips, visits to universities being considered, 'gap years' abroad, use of the Internet).

These very different socioscapes are in this study, as in other research (Ball et al., 1995; Reay, 1999), quite clearly 'classed', although they also 'abound in subtleties and complexities' (Harvey, 1989, p. 218) and would merit further research in their own right (see Clarke, 1999). They generate different 'time–space biographies' (Hagerstrand, 1975). What is produced out of these differences is what Albrow (1997) calls 'time–space social stratification . . . the frame within which inequalities of access to resources and life chances are contained today' (p. 54).

Identities: Learning to Become Somebody

'Symbolic orderings of space and time provide a framework for experience through which we learn who or what we are in society' (Harvey, 1989, p. 214).

Embedded in our discussions of families, social class, arenas of action and horizons of time and space is another of the primary organizing concepts which underpin our attempts to represent and understand these young lives. That is, identity – or more precisely as we have deployed it, identities. We eschew the purity of the singular self.

Crucially, the geographies and other possibilities for identity are not the same for all. The availability of 'fragments' is uneven. It is all to easy to play fast and loose with the concept of identities, but at the risk of that it may be possible to contrast, in terms of extremes, those young people in our study with *secure* and those with *fragile* identities. The former, while not fixed or complete, are part of a stable, if not totally predictable, transition and related to an imagined future which is often long-term and sometimes vivid. Such young people, while they are aware of risks and competition, have few real doubts about 'becoming somebody'. These are in a sense heavily 'invested' identities but still sit comfortably alongside other ways of being – clubbing, drugs, drink and sex are part of the 'natural' lifestyle of many 'academic high-fliers'. Very few young people (Rena, Ayesha, Fiona) make their social lives at home. A range of (sometimes) transient possibilities are taken up. Learning and 'life' are seamed together but not always without tensions and tears. Sometimes some identities are 'given' up in favour of others (Anne). Or new, unexpected futures are discovered (Amma). For most young people 'the unstable effect of relations' are exactly that. Parents and siblings continue to be significant others in the making up of identities. In contrast, the latter, *fragile* identities, again not fixed, are often part of a fractured transition or a set of refusals. The struggle to become somebody is frequently made up of temporary improvisations which respond to difficult and sometimes desperate circumstances. Making sense of yourself and your future is subordinated to coping with the vicissitudes of the here and now, although again young people like Debra and Ayesha also go to college and 'get qualifications'. For some such young people their 'relations' are highly unstable – the family is dissolved or rejected. Sometimes replaced by exploitative and transitory surrogates or at other times by formal agencies and state professionals.

However, not all of the young people can be encompassed within this simple heuristic and, strikingly, some of the same possibilities for identity play across this division. In the massified, 'common culture' (Willis, 1998), in the 'standardization of ways of life' (Beck, 1992, p. 90) of urban youth, there are moments when categorical and advantageous attributions dissolve – the equality of the dance floor. On the other hand, we have tried to show the way in which identities are claimed or sought and underpinned by the marking of differences – the objective classification of classifying subjects. We have also written about 'escapes' from identity; the struggles between family and community and friends and 'social life' and 'other' possibilities. For some young people these escapes are transitory; moments out of a 'normal biography'. For others, such escapes are more meaningful and more fundamental to who they might become and what they think they want to be. Motherhood can be both an escape and a claim.

One area of 'escape' which is an important discriminator within the study sample is what we might call the 'escape from learning'. For those young people whose experience of schooling has been primarily an experience of failure their 'learning identities' are 'all used up' or 'inhibiting', in Wayne's words: 'they just want to get on with their lives now'. Learning and life are antithetical, mutually exclusive. 'Choice' becomes an absence of choice, a filtering out of alternatives. Both sorts of escape, but the latter in particular, are achieved 'through the narrow eye of the negative' (Hall, 1991, p. 21).

We have also touched upon the 'performance' of identities. Particularly within what we have called the 'new urban economies', style, fashion and the body are part of ordinary employment and part of a claim to participation in 'cool careers' and fantasies about 'glossy futures'. Again, while the possibilities of and resources for identities formation are unevenly distributed, optimism continues to be a defining quality for almost all of these young people (see Wyn and Dwyer, 1999).

Finally

Despite the increasing openness of our research agenda and our attempts to identify and inter-weave a variety of themes in writing about our study sample, we are very aware of all the things we have not said and not addressed. Some of the silences are deliberate but just as this book is a selection from our voluminous data set, this chapter is a selection from the many themes and issues touched upon in the book. Both sets of selections are constrained by the space available. We can list some of the topics we wanted, but were unable, to include: domesticity, drug-use and sexual behaviour (see Macrae and Maguire, 1999), stress and anxiety, style and the body, money, poverty, religion and politics. These are issues we have written, or might write, about elsewhere. Even so we do not claim to have 'exhausted' the analytic possibilities of our data nor in any way to have fully accounted for the complex, fluid and fractured lives and identities of the young people with whom we have worked over a four year period. We leave the last word to Lucy:

> Life's different now. You don't have to go from school to college to university and then into a job for thirty or forty boring years and you don't have to wait until you're forty or something to reach the top, to be a manager. No, it's all different now. I got a university place but I'm not going just yet. I've got a job, I've got responsibility and I work hard. I'm going to make lots of money and spend it having loads of laughs and loads of experiences and that. You just go for it, grab it while you can, enjoy it, whatever it is, use it, add it to your CV and move on to something else. There's loads of opportunities and I'm just taking them while I can. My mum and dad didn't have these opportunities. Just go for it, I say.

Notes

1   Sassen (1991) describes global cities as 'sites for (1) the production of specialized services needed by complex organizations for running spatially dispersed networks of factories, offices and services outlets; and (2) the production of financial innovations and the making of markets, both central to the internationalization and expansion of the financial industry' (p. 5). But as Harloe and Fainstein (1992, p. 245) warn, there is 'no simple division between 'global cities' and 'other cities'.

2   The landscape of persons and moving groups in the global city (Appadurai, 1992, p. 585).

Appendix 1

Table A1.1 Participation in education, training and employment of 16-year olds, London Borough of Northwark 1996

Pathways	Females	%	Males	%	Total	%
	900	53	804	47	1704	100
Full-time education	674	75	574	71	1248	73
Network Training	75	8	36	5	111	7
Employed	41	5	18	2	59	3
Unemployed	83	9	124	15	207	12
Unknown	27	3	52	7	79	5
Total	900	100	804	100	1704	100

Table A1.2 Participation in education and training of 16-year olds, England 1996

Pathways	Females	%	Males	%	Total	%
	291,000	48.5	309,000	51.5	600,000	100
Full-time education	215,000	74	209,000	68	424,000	71
Part-time education	15,000	5	21,000	7	36,000	6
NVQ level 3	9,000	3	7,000	2	16,000	3
NVQ level 1 or 2	17,000	6	25,000	8	42,000	7
Not in education or training	35,000	12	47,000	15	82,000	14
Total	291,000	100	309,000	100	601,000	101

Table A1.3 Participation in education, training and employment of one cohort of 16-year olds, Northwark Park School and the Pupil Referral Unit, September 1996

Pathways	Females	%	Males	%	Total	%
	32	54	27	46	59	100
Full-time education	20	63	12	44	32	54
NVQ level 3	0	0	0	0	0	0
NVQ level 1 or 2	4	13	7	26	11	19
Employed	4	13	3	11	7	12
Unemployed	3	9	3	11	6	10
Unknown	1	3	2	7	3	5
Totals	32	101	27	99	59	100

Appendix 2

Table A2.1 Student details 1996

Project name	Ethnicity (As described by students)	Career pathway (*Indicates college)	Course	GCSEs A*–C	GCSEs D–G	Attendance Yrs 10 and 11 %	Older siblings	Siblings' career pathways (*Indicates college)	Mother's job (As described by young people)	Father's job
Delisha	Mixed race	Shop assistant		0	0	Excluded	0		Social security scrounger	Stepfather Factory work
Warren	White	Illegal work		0	0	63			Unemployed	Unemployed
Desmond	African-Carib	Northwark Park	GNVQ Intermediate	3	5	96	Sis 19 Bro 26	Phone co. Housing officer	Computers	British Rail cleaner Mechanic
Rees	White	Not working		0	4	80	Sis 26 Bro 24 Bro 27	Cook Bus driver Flats caretaker	No job	Plumber; not full-time
Kenneth	Chinese	St Faith's*	GNVQ Intermediate	4	5	95	Sis 22 Bro 20+	P/T work Univ	Makes clothes at home	Some part-time work
Leila	Bangladeshi	Burbley*	3 A-levels	6	3	97			Part-time child minder	
Kaleigh	Black	Northwark Park	GNVQ Intermediate	3	6	89		Nurse	No job	No job, very ill
Christoph	White	Streetley*	GNVQ Foundation	0	5	95	0		No job	Mechanic
Luther	Black	Youth Training	Business admin.	0	0	41				Mechanic

Romac	White	Moved away	Unknown	3	5	85	Sis 17		Hypnotherapist counsellor	Was baggage handler at BA
Zeyneba	Ethiopian	Mersley*	NVQ Level 1	0	4	96	Sis 18	Bracebridge*	Dead?	Dead?
Aaron	White	Mainwaring*	GNVQ Foundation	0	4	58	Sis 29 Bro 26 Bro 17		Sales representative	Shipping in New Zealand
Wayne	White	Streetley*	NVQ Level 1	0	5	88	0		Meals on Wheels	Van driver DJ
Sinead	White	Working in bakery Mansfield Park* next year	Performing Arts	3	6	42 In hospital	0		Occupational therapist	Civil engineer
Emma	White	Northwark Park	2 A-levels	4	0	74	Bro 17	Robert* Watson	Sells baby clothes	Film editor
Gillian	White	Working Insurance Clerk		4	4	92			Caretaker TA	
Luke	White	Northwark Park	A levels	7	2	90	0		Primary teacher	Locations officer
Earl	Black	Northwark Park	GNVQ Intermediate	3	5	98	0		No job	Fitness Instructor Graphics Exp
Tina	White	Not working		0	0	0	0		No job	Security guard
Carlene	Black	No paid work Two children		4	3	57	0		Secretary	
Marcus	Black Carib	Youth Training	Computing	0	5	87	Bro 17	Youth Training	Catering	Chef

Table A2.1 (continued)

Project name	Ethnicity As described by students	Career pathway *Indicates college	Course	GCSEs A*–C	D–G	Attendance Yrs 10 and 11 %	Older siblings	Siblings' career pathways *Indicates college	Mother's job As described by young people	Father's job
John	White	Working in laundry		0	8	82	Sis 22 Sis 20 Sis 18 Bro 23	Nursing Pizza Shop	No job	No job
Lucy	White	Riverway*	3 A-levels	6	3	92	Bro 18	Northwark Park	Teacher	Manager of Children's Home
Amma	Black	Vernon*	GNVQ Advanced	3	5	93	Sis 17	Vernon*	Hotel Housekeeper	
Anne	Chinese	Riverway*	3 A-levels	9	0	99	Sis 18 Sis 16	University A-levels at Vernon*	Restaurateur manager	Restaurateur chef
Ashraf	Indian	Mersley*	GNVQ Foundation	0	7	79			Unknown	Unknown
Debra	White	Northwark Park	1 A-level	1	2	73	0		Meals on Wheels (PT)	Stepfather Labourer
Jolene	Black	Shop work		0	7	78	Sis 21 Bro 19	College Painter and Decorator	Owned restaurant	
Hussain	Somalian	Brandon*	GNVQ Intermediate	3	6	99	Bro	Mersley* Engineering	No job	Businessman Shop

Name	Ethnicity	School	Qualification			Score	Siblings		Status	Aspiration
Kajal	White S Amer	Streetley*	GNVQ Foundation	1	6	95	0		Student	Student
Kirsty	White	St Faith's*	3 A-levels	10	0	95	Bro 18	Univ	Teacher	Sales Manager
Jordan	White	Northwark Park	3 A-levels	3	6	92	0		No job	Postman
Agesh	Indo-Caribbean	St Faith's*	3 A-levels	9	0	100	StepBro 16	St Faith's*	Nurse Age Concern	Customer Services BT
Daryl	White	Northwark Park	GNVQ Foundation	0	0	63	Autistic alcoholic bro		Recovering alcoholic in hostel	
Reggie	Caribbean	Mainwaring*	GNVQ Intermediate	7	2	98	Bro 18	No job	Auxiliary Nurse	Parking attendant
Michelle	White	Dashwood*	BTEC Equine Studies	3	6	85	0		Was cleaner, not working	Was cleaner, not working
Anthea	Black Carib	Ferrars*	GCSE retakes	0	8	97	Bro 20	Churchill* Tilney*	Teacher	Photographer Pastor
James	White	St Faith's*	3 A-levels	6	2	89	0		Blood analyst	Bricklayer
Rena	Kenyan-Asian	Burbley*	GNVQ Intermediate	6	3	88	Sis Sis	University City & Guilds	Factory work	Porter
Rachel	White	Riverway*	3 A-levels	10	0	95	0	Burbley* then Manchester	Lawyer	Architect
Dean	White	Working Fencing		1	6	59	Sis	Hair and Beauty	Accountant	Carpenter
Mehalet	Somalian	Burbley*	GNVQ Foundation	0	6	95	Bro 23 Bro 25	University University	Dead?	Dead?

Total 42

Table A2.1 (continued)

Project name	Ethnicity	Career pathway	Course	GCSEs		Attendance Yrs 10 and 11	Older siblings	Siblings' career pathways	Mother's job	Father's job
	As described by students	*Indicates college		A*–C	D–G	%		*Indicates college	As described by young people	
Michael	White	Working	Hairdresser	1	2	0			No job	Unknown
Kevin	White	Not working		0	0	0			No job	Builder
Fatima	Turkish	Bracebridge*	GNVQ Foundation	0	2	0			No job	Unknown
Nadine	White	Youth Training	Travel Agent	1	2				Cook Primary School	Owns chip shop
Karen	White	Youth Training	Hairdressing	1	0	0			Granny Cleaner	Grandad Security guard
Tony	Black	Unknown		0	1		Sis 20	No paid work Has two children	No job	Unknown
Gabrielle	White	Not working, pregnant		1	3		0		Foster mother	Foster father
Jane	White	Allen Animal Husbandry	GNVQ Foundation	1	3		0		No job	Truck driver Dead
Jessica	Black	Burbley*	NVQ Level 1	0	2				No job	No job
Jeremy	Black African	Youth Training	Sport and Leisure	1	0		0		Cleaner	Works in food shop

Name	Race									
Terry	White	Army?		0	2		Sis 21 / Sis 19	No job / Got sack	Works in pub	Part-time cleaner
Ayesha	Indo-African	Bracebridge*	NVQ Level 1	0	0		Bro 22	Has lost contact	No job	No job
Natasha	Mixed race	Not working		0	0		0		Student	Unknown
Delia	Black	Burbley	GNVQ Foundation	0	2		Sis 23 / Bro 17	Cab office / No job	Nursery teacher	Security guard
Germane	Black	Youth Training	Office work	0	3	0			Office work	No job
Gary	White	Youth Training	Catering	0	2				No job	Chef
Fiona	White	Not working		0	3		1	No paid work / Has two children	No job	No job

Total 17

Table A2.2 Summary of young people's self-described ethnicity, 1996

Self-described ethnicity	Females	%	Males	%	Total	%
	32	54	27	46	59	100
White	15	47	15	56	30	51
Black	5	16	3	11	8	14
African Caribbean	2	6	4	15	6	10
Black African	0	0	1	4	1	2
Indo-Caribbean	1	3	0	0	1	2
Indo-African	1	3	0	0	1	2
Somalian	2	6	0	0	2	3
Ethiopian	0	0	1	4	1	2
Kenyan Asian	1	3	0	0	1	2
Turkish	1	3	0	0	1	2
Bangladeshi	1	3	0	0	1	2
Indian	0	0	1	4	1	2
Mixed race	2	6	1	4	3	5
Chinese	1	3	1	4	2	3
Total	32	99	27	100	59	101

Table A2.3 Summary of domestic pathways, September 1996

Domestic pathways	Females	%	Males	%	Totals	%
	32	54	27	46	59	100
Living with parent(s)	25	78	26	97	51	86
Living with other family	1	3	0	0	1	2
With parent(s)/partner	1	3	0	0	1	2
Looked after/fostered	4	13	1	3	5	8
In mother and baby hostel	1	3	0	0	1	2
Total	32	100	27	100	59	100

Table A2.4 Summary of domestic pathways, June 1997

Domestic pathways	Females	%	Males	%	Totals	%
	32	54	27	46	59	100
Living with parent(s)	22	69	22	81	44	75
Living with other family	1	3	3	11	4	7
With parent(s)/partner	3	9	0	0	3	5
Looked after/fostered	4	13	1	4	5	8
Bedsit with babies	1	3	0	0	1	2
With friends	1	3	0	0	1	2
Young Offenders Institute	0	0	1	4	1	2
Total	32	100	27	101	59	101

Table A2.5 Summary of career pathways, May 1998

Career pathways	Females	%	Males	%	Totals	%
	32	54	27	46	59	100
A-Level	7	22	4	15	11	19
GNVQ Advanced	1	3	6	22	7	12
GNVQ Intermediate	3	9	0	0	3	5
BTec	1	3	0	0	1	2
NVQ Level 3	2	6	0	0	2	3
Full-time employment	9	28	4	15	13	22
Part-time employment	0	0	2	7	2	3
No paid employment	8	25	8	30	16	27
Unknown	1	3	3	11	4	7
Totals	32	99	27	100	59	100

Table A2.6 Summary of domestic pathways, May 1998

Domestic pathways	Females	%	Males	%	Totals	%
	32	54	27	46	59	100
Living with parent(s)	19	59	17	63	36	61
With other family	2	6	3	11	5	8
With parent(s)/partner	3	9	3	11	6	10
With partner	3	9	2	7	5	8
Looked after/fostered	2	6	0	0	2	3
Council flat/bedsit	2	6	1	4	3	5
Hostel	1	3	0	0	1	2
Young Offenders Institute	0	0	1	4	1	2
Total	32	100	27	100	59	99

Table A2.7 Young people's self-described ethnicity, career and domestic pathways, February
1999

Project name	Ethnicity self-described	Career pathways	Domestic pathways
Delisha	Mixed race	FE GNVQ Intermediate	Living at home with mother, stepfather and younger siblings
Warren	White	Occasional work as DJ	Living with father
Desmond	African-Carib	FE GNVQ Advanced	Parents have moved back to Jamaica. Desmond has tenancy of council property property (family home) with older sister
Rees	White	Working in Sainsbury	Sometimes living at home with both parents, sometimes with girlfriend at her mother's home
Kenneth	Chinese	HE	Living at home with both parents and older sister and brother
Leila	Bangladeshi	FE Re-taking A-levels	Living at home with mother and younger sister
Kaleigh	Black	Working on newspaper	Living at home with both parents and two older sisters
Christoph	White	Part-time work in Sainsbury	Living with girlfriend at her mother's home
Luther	Black	No paid work	Recently out of Young Offenders Institute. Living with partner and their one child in her council flat
Romac	White	Part-time work on market stall	Moved from London (where he was living with his mother) to High Wycombe to live with his father
Zeyneba	Somalian	FE GNVQ Advanced	Refugee; moved out of care into council flat on her own
Aaron	White	Hopes to enter HE in Australia	Moved from London where he was living with his mother to Africa to be with his father
Wayne	White	Part-time DJ	Living at home with both parents
Sinead	White	Working in Iceland	Living at home with mother and younger sister
Emma	White	Part-time work with film editor	Living at home with both parents
Gillian	White	No paid work One child	Living with partner and baby in council flat
Luke	White	HE	Living at home with both parents and younger brother
Earl	Black	Gap year. Part-time office work	Living at home with mother, stepfather and younger brother

Project name	Ethnicity self-described	Career pathways	Domestic pathways
Tina	White	No paid work	Living with partner
Carlene	Black	No paid work Two children	Living on own in council flat. Visited by father of children
Marcus	Black Carib	Works with computers	Living with partner
John	White	Working in laundry	Living with father and large extended family
Lucy	White	Gap year. Part-time bar work	Living with partner in Devon where he is a first-year undergraduate
Amma	Black	FE GNVQ Advanced	Living at home with mother and younger sister
Anne	Chinese	Waitress in bar	Living at home with both parents and two older sisters
Ashraf	Indian	HE London	Living with large extended family
Debra	White	FE GNVQ Foundation	Ran away from home, lived in hostel, currently in Housing Association flat, being threatened with eviction
Jolene	Black	No paid work	Living at home with mother
Hussain	Ethiopian	FE HND	Refugee; living with uncle
Kajal	White South American	FE GNVQ Advanced	Refugee; living at home with mother, two younger brothers and younger sister
Kirsty	White	HE Sussex	Living in shared house with other students
Jordan	Mixed race	HE London	Living at home with both parents and younger two brothers
Agesh	Indo-Caribbean	HE Sussex	Living in halls of residence
Daryl	White	No paid work	Living at home with mentally ill father
Reggie	Caribbean	HE London	Living with mother and six younger sisters and brothers
Anthea	Black Carib	FE A-levels	Living at home with both parents and younger sister
James	White	Working in Sainsbury	Living partly with father, partly with girlfriend's parents
Rena	Kenyan-Asian	Working in Hair and Beauty	Living at home with both parents and two older sisters
Rachel	White	Gap year. Full-time work in Tesco	Living with partner
Dean	White	Working in Fence building	Living with both parents

Table A2.7 (continued)

Project name	Ethnicity self-described	Career pathways	Domestic pathways
Mehalet	Somalian	No paid work One child	Refugee; moved from care into council flat where she now lives with partner (a student and also Somalian refugee) and baby.
Michael	White	Hairdresser	Living with partner
Nadine	White	Works in travel agent	Partly living at home, partly with boyfriend
Karen	White	No paid work	Lived with grandmother, went off with boyfriend; whereabouts currently unknown to family who are unconcerned: 'she'll come back when she's ready'
Gabrielle	White	No paid work One child	Moved out of care into bedsit with child. Awaiting a council flat. Father of baby living in bedsit some of the time
Jeremy	Black African	Works in Sports Centre	Living with partner
Ayesha	Indo-African	Office work Modern apprentice-ship	Moved out of care into bedsit where she lives alone
Delia	Black	Shop work	Living at home with mother and younger siblings
Germane	Black	No paid work	Living at home with mother
Fiona	White	Nanny	Living at home with both parents and younger brother
Total 50			

Table A2.8 Summary of career pathways, February 1999

Career pathways	Females	%	Males	%	Totals	%
	27	54	23	46	50	100
Further Education	6	22	3	13	9	18
Higher Education	3	11	5	22	8	16
Full-time employment	8	30	7	30	15	30
Part-time employment	2	7	4	17	6	12
Gap year/full-time work	1	4	0	0	1	2
Gap year/part-time work	1	4	1	4	2	4
No paid work	6	22	3	13	9	18
Total	27	100	23	99	50	100

Table A2.9 Summary of domestic pathways, February 1999

Domestic Pathways	Females	%	Males	%	Totals	%
	27	54	23	46	50	100
Living with parent(s)	13	48	14	61	27	54
With other family	0	0	2	9	2	4
With partner	6	22	5	22	11	22
With parent(s)/partner	1	4	2	9	3	6
On own/partner	1	4	0	0	1	2
Council flat on own	4	15	0	0	4	8
University accommodation	2	7	0	0	2	4
Total	27	100	23	101	50	100

Table A2.10 Socially, educationally and/or economically excluded young people, April 1999

Project name	Ethnicity self-described	Educational status	Current pathway	Life summary
Warren	White	No qualifications	No paid work	Was school truant; has never had paid work; was in care, then in hostel; currently lives with unemployed father. Both parents mentally ill; mother frequently hospitalized.
Luther	Black	No qualifications	No paid work	Has never had paid work; spent time in Young Offenders' Institution. Lives with partner in her council flat with their baby.
Zeyneba	Black	GNVQ Intermediate	GNVQ Advanced	Refugee; moved from council care into council flat on her own. Parents missing, presumed dead.
Wayne	White	5 GCSEs grades D–G	Occasional work as a DJ	Lives with both parents; father is a part-time DJ; mother unemployed; Wayne gets occasional DJ work from father.
Gillian	White	4 GCSEs grades A–C	No paid work; full-time mother	Was fairly promising A-level student; lives with unemployed partner and baby in council flat.
Tina	White	No qualifications	No paid work	Was school refuser; 'left' school during Year 10; worked part-time for few months in Blockbuster video shop; lives with partner (also school refuser) who works as a builder with his father.
Carlene	Black	4 GCSEs grades A–C	No paid work; full-time mother	Had first child at 15 and second at 16; lives with children in council flat. Visited by father of children.
Debra	White	1 GCSE (Art) grade A–C	No paid work	Mother was abused as child and, in turn, abused Debra who often ran away from home; lived in hostel; currently in Housing Association flat, being threatened with eviction.
Kajal	White South American	GNVQ Intermediate	GNVQ Advanced	Refugee; lives in council flat with mother and 3 younger siblings; feels responsible for family as she is oldest and mother speaks little English.
Daryl	White	No qualifications	No paid work	Has never had a job; alcoholic mother is in mental hospital; heroin addict brother in prison; lives at home with employed father.

Project name	Ethnicity self-described	Educational status	Current pathway	Life summary
Mehalet	Black	GNVQ Foundation	No paid work; full-time mother	Refugee; moved from care into council flat ; lives with baby and partner (Somalian, unemployed refugee). Father presumed dead, mother recently 'found' in Australia.
Gabrielle	White	1 GCSE (Art) grade A–C	No paid work; full-time mother	Both parents alcoholic; has been 'mother' to 7 younger siblings most of her life; put herself into care while attending the PRU; then moved into bedsit with own baby; awaiting council flat; unemployed father of baby visits occasionally.
Jeremy	Black African	1 GCSE (Art) grade A–C	No paid work	Started NVQ 1 but left early; almost illiterate; has had several, low paid jobs; often in trouble with police; lives partly with mother and partner.
Ayesha	Indo-African	NVQ level 1	Office work	Ran away from home and from foster parents; squatted in empty flats; abused by men; took drugs; several suicide attempts; moved into bedsit where she lives alone.
Germane	Black	3 GCSEs grade D–G	No paid work	Started NVQ 1 but left early, has never had a job but is not short of money; several brushes with police; lives at home with mother.

Total 15

Note

A sizeable proportion of our sample could be described as socially, educationally and/or economically excluded. For example, 12 of the 15 described above have direct contact with a variety of state welfare professionals and two have indirect contact (they live in households dependent on state welfare benefits). Some of the group are extremely vulnerable. For example, one has attempted suicide on several occasions; two have alcoholic parents; one has a seriously mentally ill mother; one lives with a mentally ill father; three are refugees; two (that we know about) have been abused by adults; five have young children; two have been homeless; five have been looked after by the local authority; eight were poor school attenders; two were excluded from mainstream education; four attended the Pupil Referral Unit (PRU); two have no access to immediate family and three have been in serious trouble with the police. While the refugees should be regarded positionally as working-class, their backgrounds are mainly professional middle-class and their cultural capital often reflects this. The other young people are from working-class backgrounds (see above for young people's parents' current career pathways).

Table A2.11 Summary of self-described ethnicity of 'excluded' group, April 1999

Ethnicity self-described	Females	Males	Total
White	5	3	8
Black	3	3	6
Indo-African	1	0	1
Total	9	6	15

Table A2.12 Summary of educational status of 'excluded' group, April 1999

Educational status	Females	Males	Total
No qualifications	1	3	4
GCSEs grades D–G	0	2	2
One GCSE (Art) grade A–C	2	1	3
Four GCSEs grades A–C	2	0	2
NVQ level 1	1	0	1
GNVQ Foundation	1	0	1
GNVQ Intermediate	2	0	2
Total	9	6	15

Table A2.13 Summary of career pathways of 'excluded' group, April 1999

Career pathways	Females	Males	Total
No paid work	6	5	11
Occasional/part-time work	0	1	1
Full-time work	1	0	1
Students	2	0	2
Total	9	6	15

Table A2.14 Summary of domestic pathways of 'excluded' group, April 1999

Domestic pathways	Females	Males	Total
Living with both parents	0	1	1
Living with mother	1	1	2
Living with father	0	2	2
Living with mother or partner	0	1	1
Living with partner	1	0	1
Living with partner and baby	2	1	3
Living on own with baby/babies	2	0	2
Living on own	3	0	3
Total	9	6	15

Table A2.15 Summary of state welfare benefits received by 'excluded' group, April 1999

State welfare benefits	Females	Males	Total
Housing benefit	7	0	7
Child allowance	4	0	4
New Deal	1	5	6
Unemployed but not registered	1	1	2
Total	13	6	19

Note
Numbers in Table 2.15 do not tally because some young people are in receipt of more than one benefit. Others (not indicated above), although not direct recipients of state benefits, live in homes which are. All households currently receive some sort of financial aid from the state.

Table A2.16 Summary of 'excluded' group's parents' career pathways, April 1999

Parents' career pathways	Mothers	Fathers	Total
No paid work	8	5	13
Occasional/part-time work	2	1	2
Full-time work	3	1	5
Not known (by young person)	1	6	7
Missing, presumed dead	1	2	3
Total	15	15	30

Notes
1 Of the three mothers in full-time work, two are cleaners (one has three cleaning jobs) and one is an office worker. The one employed father has recently secured work in a Job Centre. Of the parents who work part-time, one mother sells baby clothes and the other is a cleaner; the father is a part-time DJ.
2 In the seven cases where a parent's career pathway is 'not known', this is because the young person has no contact with that parent.

Table A2.17 Young people's self-described ethnicity, career and domestic pathways, October 1999

Project name	Ethnicity self-described	Career pathways	Domestic pathways
Delisha	Mixed race	No paid work	Living at home with mother, stepfather and younger siblings
Warren	White	Occasional work as DJ	Living with father
Desmond	African-Caribbean	Working in office	Living in council flat with partner, older sister and her partner
Rees	White	Working in Sainsburys	Living with partner
Kenneth	Chinese	HE London	Living at home with both parents and older sister and brother
Leila	Bangladeshi	HE London	Living at home with mother and younger sister
Kaleigh	Black	Working on newspaper	Living at home with both parents and two older sisters
Christoph	White	No paid work	Living with mother
Luther	Black	No paid work	Living with partner and their one child in her council flat. Partner pregnant again
Romac	White	Part-time bar work	Living with father in High Wycombe
Zeyneba	Ethiopian	Occasional unskilled work	Married to a refugee; living in council flat
Aaron	White	Unknown	Unknown
Wayne	White	Part-time DJ	Living at home with both parents
Sinead	White	Sales administrator	Living at home with mother and younger sister
Emma	White	Working in office	Living at home with both parents
Gillian	White	No paid work One child	Living with partner and baby in council flat
Luke	White	HE London	Living at home with both parents and younger brother
Earl	Black	Working in graphics	Living at home with mother, stepfather and younger brother
Tina	White	No paid work	Living with partner
Carlene	Black	No paid work Two children	Living on own in council flat, visited by father of children
Marcus	Black Caribbean	Working with computers	Living with partner
John	White	No paid work	Living with father and large extended family
Lucy	White	Working in Tescos	Living with both parents, older brother and younger sister and brother

Project name	Ethnicity self-described	Career pathways	Domestic pathways
Amma	Black	HE London	Living at home with mother and younger sister
Anne	Chinese	Waitress in bar	Living at home with both parents and two older sisters
Ashraf	Indian	HE London	Living with large extended family
Debra	White	No paid work	Living on own in council flat
Jolene	Black	No paid work	Living at home with mother
Hussain	Somalian	Unknown	Unknown
Kajal	White South American	Working in Chemist	Refugee; living at home with mother, two younger brothers and younger sister
Kirsty	White	HE Sussex	Living in shared house with other students
Jordan	Mixed race	HE London	Living at home with both parents and two younger brothers
Agesh	Indo-Caribbean	HE Sussex	Living in shared house with other students
Daryl	White	No paid work	Living at home with mentally ill father
Reggie	Caribbean	HE London	Living with mother and six younger sisters and brothers
Anthea	Black Caribbean	Working in marketing	Living at home with mother and younger sister
James	White	Working with computers	Living with father
Rena	Kenyan-Asian	Working in Hair and Beauty	Living at home with both parents and two older sisters
Rachel	White	Working in Tesco	Living with four young women
Dean	White	No paid work	Living with both parents
Mehalet	Somalian	No paid work One child	Living in council flat with partner and child
Michael	White	Hairdresser	Living with partner
Nadine	White	No paid work One child	Living in council flat with baby
Karen	White	No paid work One child	Living in council flat with baby
Gabrielle	White	No paid work One child	Living in council flat with baby
Jeremy	Black African	Working in sports shop	Living with mother

Table A2.17 (continued)

Project name	Ethnicity self-described	Career pathways	Domestic pathways
Ayesha	Indo-African	No paid work	Living on own in council flat
Delia	Black	Working in office	Living at home with mother and younger siblings
Germane	Black	No paid work	Living at home with mother
Fiona	White	Nanny	Living at home with both parents and younger brother
Total 50			

Table A2.18 Summary of domestic pathways, October 1999

Domestic pathways	Females	%	Males	%	Totals	%
	27	54	23	46	50	100
Living with parent(s)	14	52	16	70	30	60
With partner	3	11	5	22	8	16
Married	1	4	0	0	1	2
Council flat on own	6	22	0	0	6	12
Shared house with friends	3	11	0	0	3	6
Unknown	0	0	2	9	2	4
Total	27	100	23	101	50	100

Appendix 3

We certainly would not want to deny the obvious evidence of continuing scope for making significant choices – although choice-making in itself differs between groups. However we would also want to point to the clear and obvious evidence of the continuing significance of the structural *limitations* upon young people's opportunities. We test this out to some extent by looking across the sample as a whole at 'origins', attainments and current destinations.

Table A3.1 Student 'origins', attainments, destinations and social class, October 1998

Project name	Mother	Father	GCSEs A*–C	Destinations June 1998
	Social class groups 3M–5			
Delisha	Play group leader	Factory worker	0	B.Tec national, computing
Warren	Unemployed	Unemployed	0	Unemployed
Desmond	Computers	Cleaner	3	GNVQ intermediate
Rees	Unemployed	Plumber	0	Working in food shop
Kenneth	Homeworker	Unemployed	4	GNVQ advanced
Leila	Childminder	Unknown	6	A-levels
Kaleigh	Unemployed	Unemployed/ill	3	Office work
Christoph	Unemployed	Mechanic	0	GNVQ intermediate
Luther	Not known	Not known	0	Unemployed/father
Romac	Hypnotherapist	Baggage handler	3	Working on market stall
Zeyneba*	Presumed dead	Presumed dead	0	GNVQ advanced
Wayne	Van driver	Unemployed	0	DJ-ing
Gillian	Caretaker/cleaner	Unknown	4	A-levels/home with baby
Earl	Unemployed	Fitness instructor	3	GNVQ advanced
Tina	Unemployed	Security guard	0	Unemployed
Carlene	Secretary	Unknown	4	Home with two babies
Marcus	Caterer	Chef	0	Computer engineer

Table A3.1 (continued)

Project name	Mother	Father	GCSEs A*–C	Destinations June 1998
	Social class groups 3M–5			
John	Unemployed	Unemployed	0	Driver's mate/ unemployed
Amma	Housekeeper	Unknown	3	B.Tec Performing Arts
Ashraf	Not known	Not known	0	GNVQ advanced
Debra	Part-time van driver	Labourer	1	1 A-level/unemployed
Jolene	Unemployed	Unknown	0	Working in foodshop
Michael	Unemployed	Unknown	1	Hairdressing + NVQ
Kevin	Unemployed	Builder	0	Unemployed
Fatima	Unemployed	Unknown	0	Office work
Nadine	Cook	Chip shop owner	1	Travel clerk/unemployed
Karen	Cleaner†	Security guard	1	Hairdressing/baby
Tony	Unemployed	Unknown	0	Unknown
Gabrielle	Unemployed	Unemployed	1	Dental assistant/baby
Jane	Unemployed	Dead	1	NVQ/unemployed
Jessica	Cleaner	Bus driver	0	Office work
Jeremy	Cleaner	Shop assistant	1	Works in sports centre
Terry	Barmaid	Part-time cleaner	0	Army
Ayesha	Barmaid	Unknown	0	NVQ level 3
Natasha	Student	Unknown	0	Unemployed
Gary	Unemployed	Unemployed	0	Catering NVQ 3
Fiona	Unemployed	Unemployed	0	Nanny
Kajal*	Student	Student	1	GNVQ advanced
Jordan	Unemployed	Postman	3	A-levels
Michelle	Cleaner	Parking attendant	3	Working with horses
James	Lab technician	Bricklayer	6	A-levels/warehouse
Rena	Factory worker	Porter	6	GNVQ intermediate
Mehalet*	Part-time saleswork	Presumed dead	0	GNVQ advanced
Daryl	Unemployed	Unemployed	0	Unemployed
	Social Class groups 1–3N			
Aaron	Sales representative	Shipping agent	0	GNVQ advanced
Emma	Sells baby clothes	Film editor	4	A-levels/part-time work
Sinead	Occup. therapist	Dead	3	Working in food shop
Luke	Primary teacher	Locations officer	7	A-levels
Lucy	Teacher	Carehome manager	6	A-levels
Anne	Restaurant owner	Chef/owner	9	A-levels
Hussain	Unemployed	Shop manager	3	GNVQ advanced

Project name	Mother	Father	GCSEs A*–C	Destinations June 1998
	Social Class groups 1–3N			
Delia	Nursery teacher	Unknown	0	Working in clothes shop
Germane	Office worker	Unknown	0	Unemployed
Kirsty	Teacher	Sales manager	10	A-levels
Agesh	Nurse	Customer services	9	A-levels
Reggie	Auxiliary nurse	Unknown	7	GNVQ advanced
Anthea	Teacher	Photographer	0	A-levels
Rachel	Solicitor	Architect	10	A-levels
Dean	Accountant	Carpenter	1	labourer

Notes
* = Refugees   † = Grandparents
Unknown = unknown to young person
Not known = not known to research team

Any general description and discussion here has to be based on a recognition of the crudeness of the categories employed and the smallness of the sub-groups. As Pearce and Hillman (1998) note: 'Attainment at 16 is the strongest predictor of both future participation in education and labour market prospects' (p. 35).

The GCSE A*–C grade passes per student were 1.3 for the working-class group and 4.6 for the middle-class group. It is perhaps not surprising then that while five (11.4 per cent) of the working class group began A-level courses, three dropped out. Eight (53.3 per cent) of the middle-class group were doing A-levels, seven of whom completed their courses. The A-level route is still dominated here by the offspring of the middle-class. Furthermore, at this point, 11 (25 per cent) of the working-class group are unemployed (this does not include four who are full-time mothers), and only one (6.6 per cent) of the middle-class. Three (20 per cent) of the middle-class group are not on post-16 courses of some kind, compared with 27 (61.4 per cent) of the working-class group. Significantly, eight (18 per cent) of the working-class group with three or more GCSE A*–C passes are not doing A-level courses – 'self-exclusion' perhaps?

While realizing the fragility of these comparisons, the continuing salience of class as a discriminating factor in routes, opportunities and positioning in the 'economy of student worth' in the post-16 education, training and labour market seems very clear.

References

Aggleton, P. (1987). *Rebels Without a Cause? Middle-class Youth and the Transition from School to Work*. London, New York and Philadelphia: Falmer Press.

Ainley, P. and Bailey, B. (1997). *The Business of Learning: Staff and Student Experiences of Further Education in the 1990s*. London: Cassell.

Albrow, M. (1997). 'Travelling beyond local cultures: socioscapes in a global city'. In J. Eade (ed.), *Living the Global City: Globalization as a Local Process*. London: Routledge.

Alheit, P. (1994). *Taking the Knocks: Youth Unemployment and Biography*. London: Cassell.

Alheit, P. (1999). 'On a contradictory way to the "learning society": a critical approach', *Studies in the Education of Adults*, **31**(1), 66–82.

Allatt, P. (1993). 'Becoming privileged: the role of family processes'. In I. Bates and G. Riseborough (eds), *Youth and Inequality*. Buckingham: Open University Press.

Appadurai, A. (1992). 'Disjuncture and difference in the global cultural economy'. In M. Featherstone (ed.), *Global Culture: Nationalism, Globalisation and Modernity*. London: Sage.

Apple, M. (1986). *Teachers and Texts: a Political Economy of Class and Gender Relations in Education*. New York: Routledge.

Baethge, M. (1989). 'Individualization as hope and as disaster'. In K. Hurrelmann and U. Engel (eds), *The Social World of Adolescents: International Perspectives*. New York: Walter de Gruyter.

Ball, S. J., Bowe, R. and Gewirtz, S. (1995). 'Circuits of schooling: a sociological exploration of parental choice of school in social class contexts', *Sociological Review*, **43**(1), 52–78.

Ball, S. J. and Vincent, C. (1998). 'I heard it on the grapevine: "hot" knowledge and school choice'. *British Journal of Sociology of Education*, **19**(3), 377–400.

Ball, S. J., Bowe, R. and Gewirtz, S. (1996). 'School choice, social class and distinction: the realisation of social advantage in education', *Journal of Education Policy*, **11**(1), 89–112.

Ball, S. J., Maguire, M. and Macrae, S. (1997). The post-16 education market: ethics, interests and survival. Paper presented at the BERA Conference, University of York, 11–14 September.

Ball, S. J. (1998). 'Ethics, self interest and the market form in education'. In A. Cribb (ed.), *Markets, Managers and Public Service?* Occasional Paper No. 1. London: Centre for Public Policy Research, King's College London.

Ball, S. J. (1998). 'It's becoming a habitus: identities, youth transitions and socio-economic change'. Paper presented at the BERA Conference, Queens University, Belfast, 27–30 August.

Ball, S. J., Maguire, M. and Macrae, S. (1998). 'Race, space and the further education marketplace', *Race, Ethnicity and Education*, **1**(2), 171–89.

Ball, S. J., Macrae, S. and Maguire, M. (1999). 'Young lives, diverse choices and imagined futures in an education and training market', *International Journal of Inclusive Education*, **3**(3), 195–224.

Ball, S. J., Maguire, M. and Macrae, S. (1999). Space, choice and risk in the London education market. Paper presented at the AERA Conference, University of Montreal, 19–23 April.

Ball, S. J., Macrae, S. and Maguire, M. (1999). 'Young lives at risk in the "futures" market: some policy concerns from on-going research'. In F. Coffield (ed.), *Speaking Truth to Power: Research and Policy on Lifelong Learning*. Bristol: Policy Press.

Banks, M. H. (1992). 'Youth employment and training'. In J. C. Coleman and C. Warren-Adamson (eds), *Youth Policy in the 90s: the Way Forward*. London: Routledge.

Banks, M., Bates, I., Breakwell, G., Bynner, J., Emler, N., Jamieson, L. and Roberts, K. (1992). *Careers and Identities*. Buckingham: Open University Press.

Bartlett, W. and Le Grand, J. (1993). *Quasi Markets and Social Policy*. London: Macmillan.

Bartlett, W., Roberts, J. A. and Le Grand, J. (1998). 'The development of quasi-markets in the 1990s'. In J. C. Coleman and C. Warren-Adamson (eds), *Quasi-Market Reforms in the 1990s: a Revolution in Social Policy* (pp. 1–16). Bristol: Policy Press.

Bates, I. (1993). 'A job which is "right for me"?' In I. Bates and G. Riseborough (eds), *Youth and Inequality*. Buckingham: Open University Press.

Bates, I. and Riseborough, G. (eds) (1993). *Youth and Inequality*. Buckingham: Open University Press.

Beck, U. (1992). *Risk Society: Towards a New Modernity*. Newbury Park, CA: Sage.

Becker, G. (1964). *Human Capital*. New York: National Bureau of Economic Research.

Bernstein, B. (1996). *Pedagogy, Symbolic Control and Identity: Theory, Research, Critique*. London: Taylor Francis.

Bettis, P. J. and Stoeker, R. (1993). 'New urban sociology and critical education theory: framework for urban school reform in an era of deindustrialisation'. Paper presented at the American Educational Research Association, Conference. Atlanta, Georgia, USA, April.

Bettis, P. J. (1996). 'Urban students, liminality and the postindustrial context'. *Sociology of Education*, **69**(2), 105–25.

Bloomer, M. and Hodkinson, P. (1997). *Moving into FE: the Voice of the Learner*. London: Further Education Development Agency.

Boudon, R. (1982). *The Unintended Consequences of Social Action*. London: Macmillan.

Boulton, M. G. (1983). *On Being a Mother: a Study of Women with Pre-school Children*. London: Tavistock.

Bourdieu, P. (1977). Towards a Theory of Practice. Cambridge: Cambridge University Press.

Bourdieu, P. (1986). *Distinction: a Social Critique of the Judgement of Taste*. London: Routledge.

Bourdieu, P. (1990). *The Logic of Practice*. Cambridge: Polity Press.

Bourdieu, P. and Passeron, J.-C. (1990). *Reproduction in Education, Society and Culture*. London: Sage.

Bourdieu, P. and Wacquant, L. J. D. (1992). *An Invitation to Reflexive Sociology*. Chicago: University of Chicago Press.

Brake, M. (1990). 'Changing leisure and cultural patterns among British youth'. In L. Chisholm, P. Buchner, H. H. Kruger and P. Brown (eds), *Childhood, Youth and Social Change: a Comparative Perspective*. London: Falmer Press.

Brannen, J. (1996). 'Discourses of adolescence: young people's independence and autonomy within "families" '. In J. Brannen and M. O'Brien (eds), *Children in 'Families': Research and Policy*. London: Falmer Press.

Branson, J. (1991). 'Gender, education and work'. In D. Corson (ed.), *Education for Work: Background to Policy and Curriculum*. Cleveden: Multilingual Matters; Buckingham: Open University.

Brice Heath, S. and McLaughlin, M. W. (eds) (1993). *Identity and Inner-City Youth: Beyond Ethnicity and Gender*. New York and London: Teachers College Press, Columbia University.

Britzman, D. (1997). 'Tangles of implication', *International Journal of Qualitative Studies in Education*, **10**(1), 31–7.

Buffoni, L. (1997). 'Rethinking poverty in globalised conditions'. In J. Eade (ed.), *Living the Global City: Globalisation as a Local Process*. London: Routledge.

Bynner, J. and Ashford, S. (1994). 'Politics and participation: some antecedents of young people's attitudes to the political system and political activity', *European Journal of Social Psychology*, **24**, 223–36.

Bynner, J. and Parsons, S. (1997). *It Doesn't Get Any Better: the Impact of Poor Basic Skills on the Lives of 37 Year-Olds*. London: Basic Skills Agency.

Bynner, J., Ferri, E. and Shepherd, P. (eds) (1997). *Twenty-Something in the 1990s: Getting On, Getting By, Getting Nowhere*. Aldershot: Ashgate.

Carvel, J. (1999). 'Second chance for drop-outs'. *The Guardian*, p. 7, 13 July.

Castells, M. (1998). *End of Millennium*. Malden, Mass; Oxford: Blackwell.

Charter, D. (1997). Lifestyle is worth more than pay, say students. *The Times*, p. 4, 22 October.

Chisholm, L. (1995). 'Cultural semantics: occupations and gender discourse'. In P. Atkinson, B. Davies and S. Delamont (eds), *Discourse and Reproduction*. Creskill, NJ: Hampton Press.

Chisholm, L. and Hurrelmann, K. (1995). 'Adolescence in mid-Europe: pluralized transition patterns and their implications for personal and social risks', *Journal of Adolescence*, **18**(2), 129–58.

Clarke, D. (1999). 'Work hard, play hard: consumption, lifestyle and the city'. *Research Counts* (Vol. UpDates (dave@geog.leeds.ac.uk), Swindon: ESRC.

Clywd, A. (1994). *Children at Risk: an Analysis of Illegal Employment of Children in Great Britain*. London: The Labour Party.

Cockett, R. (1996). 'Thatcher's final victory: a Labour win'. *New Statesman*, pp. 56–7, 20 December.

Coffield, F. (1996). 'Nine learning fallacies and their replacement by a national strategy for lifelong learning'. In F. Coffield (ed.), *A National Strategy for Lifelong Learning*. Newcastle: Department of Education, University of Newcastle.

Coffield, F. (1999). *Breaking the Consensus: Lifelong Learning as Social Control*. Newcastle: Department of Education, University of Newcastle.

Connell, R. W. (1989). 'Cool guys, swots and wimps: the interplay of masculinity and education', *Oxford Review of Education*, **15**(3), 291–303.

Corbett, J. (ed.) (1990). *Uneasy Transitions: Disaffection in Post-compulsory Education and Training*. Basingstoke: The Falmer Press.

Craib, I. (1998). *Experiencing Identity*. London; Thousand Oaks; New Delhi: Sage.

Crompton, R. (1998). *Class and Stratification: an Introduction to Current Debates*. (2nd edn.) Oxford: Polity Press.

de Certeau, M. (1984). *The Practice of Everyday Life*. Berkeley, CA: University of California Press.

Demos (1999). *The Real Deal*. London: Demos (in association with Centre Point, Save the Children and Pilotlight).

Desai, R. (1994). 'Second-hand dealers in ideas: think-tanks and Thatcherite hegemony', *New Left Review*, **203** (January/February), 27–64.

DfEE (1998). Green Paper. *The Learning Age: a Renaissance for a New Britain*. London: The Stationery Office.

DfEE (1999). White Paper. *Learning to Succeed: a New Framework for Post-16 Learning*. London: DfEE.

Dixon, C. (1996). 'Having a laugh, having a fight: masculinity and the conflicting needs of the self in design and technology', *International Studies of Sociology of Education*, **6**(2), 147–66.

DSS (1995). *Households Below Average Income: a Statistical Analysis 1979–1992/3*. London: HMSO.

Du Bois-Reymond, M. (1998). ' "I don't want to commit myself yet": young people's life concepts', *Journal of Youth Studies*, **1**(1), 63–79.

Dunnell, K. (1979). *Family Formations 1976*. London: OPCS and HMSO.

Durrschmidt, J. (1997). 'The delinking of locale and milieux: on the situatedness of extended milieux in a global environment'. In J. Eade (ed.), *Living the Global City: Globalization as a Local Process*. London: Routledge.

Dwyer, P. and Wyn, J. (1998). 'Post-compulsory education policy in Australia and its impact on participant pathways and outcomes in the 1990s', *Journal of Education Policy*, **13**(3), 285–300.

Eade, J. (ed.) (1997). *Living the Global City: Globalization as a Local Process*. London: Routledge.

Edwards, T., Fitz, J. and Whitty, G. (1989). *The State and Private Education: an Evaluation of the Assisted Places Scheme*. Lewes: Falmer.

Ely, M., Vinz, R., Downing, M. and Anzul, M. (1997). *On Writing Qualitative Research: Living by Words*. London: Falmer Press.

Evans, K. and Heinz, W. R. (1994). *Becoming Adults in England and Germany*. London: Anglo-German Foundation.

Falk, P. and Campbell, C. (eds) (1997). *The Shopping Experience*. London: Sage.

Featherstone, M. (1991). *Consumer Culture and Postmodernism*. London: Sage.

Ferguson, H. (1992). 'Watching the world go round: atrium culture and the psychology of shopping'. In R. Shields (ed.), *Lifestyle Shopping: the Subject of Consumption*. London: Routledge.

Ferri, E. and Smith, K. (1997). 'Where you live and who you live with'. In J. Bynner, E. Ferri and P. Shepherd (eds), *Twenty-Something in the 1990s: Getting On, Getting By and Getting Nowhere*. Aldershot: Ashgate.

Fornas, J. A. and Bolin, G. (1995). *Youth Culture in Late Modernity*. London; New Delhi: Sage.

Foskett, N. and Hesketh, A. (eds) (1996). 'Student decision-making and the post-16 market place'. In *Markets in Education: Policy, Process and Practice* (vol. 2). Southampton: Heist.

Foucault, M. (1970). *The Order of Things*. New York: Pantheon.

Foucault, M. (1986). *Death and the Labyrinth: the World of Raymond Roussel*. New York: Doubleday.

Furlong, A. (1992). *Growing Up in a Classless Society? School to Work Transitions*. Edinburgh: University Press.

Furlong, A. and Cartmel, F. (1997). *Young People and Social Change: Individualization and Risk in Late Modernity*. Milton Keynes: OUP.

Gamble, A. (1994). *Free Economy and the Strong State: Politics of Thatcherism*. London: Macmillan.

Gamble, A. (1995). 'The crisis of Conservatism', *New Left Review*, **214** (November/December), 3–25.

Gamble, A. and Kelly, G. (1996). 'The new politics of ownership', *New Left Review*, **220** (November/December), 62–97.

Gecas, V. and Burke, P. J. (1995). 'Self and identity'. In K. S. Cook, G. A. Fine and J. S. House (eds), *Sociological Perspectives on Social Psychology*. Boston: Allyn and Bacon.

Gewirtz, S., Ball, S. J. and Bowe, R. (1993). 'Values and ethics in the marketplace: the case of Northwark Park', *International Journal of Studies in Education*, **3**(2), 233–53.

Gewirtz, S., Ball, S. J. and Bowe, R. (1995). *Markets, Choice and Equity*. Buckingham: Open University Press.

Giddens, A. (1971). *Capitalism and Modern Social Theory*. Cambridge: Cambridge University Press.

Giddens, A. (1991). *Modernity and Self-Identity: Self and Identity in the Late Modern Age*. Oxford: Polity.

Gillham, B. (1997). *The Facts about Teenage Pregnancies*. London: Cassell.

Glaser, B. G. and Strauss, A. L. (1967). *The Discovery of Grounded Theory*. New York: Aldine Publishing Co.

Gordon, I. and Sassen, S. (1992). 'Restructuring the urban labour markets'. In S. S. Fainstein, I. Gordon and M. Harloe (eds), *Divided Cities: New York and London in the Contemporary World*. Oxford, UK and Cambridge USA: Blackwell.

Grace, G. (1978). *Teachers, Ideology and Control: a Study in Urban Education*. London: Routledge and Kegan Paul.

Grace, G. (1994). 'Urban education and the culture of contentment: the politics, culture and economics of inner-city schooling'. In N. P. Stronquist (ed.), *Education in Urban Areas: Cross-national Dimensions*. Westport, Connecticut; London: Praeger.

Griffin, C. (1985). *Typical Girls? Young Women from School to the Job Market*. London; Boston; Melbourne and Henley: Routledge and Kegan Paul.

Grossberg, L. (1996). 'Identity and cultural studies: is that all there is?' In S. Hall and P. du Gay (eds), *Questions of Cultural Identity*. London: Sage.

Hagerstrand, T. (1975). 'Survival and arena: on the life history of individuals in relation to their geographical environment'. In T. Carlstein, D. Parkes and M. Thrift (eds), *Human Activity and Time Geography*. London: Edward Arnold.

Hall, S. and Martin, J. (eds) (1983). *The Politics of Thatcherism*. London: Lawrence and Wishart.

Hall, S. (1988). *Thatcherism and the Crisis of the Left: the Hard Road to Renewal*. London: Verso.

Hall, S. (1991). 'The local and the global: globalisation and ethnicity'. In A. King (ed.), *Culture, Globalisation and the World-System*. London: Macmillan.

Hall, S. (1992). 'New ethnicities'. In J. Donald and A. Rattansi (eds), *'Race', Culture and Difference*. London: Sage.

Hall, S. (1996). 'Who needs identity?' In S. Hall and P. E. du Gay (eds), *Questions of Cultural Identity*. London; New Delhi: Sage.

Halpern, D. (1998). *Social Capital, Exclusion and Poverty*. London: Nexus/Fabian Society.

Harloe, M. and Fainstein, S. S. (1992). 'Conclusion: the divided cities'. In S. S. Fainstein, I. Gordon and M. Harloe (eds), *Divided Cities: New York and London in the Contemporary World*. Oxford: Blackwell.

Harvey, D. (1973). *Social Justice and the City*. London: Edward Arnold.

Harvey, D. (1989). *The Condition of Postmodernity*. Oxford: Basil Blackwell.

Haywood, C. and Mac An Ghaill, M. (1996). 'What about the boys? Gendered local labour markets and the recomposition of working-class masculinities', *British Journal of Education and Work*, **9**(1), 19–30.

Hebdige, D. (1988). *Hiding in the Light: on Images and Things*. London: Routledge.

Hendry, L., Shucksmith, J., Love, J. and Glendinning, A. (1993). *Young People's Leisure and Lifestyles*. London: Routledge.

Hewitt, R. (1990). 'Youth, race and language in contemporary Britain'. In L. Chisholm, P. Buchner, H. H. Kruger and P. Brown (eds), *Childhood, Youth and Social Change: a Comparative Perspective*. London: Falmer.

Hills, J. (1995). *Joseph Rowntree Inquiry into Income and Wealth*. York: Joseph Rowntree Foundation.

HMSO (1999). *Social Trends 29*. London: HMSO.

HM Treasury (1999). *The Modernization of Britain's Tax and Benefit System*. Report No. 4. London: The Treasury.

Hobcraft, J. (1998). *Intergenerational and Life-Course Transmission of Social Exclusion: Influences of Childhood Poverty, Family Disruption and Contact with the Police*. London: Centre for Analysis of Social Exclusion, London School of Economics.

Hodkinson, P., Sparkes, A. C. and Hodkinson, H. (1996). *Triumphs and Tears: Young People, Markets and the Transition from School to Work*. London: David Fulton.

Hodkinson, P. (1999). 'The origins of a theory of career decision-making: a case study of hermeneutical research', *British Educational Research Journal*, **24**(5), 557–72.

Hollands, R. (1995). *Friday Night, Saturday Night: Youth Cultural Identification in the Post-industrial City*. Newcastle: University of Newcastle.

Hoogvelt, A. M. M. (1997). *Globalisation and the Post-Colonial World: the New Political Economy of Development*. Basingstoke: Macmillan.

Hurrelmann, K. E. (ed.) (1994). *International Handbook of Adolescence*. Westport, US: Greenwood Press.

Hutton, W. (1995). *The State We're In*. London: Cape.

Irwin, S. (1995). *Rights of Passage: Social Change and the Transition from Youth to Adulthood*. London: University College London Press.

Jacobson, L. D., Wilkinson, C. and Pill, R. (1995). 'Teenage pregnancy in the UK in the 1990s: the implication for primary care', *Family Practice*, **12**(2), 232–36.

Jones, G. and Wallace, C. (1992). *Youth, Family and Citizenship*. Buckingham: Open University Press.

Kidd, L. (1992). 'Significant change or lost opportunity?' In T. Whiteside, A. Sutton and T. Everton (eds), *16–19 Changes in Education and Training*. London: David Fulton.

Kingdom, J. (1992). *No such thing as Society? Individualism and Community*. Buckingham: Open University Press.

Langouët, G. and Léger, A. (2000). 'Public and private schooling in France: an investigation into family choice', *Journal of Education Policy*, **15**(1), 41–9.

Larson, C. L. (1997). 'Re-presenting the subject: problems in personal narrative inquiry', *International Journal of Qualitative Studies in Education*, **10**(4), 455–70.

Lash, S. and Urry, J. (1994). *Economies of Signs and Space*. London: Sage.

Lather, P. (1994). 'Feminist efforts toward a double science: researching the lives of women with HIV/AIDS'. Paper presented at AERA Conference, San Francisco.

Lather, P. (1995). 'Textuality as praxis'. Paper presented at the AERA Conference, New Orleans.

Lather, P. (1997). 'Drawing the line at angels: working the ruins of feminist ethnography', *Qualitative Studies in Education*, **10**(3), 285–304.

Lather, P. (1999). 'Authorship/ownership/methods and ethics in research on teaching and teacher education'. Paper presented at AERA Conference, Montreal, 19–23 April.

Lavalette, M. (1996). 'Thatcher's working children: contemporary issues of child labour', in J. Pilcher and S. Wagg (eds.), *Thatcher's Children? Politics, Childhood and Society in the 1980s and 1990s*. London: Falmer.

Lees, S. (1993). *Sugar and Spice: Sexuality and Adolescent Girls*. London: Penguin Books.

Lloyd, J. (1996). 'Cakes, ale and virtue', in *New Statesman*, 20 December, pp. 38–9.

Lucey, H. (1996). 'Transitions to womanhood: constructions of success and failure for middle and working-class young women'. Paper presented at the British Youth Research: the New Agenda Conference. University of Glasgow, 26–8 January.

Mac An Ghaill, M. (1994). *The Making of Men*. Buckingham: Open University Press.

Mac An Ghaill, M. (1996). 'Class, culture and difference in England: deconstructing the institutional norm', *Qualitative Studies in Education*, **9**(3), 297–309.

MacDonald, R. E. (1997). *Youth, the 'Underclass' and Social Exclusion*. London and New York: Routledge.

MacLure, M. (1995). *Telling Transitions: Boundary Work in Narratives of Becoming an Action Researcher*. Norwich: CARE, University of East Anglia.

Macrae, S., Maguire, M. and Ball, S. J. (1996). 'Opportunity knocks: "choice" in the post-16 education and training market'. In *Markets in Education: Policy, Process and Practice*, vol. 2. Southampton: Heist.

Macrae, S., Maguire, M. and Ball, S. J. (1997a). 'Competition, choice and hierarchy in a post-16 education and training market'. In S. Tomlinson (ed.), *Education 14–19: Critical Perspectives*. London: Athlone Press.

Macrae, S., Maguire, M. and Ball, S. J. (1997b). 'Whose "learning" society? A tentative deconstruction', *Journal of Education Policy*, **12**(6), 499–509.

Macrae, S. and Maguire, M. (1999). 'All change, no change: gendered regimes in the post-16 market'. In J. Salisbury and S. Riddell (eds), *Gender, Policy and Educational Change: Shifting Agendas in the UK and Europe*. London: Routledge.

Maden, M. (1996). Divided cities: 'dwellers in different zones, inhabitants of different planets'. *The TES/Greenwich Education Lecture*.

Mandelson, P. (1997). *Tackling Social Exclusion*. London: The Fabian Society.

Mann, M. (1995). 'Sources of variation in working-class movements in twentieth-century Europe', *New Left Review*, **212**(July/August), 14–54.

Marginson, S. (1997). 'Subjects and subjugation: the economics of education as power knowledge', *Discourse*, **18**(2), 215–25.

McCrone, D. (1994). 'Getting by and making out in Kirkcaldy'. In M. Anderson, F. Bechhofer and J. Gershuny (eds), *The Social and Political Economy of the Household*. Oxford: Oxford University Press.

McRobbie, A. and Nava, M. (eds) (1984). *Gender and Generation*. Basingstoke: MacMillan.

McRobbie, A. (1991). 'Teenage mothers: a new social state?' In A. McRobbie (ed.), *Feminism and Youth Culture: from Jackie to Just Seventeen* (pp. 220–42). London: Macmillan.

Milbourne, L. (1999). 'Life at the margin: education of young people, social policy and the meanings of social exclusion'. Paper presented at the BERA Conference, University of Sussex, 2–5 September.

O'Bryne, D. (1997). 'Working-class culture: local community and global conditions'. In J. Eade (ed.), *Living the Global City: Globalization as a Local Process*. London: Routledge.

OECD. (1994). *School, a Matter of Choice*. Paris: OECD.

Oppenheim, C. (1998). 'Poverty and social exclusion: an overview'. In C. Oppenheim (ed.), *An Inclusive Society: Strategies for Tackling Poverty*. London: IPPR.

Pandya, N. (1999). Ethnic minorities are losing out under the New Deal. *The Guardian*, p. 25, Saturday 22 May.

Pearce, N. and Hillman, J. (1998). *Wasted Youth: Raising Achievement and Tackling Social Exclusion*. London: Institute for Public Policy Research.

Perkin, H. (1989). *The Rise of Professional Society: England since 1800*. London: Routledge.

Phoenix, A. (1991). *Young Mothers*. Cambridge: Polity Press.

Pilcher, J. and Wagg, S. (eds) (1996). *Thatcher's Children? Politics, Childhood and Society in the 1980s and 1990s*. London: Falmer.

Polhemus, T. (1994). *Streetstyle*. London: Thames and Hudson.

Power, S., Whitty, G., Edwards, T. and Wigfall, V. (1998). 'Education and the formation of middle-class identities'. Paper presesented at the European Conference on Educational Research. University of Ljubljana, Slovenia, 17–20 September.

Prout, A. (1999). 'Children – a suitable case for inclusion?' Annual Lecture, CPPR, King's College London.

QPID (1998). *TECs and CCTEs Working Towards Achieving Social and Economic Inclusion*. Sheffield: Training and Enterprise Council and Department for Education and Employment.

Quicke, J. (1993). 'A yuppie generation'. In I. Bates and G. Riseborough (eds), *Youth and Inequality*. Buckingham: Open University Press.

Rabinow, P. (ed.) (1987). *The Foucault Reader*. Harmondsworth: Penguin.

Reay, D. (1995a). 'A silent majority: mothers in parental involvement', *Women's Studies International Forum (Special Edition)*, **18**(3), 337–48.

Reay, D. (1995b). 'They employ cleaners to do that: habitus in the primary classroom'. *British Journal of Sociology of Education*, **16**(3), 353–71.

Reay, D. and Ball, S. J. (1997). 'Spoilt for choice: The working classes and education markets'. *Oxford Review of Education*, **23**(1), 89–101.

Reay, D. (1998). Emotional capital: a useful extension of Bourdieu's conceptual framework. Unpublished paper, School of Education, King's College London.

Reay, D. and Ball, S. J. (1998). 'Making their minds up: family dynamics of school choice', *British Educational Research Journal*, **24**(4), 431–48.

Redhead, S. (1993). *Rave Off: Politics and Deviance in Contemporary Youth Culture*. Manchester: University of Manchester Press.

Rees, G., Fevre, R., Furlong, J. and Gorard, S. (1997). 'History, place and the learning society: towards a sociology of lifetime learning'. *Journal of Education Policy*, **12**(6), 485–98.

Roberts, K. (1968). 'The entry into employment: an approach towards a general theory'. *Sociological Review*, **16**(2), 165–84.

Roberts, K. and Parsell, G. (1991). 'Young people's sources and levels of income and patterns of consumption in Britain in the late 1980s', *Youth and Policy*, **35** (December), 20–35.

Roberts, K. (1993). 'Career trajectories and the mirage of increased social mobility'. In I. Bates and G. Riseborough (eds), *Youth and Inequality*. Buckingham: Open University Press.

Roberts, K. and Parsell, G. (1994). 'Youth cultures in Britain: the middle-class take-over', *Leisure Studies*, **13**, 33–48.

Roberts, K., Clarke, S. C. and Wallace, G. (1994). 'Flexibility and individualisation: a comparison of transitions into employment in England and Germany'. *Sociology*, **28**(1), 31–54.

Robertson, R. (1992). *Globalisation*. London: Sage.

Rose, N. (1992). 'Governing the enterprising self'. In P. Hellas and P. Morris (eds), *The Values of the Enterprise Culture*. London: Routledge.

Sassen, S. (1991). *The Global City*. Princeton: Princeton University Press.

Savage, M., Barlow, J. Dickens, P. and Fielding, T. (1992). *Property, Bureaucracy and Culture: Middle-class Formation in Contemporary Britain*. London: Routledge.

Schuller, T. and Field, J. (1998). 'Social capital, human capital and the learning society', *International Journal of Lifelong Education*, **17**(4), 226–35.

Shields, R. (1992). 'Consumption cultures and the fate of community'. In R. Shields (ed.), *Lifestyle Shopping: the Subject of Consumption*. London: Routledge.

Sing-Raud, H. (1998). 'Asian women undergraduates: British universities and the dangers of creedism'. Paper presented at the European Conference on Educational Research, University of Ljubljana, Slovenia, 17–20 September.

Skelton, T. and Valentine, G. (eds) (1998). *Cool Places: Geographies of Youth Cultures*. London: Routledge.

Smith, M. K. (1994). *Local Education: Community, Conversation, Praxis*. Buckingham: Open University Press.

Strauss, A. L. (1962). 'Transformation of identity'. In A. M. Rose (ed.), *Human Behaviour and Social Processes: an Interactionist Approach*. London: Routledge and Kegan Paul.

Strauss, A. L. (1987). *Qualitative Data Analysis*. New York: Cambridge University Press.

Tsolidis, G. (1996). 'Feminist theorisation of identity and difference', *British Journal of Sociology of Education*, **17**(3), 267–77.

Van Maanen, J. (1995). 'An end to innocence: the ethnography of ethnography', in J. Van Maanen (ed.) *Representation in Ethnography*. Thousand Oaks, CA: Sage.

Wainwright, M. (1999). 'Shangri-La tracked down to Leeds'. *The Guardian*, p. 13, Thursday 1 April.

Walkerdine, V. (1997). *Daddy's Girl: Young Girls and Popular Culture*. Basingstoke: Macmillan Press.

Wallace, C. (1987). 'From generation to generation: the effects of employment and unemployment upon the domestic life-cycle of young adults'. In P. Brown and D. Ashton (eds), *Education, Unemployment and Labour Markets*. Lewes: Falmer Press.

Westwood, S. (1990). 'Racism, black masculinity and the politics of space'. In J. Hearn and D. Morgan (eds), *Men, Masculinities and Social Theory*. London: Unwin Hyman.

Wexler, P. (1992). *Becoming Somebody: Toward a Social Psychology of School*. London: Falmer Press.

White, S. (1998). *Interpreting the 'Third Way': a Tentative Overview*. Cambridge, MA: Dept of Political Science, MIT.

Wilkinson, R. G. (1996). *Unhealthy Societies: the Afflictions of Inequality*. London: Routledge.

Willis, P. (1977). *Learning to Labour: How Working-class Kids get Working-class Jobs*. Farnborough: Saxon House.

Willis, P. (1998). 'Notes on a common culture', *European Journal of Cultural Studies*, **1**(2), 163–76.

Wright-Mills, C. (1970). *The Sociological Imagination*. Harmondsworth: Penguin.

Wyn, J. and Dwyer, P. (1999). 'New directions in research on youth in transition'. *Journal of Youth Studies*, **2**(1), 5–21.

Zinneker, J. (1990). 'What does the future hold? Youth and sociocultural change in the FRG'. In L. Chisholm, P. Buchner, H. Kruger and P. Brown (eds), *Childhood, Youth and Social Change: a Comparative Perspective*. London: Falmer Press.

Author Index

Subject Index